A HANDBOOK
OF EDUCATIONAL
TECHNOLOGY

A HANDBOOK OF EDUCATIONAL TECHNOLOGY

FRED PERCIVAL & HENRY ELLINGTON

NP
Kogan
Page

Copyright © Fred Percival and Henry Ellington 1984
All rights reserved

First published in Great Britain in 1984 by
Kogan Page Ltd, 120 Pentonville Road, London N1 9JN

British Library Cataloguing in Publication Data

Percival, Fred
    Handbook of educational technology.
    1. Educational technology
    I. Title   II. Ellington Henry
    371.3'07'8   LB1028.3
ISBN 0-85038-569-5

First published in the United States of America in 1984 by
Nichols Publishing Company, PO Box 96, New York, NY10024

Library of Congress Cataloging in Publication Data

Percival, Fred
    Handbook of educational technology.
    1. Educational technology — Handbooks, manuals, etc.
    I. Ellington, Henry.   II. Title.
    LB1028.P39 1983   371.3'07'8   82-24655
ISBN 0-89397-150-2

Printed in Great Britain by Billings & Sons Limited, Worcester

Contents

Acknowledgements

Acknowledgements
We would like to acknowledge the help that we have received from the following people in producing this book:

- [ ] our colleagues Eric Addinall and Barry Murton, for advice and constructive criticism;
- [ ] the two (anonymous) readers to whom the original MS was sent by Kogan Page, whose constructive criticism was of considerable help in producing the final published version of the book;
- [ ] Una Baillie and Margaret Geddes, for typing the MS of this book and for all the other secretarial support they have given us in our work;
- [ ] our Kogan Page editor Jane Wilkinson.

We apologize to female readers for the fact that we have made exclusive use of male pronouns throughout this book. We would, however, like to assure them that this has no sinister male chauvinist overtones, but is done purely in order to avoid breaking up the flow of the text by constant use of the rather ugly 'he/she' and 'his/her'. Thus, wherever the words 'he' or 'his' occur, they should be taken as covering both the masculine and feminine genders.

Introduction

Since educational technology emerged as a discipline in its own right in the years following the end of the Second World War, whole libraries of books have been written on virtually every aspect of the subject. Despite this wealth of material, however, there has been a noticeable lack of books that can be used as a basic 'primer' in the field, that is, books that give a simple overview of the main aspects of educational technology and explain how adopting an educational technology-based approach can help to improve the efficiency and effectiveness of the average teacher or lecturer.

This book has been written in an attempt to fill this gap, and we see it as having two main roles, namely, as a handbook for practising teachers and lecturers who want to learn something about the principles and practice of educational technology so that they can use it in their day-to-day work, and as a basic text for trainee teachers and students of education who are studying educational technology as part of their courses. The book should also prove useful as an introductory text for students of educational technology.

Since the book is not based on any particular educational system, and deals with the various topics covered in fairly general terms, we also hope that it will prove just as helpful to American, Australian and other English-speaking readers as it does to those in Britain.

The main text of the book consists of 11 chapters, each of which deals with a different aspect of educational technology.

Chapter 1 gives a broad introduction to educational technology, explaining what is meant by the term, introducing the 'systems approach' that underlies its thinking, and outlining a brief historical account of the way in which the field has developed since the late 1940s.

Chapter 2 then describes two fundamentally different approaches to education, within the context of which virtually all important developments in educational technology have taken place — the traditional 'teacher/institution-centred' approach and the more recent 'student-centred' approach.

Chapter 3 deals with the subject of educational objectives, the formulation of which should constitute the starting point of any systematic approach to course or curriculum design. It explains the difference between 'aims' and 'objectives', offers guidance on how objectives should be written, and discusses the different types of objectives.

The next three chapters deal with the three main types of teaching methods that can be employed in implementing a course or programme of instruction, Chapter 4 dealing with 'mass instruction' techniques, Chapter 5 with 'individualized learning' techniques and Chapter 6 with 'group learning' techniques. In each case, a general discussion of the various methods that can be used and an analysis of their respective strengths and weaknesses is followed by a review of the different media and techniques that can be used to support them or put them into practice.

Chapters 7 and 8 then deal with the related topics of student assessment and course evaluation, explaining the overall role of each in the instructional process and describing the various techniques that can be used to carry them out.

Chapters 9 and 10 deal with two aspects of educational technology that have become progressively more important during the last 20 years and seem certain to become even more important during the next, looking at the role and organization of resources centres and at the various ways in which computers can be used in education.

Finally, Chapter 11 takes a glimpse into the future, trying to identify the main trends that underlie current educational technology and making informed guesses as to how these will have affected the overall educational scene by the year 2000.

The book also contains four reference sections, which have been included in order to increase its usefulness as a handbook.

The first is a comprehensive glossary of terms used in educational technology, defining over 800 words and phrases that teachers and lecturers are likely to come across in the course of their work; these not only cover the 'hardware' and 'software' aspects of educational technnology, but also the highly important intangible aspects of the subject (sometimes described as the 'underwear').

The second is a wide-ranging bibliography that lists over 350 books, papers and articles relating to the subjects covered in the individual chapters. This will enable readers to study in greater depth any topic or topics in which they are particularly interested. Full bibliographic details about all books, articles or other publications specifically referred to in the main text are given in the Bibliography under the appropriate chapter heading.

The third is a country-by-country list of some of the main professional bodies, associations and other organizations that are involved in the educational technology field and the various specific aspects thereof.

The fourth and final section is a detailed keyword index to the material covered in the main text.

CHAPTER 1

The Nature of Educational Technology

Introduction

To most people, the term 'educational technology' is, at best, confusing, and, at worst, downright off-putting. To some, the term is associated solely with the technical equipment and media of education — such as overhead projectors, television, tape-slide programmes, etc. Others take the view that educational technology involves a clinical, systematic analysis of the entire teaching/learning process in an attempt to maximize its effectiveness. Indeed, extreme proponents of the latter view have sometimes been accused of treating learners more like 'impersonalized battery hens' than as 'people with inquiring minds who thrive on intellectual stimulation and human contact' — a view with which we have some sympathy.

Largely because of this confusion over its meaning, there can be little doubt that educational technology has now become a rather unhelpful jargon expression. Indeed, many practitioners working in the field are embarrassed by it, and, in some cases, have even made an attempt to disown it; several former 'educational technology units' in colleges and polytechnics have, for example, recently been re-named as 'educational development units', 'learning units', or something similar. No one has so far managed to come up with a better name, however, so we appear to be stuck with it for the time being, and, for this reason, we will continue to use the term 'educational technology' throughout this book.

The perceptions of what constitutes 'educational technology' have evolved over a period of about 30 years, and its exact nature is not easily explained. Indeed Kenneth Richmond, in his excellent book *The Concept of Educational Technology* (1970) devotes the first 70 pages to a discussion of what educational technology is, and of the different connotations of the word 'technology'.

In this chapter, we will describe some of the general 'aspects' of educational technology, and trace its historical development. We will begin by discussing two quite different perceptions of educational technology, namely the idea of the 'technology *in* education' and the idea of a 'technology *of* education'.

Technology *in* Education

'Technology *in* education' embraces every possible means by which information can be presented. It is concerned with the 'gadgetry' of education and training, such as television, language laboratories and the various projected media, or, as someone once said, 'everything from computers to dinner ticket dispensers'. In other words, technology *in* education is basically the popular impression of what educational technology is all about, namely, *audiovisual aids*.

The general field of audiovisual aids is itself composed of two related but distinguishable areas, namely, *hardware* and *software*. The hardware side is concerned with the actual equipment — overhead projectors, slide projectors, tape recorders, videocassette recorders, television monitors, microcomputers, etc. The software side, on the other hand, is concerned with the various items that are used in conjunction with this equipment — such as overhead transparencies, slides, audiotapes, videorecordings and computer programs.

Technology *in* education is obviously one very important aspect of educational technology. Indeed, historically, many of the college-based educational technology units evolved from units which were previously called 'audiovisual aids units'. By making appropriate use of hardware along with suitable software, it is often possible to improve the efficiency or quality of learning in a given situation, and this was the basis of the first developments in educational technology, as we shall see later.

One of the earliest phases in the evolution of educational technology was the 'hardware phase', in which a great deal of work was done in developing effective instructional equipment which was also reliable, serviceable and within the budgets of schools, colleges and training establishments. However, when such hardware eventually became generally available, it was found that there was a shortage of suitable software to use with it; this triggered off a subsequent 'software phase', in which particular attention was paid to the development of suitable learning materials, often based on the contemporary theories of learning and perception. Thus, even within this early development of educational technology, we can identify changes in the interpretation of the term 'technology'.

Initially, this had distinctly engineering connotations, since the main thrust of educational technology was concerned with the development of items of optical and electronic equipment for educational purposes; subsequently, it became much more associated with psychology and learning theory as the main thrust changed to the development of suitable software for use with this equipment.

However, at this stage in the development of educational technology, many people became aware that there was much in education and training which could be improved by thinking more carefully about *all* aspects of the design of teaching/learning situations. Such considerations led to a new interpretation of 'educational technology' as the entire technology *of* education rather than merely as the use of technology *in* education, with the latter being regarded as merely a part of the former rather than the whole field as had previously been the case. Let us now examine this new interpretation in more detail.

The Technology *of* Education

It could be argued that the principal role of educational technology is to help improve the overall efficiency of the teaching/learning process. In education and training, improved efficiency can manifest itself in many ways, for example:

(a) increasing the quality of learning, or the degree of mastery;
(b) decreasing the time taken for learners to attain desired goals;
(c) increasing the capacity of teachers in terms of numbers of learners taught, without reducing the quality of learning;
(d) reducing costs, without affecting quality.

It is a value judgement as to which of the above examples are more important, and, indeed, such a judgement must be made in terms of the educational, financial and political aspects of individual situations. They are not necessarily mutually exclusive, but (to quote a hypothetical example) it might be found that certain measures that could well improve the quality of learning in a particular situation would also involve an increase in expenditure, so that a decision based on the likely cost-effectiveness of the measures would have to be made.

However, given well-defined criteria by which an improvement in the efficiency of an educational system, situation or process can be gauged, then decisions regarding the exact measures by which this can best be achieved can often be reached by applying a 'technology *of* education' approach. Recommendations for improvement are thus based on a study of the particular system *as a whole*, together with knowledge of appropriate educational research findings and theories of learning. In many cases, ideas and practices drawn from such diverse fields as psychology, sociology, business management and systems analysis are combined with developments in more technical fields such as optics, reprography, acoustics and microelectronics in order to produce the optimum learning or teaching system.

These aspects, which are all part of the technology *of* education, are sometimes called the 'intangible' aspects (or the 'underwear', as opposed to the hardware and software already described). In this case, the emphasis is on the *techniques* of teaching and learning rather than on audiovisual aids *per se*. Although the 'intangible' aspects of educational technology are, by definition, less obvious than the 'hardware' and 'software' aspects, they are, nevertheless, just as important (indeed, most educational technologists would say more important) when it comes to solving a particular problem.

A 'technology *of* education' approach to educational technology thus involves a systematic, scientific approach to a problem, together with the application of appropriate scientific research, both from 'hard' sciences such as physics and electronics and from social sciences such as psychology and sociology. In applying a technology *of* education approach, changes are not made to a system for their own sake, but only for good educational reasons that are generally based on scientific research. Such changes may not always work as intended, but even unexpected outcomes may prove useful to the people involved (and to others) when future developments are being planned.

It is as a technology *of* education that most practitioners view educational technology today. Within this concept, technology *in* education is seen mainly as one of the possible means to an end, with appropriate hardware and software being selected or designed to back up the particular strategy that it is decided to adopt in order to achieve a given set of educational aims or objectives. In some cases, this may involve the use of highly sophisticated equipment such as video or computers; in others, duplicated worksheets may be all that are required. Here it is important that the educational development or innovation has been *systematically* and *scientifically* planned and executed. It is this 'systems approach' to educational technology which is at the heart of the technology *of* education.

The relationships between the various aspects of educational technology discussed so far are shown in schematic form in Figure 1.1.

The Systems Approach

The systems approach to the design and analysis of teaching/training situations is the basis of the great majority of modern educational technology-related developments. However the terms 'system' (which we have already used in a number of contexts) and 'systems approach' are jargon terms, and can have a variety of interpretations. Let us therefore first take a look at these terms in order to define the way in which we are to use them.

In an educational technology context, a *system* is any collection of interrelated parts that together constitute a larger whole. These component parts, or *elements*, of the system are intimately linked with one another, either directly or indirectly, and any change in one or more elements may affect the overall performance of the system, either beneficially or adversely. A simple system is illustrated schematically in Figure 1.2.

In Figure 1.2 the system consists of four distinct elements A, B, C, D which are related to or dependent upon each other as indicated.

Figure 1.1 **The relationships between
the different aspects of educational technology**

Note that some interrelationships may be two-way, while others may be one-way only. These elements may themselves be capable of further breakdown into other smaller components, and may thus be regarded as *sub-systems* of the overall system.

The processes of education and learning can be considered to be very complex systems indeed. The input to a given educational or learning system consists of people, resources and information, and the output consists of people whose performance has (it is to be hoped) improved in some desired way. A schematic representation of systems of this type is shown in Figure 1.3.

In such a system, the educational or learning process may be so complex that it can only be considered as a 'black box' whose mechanisms are not fully understood. However, research into the nature of the learning process has thrown *some* light on what happens inside the 'black box'. This has enabled educational technologists to structure the input to systems of this type in such a way as to try to improve the output through increasing the efficiency of the learning process, thus leading to a systems approach to course design based on existing knowledge of how people learn. Such a systems approach attempts to mould the input to a course in such a way as to enable the optimum assimilation of knowledge and skills to take place during the learning

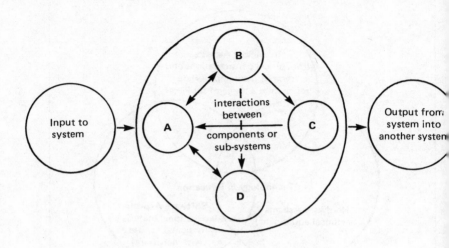

Figure 1.2 **A typical system**

process and hence maximize the quality of the output. It is to the various aspects of such a systems approach to the design of courses, lessons and training programmes that we will be paying particular attention in later chapters of this book.

A simple system for the design of teaching/learning situations is given in Figure 1.4. We have deliberately chosen an extremely basic

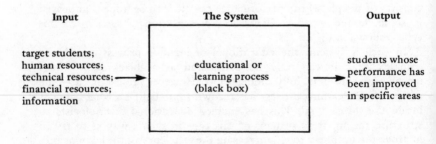

Figure 1.3 **The 'systems' model of the educational or learning process**

Figure 1.4 **A simplified systems approach to course design**

example of a systems approach to course design. Other writers (for example, Romiszowski, in his books *The Selection and Use of Instructional Media: a Systems Approach* (1974) and *Designing Instructional Systems* (1981)) have described more sophisticated systems, but we feel that these would be unnecessarily complicated for our present purposes. The components of the system all have sub-sections, which we will discuss in detail in later chapters.

In this simple model, having first taken into account relevant levels of skills and pre-knowledge which the potential learners should possess, we start with the formulation of the objectives, or desired learning outcomes of the course, for a given target population of students. We will look in detail at the nature and role of objectives in Chapter 3. Having specified the objectives (that is, exactly what we are trying to achieve in the course) we are then in a better position to select appropriate teaching/learning methods by which the objectives have a reasonable chance of being achieved. There are far more teaching methods available to choose from than most people realize — a recent book by Andrej Huczynski lists descriptions of no less than 303 different educational and training methods! The exercise of attempting to match appropriate methods to given objectives is normally done on the basis of a combination of research and experience. The strengths and weaknesses of a range of different teaching methods will be discussed in detail in Chapters 2, 4, 5 and 6.

The next element in the system is the actual implementation of the course. This involves all the logistical arrangements associated with running a course, including structuring and pacing, teaching strategies, selecting appropriate media, and ensuring that all aspects of the course run as smoothly as possible.

The combined result of these first three steps is that a *learning experience* is provided for the target students. How efficient and useful the pre-planning has been can be measured by studying student performance in post-course *assessments*. These assessments should be closely related to the original specified course objectives. Poorly-achieved course objectives should lead the course designers to examine the entire system in order to identify places where improvements can be made. This could involve a change in the original objectives, a revised assessment of students' pre-knowledge, a critical review of the teaching methods used, an examination of the course structure and organization, a consideration of the assessment methods used, or a combination of some or all of these. These deliberations, together with feedback on the course from staff, students, employers, etc can lead to an *evaluation* of the entire concept of the course, which should, in turn, form the basis of on-going cyclical *course development* process. The topics of assessment and evaluation will be discussed in Chapter 7 and Chapter 8 respectively.

The systems approach to course design is therefore no more

mysterious than an attempt to tackle course design through a process of logical development and on-going monitoring and evaluation in order to allow continuous evolution of the course to take place. As indicated earlier, more complicated systems approaches to course design do exist, but these all contain the core elements indicated in Figure 1.4.

Definitions of Educational Technology

We have so far discussed the perception of educational technology from a number of different stances, namely, technology *in* education, technology *of* education, and the systems approach. A number of definitions of educational technology have been produced by different bodies and organizations, and three of these are given below, in order of increasing detail.

Definition 1

'Educational technology is the development, application and evaluation of systems, techniques and aids to improve the process of human learning'.

Council for Educational Technology for the United Kingdom (CET)

Definition 2

'Education technology is the application of scientific knowledge about learning, and the conditions of learning, to improve the effectiveness and efficiency of teaching and training. In the absence of scientifically established principles, educational technology implements techniques of empirical testing to improve learning situations'.

National Centre for Programmed Learning, UK

Definition 3

'Educational technology is a systematic way of designing, implementing and evaluating the total process of learning and teaching in terms of specific objectives, based on research in human learning and communication and employing a combination of human and non-human resources to bring about more effective instruction'.

Commission on Instructional Technology, USA

All three definitions are similar in that each emphasizes the primary function of educational technology as *improving the efficiency of the process of learning.* As discussed earlier, this is normally done on the basis of what is known as a result of research into the nature of the learning process. Each of the definitions implies a technology *of* education interpretation of the role of educational technology, involving a cyclical, systems approach to the design of teaching/learning situations and the use of whatever methods and techniques are judged to be appropriate in order to achieve one's desired objectives. Note also the strong emphasis on testing and evaluation implicit in each of the definitions.

Educational technology, via the systems approach to course design, should therefore be flexible enough to react to new knowledge about the process of human learning, and also to new developments in teaching/learning approaches and methods. Examination of the historical development of the main concerns of educational technology provides an interesting insight into the nature of the subject, so we will now conclude this opening chapter by carrying out such a study.

Development of the Main Concerns of Educational Technology: The Elton Model

One of the most useful overall pictures of the development of educational technology is that given by Professor Lewis Elton (1977). He identifies three broad lines along which the field has evolved, namely, *mass communication*, *individualized learning*, and *group learning.* Furthermore, he believes that each of these strands has consisted of successive *research*, *development* and *use* phases, as shown schematically in Figure 1.5.

In essence, Professor Elton believes that educational technology has undergone a progressive change of emphasis since the end of the Second World War, when it first emerged as a discipline in its own right. Initially, there was a concentration on the techniques of mass communication, then a change to individualized learning, and finally, during recent years, a move towards group learning. In each case, he identifies three broad, overlapping stages in the development, starting with a *research* phase, in which the basic concepts and techniques are developed, then progressing to a *development* phase, in which these basic concepts and techniques are converted into practical teaching and learning techniques together with their associated support materials, and finally leading to a third phase in which the techniques start to achieve widespread *use*. The combined research and development phases have in each case tended to last for roughly 25 years, after which the on-going 'use' phase continues indefinitely. Let us now look at these three major phases in the development of educational technology – the 'mass communication', 'individualized learning' and 'group learning' phases – in greater detail.

The 'Mass Communication' Phase

The first major area of development in educational technology was in

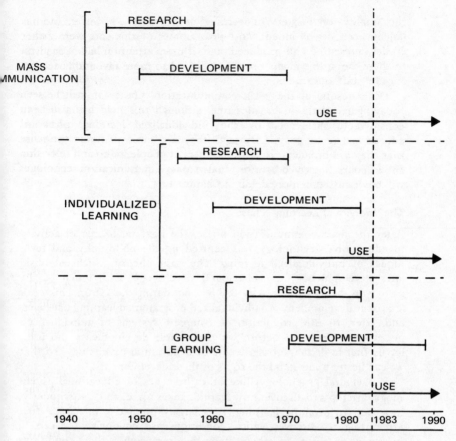

Figure 1.5 **The historical development of the main concerns
of educational technology** (after Elton)

the field of mass communication or mass instruction. The main impetus
of this phase came from a desire to try to achieve economies of scale
through the use of the hardware equipment which was being developed
at the time. The development of this hardware led to the notion that
more people could be educated or trained without necessarily increasing the number of teachers and trainers.

One of the results of this phase was the relatively widespread use of
closed circuit television (CCTV) in an attempt to improve the teaching
efficiency of educational and training establishments in terms of the
number of students taught by a given complement of staff. For
example, colleges or universities with very large classes, or with lectures
which were repeated to different classes, used CCTV to record the
lectures, and subsequent classes were then shown the videotaped
lectures via TV monitors. This practice was not very successful from

the 'quality' or 'mastery of learning' point of view, however, and has largely been discontinued. Most programmes of this sort were rather crudely presented and produced, and, if more attention had been given to these areas, this might possibly have led to more favourable acceptance by staff and students.

Other results of the 'mass communication' phase can still be seen today, particularly in broadcasting, although this field has also been considerably influenced by the 'individualized learning' phase of educational technology. (Although they are 'mass media' in the sense that they are broadcast to large numbers of people, radio and television are, of course, received by individuals.) Mass communication techniques will be discussed in more detail in Chapter 4.

The 'Individual Learning' Phase

After the mass communication phase, the next main area of activity in educational technology was centred on the philosophy and techniques of individualized learning. The basic theory which catalyzed later developments was behavioural psychology, with much of the early work being pioneered by B F Skinner during the 1950s. This work led to the development of individualized programmed learning packages, and, later, to the production of complete systems of individualized instruction. However, before we trace these developments and uses, let us first look at the basic tenets of behavioural psychology, so that we can better understand the roots of these developments.

Behavioural psychology, like other branches of educational psychology, attempts to discover how learning takes place, and, consequently, how best to promote learning. It is largely predictive in nature, first attempting to discover which conditions are conducive for certain behaviour to occur, and then attempting to reproduce these conditions in order to bring about the desired behaviour.

Behavioural psychology theory is based on what is commonly referred to as *stimulus and response*, that is, it assumes that learning has occurred when a specific response is elicited from a learner when he is placed in a particular situation and given a particular stimulus. Learning of relatively complex behaviour can (it is claimed) be achieved through an appropriate series of stimulus-response situations. At each stage, the learner must actively participate by performing a set task, after which he is then supplied with immediate feedback in the form of the correct answer. This is known as *successive reinforcement*. Skinner also argued that each successive stimulus-response step should be small enough to ensure that the learner is almost always correct in his response. Use of these small steps, plus successive reinforcement, led to what behavioural psychologists believed was an efficient way of 'shaping behaviour'.

Skinner's original work was with animals, mostly with pigeons. His later work, which evolved from this, was with humans. Many people have since rejected or at least considerably adapted Skinner's model, but it is important to remember that his work led to the beginnings of individualized learning, which now exists in many forms in the education and training fields. We shall look at some of these in more detail in Chapters 2 and 5.

The first application of Skinner's research to the classroom situation came in the form of *linear programmed learning*. In this type of programmed learning, the subject matter is broken down into a sequence of small steps (or frames) logically following upon one another. Each of the steps represents only a very small part of the concept or skill to be taught. In order to reward the learner, and so, in turn, reinforce the learning process, each step contains a certain amount of information and requires the student to respond to a question about the information, while the small size of the step practically guarantees the correctness of the desired response. Immediate feedback on the correctness (or otherwise) of the response is designed to provide suitable reinforcement. Ideally, it should be virtually impossible to take a step without having successfully taken the previous ones. There is thus only one possible path which a student can take through the frames, hence the name *linear* programmed learning (see Figure 1.6).

Skinner's 'essential' ingredients for programmed learning were the use of small steps, the degree of interaction with the programme, and the 'linear' nature of the sequence. The evidence for the need to use very small steps has subsequently been challenged from a theoretical standpoint, and, in practice, such an approach can very often lead to boredom on the part of the learner. It is now accepted that the optimum step size in learning programmes is governed by a large

STARTING
POINT   STIMULUS/RESPONSE STEPS
'RE-KNOWLEDGE) → → → → → → → → → → → GOAL

Figure 1.6 **The basic structure
of a linear programmed learning sequence**

number of considerations, and, as a result, large and/or difficult steps are often incorporated into modern learning programmes, which may also contain a lesser degree of reinforcement than the early programmes developed by Skinner and his followers.

In the 1960s, another form of programmed learning known as *branching programmed learning* was developed. This involved the use of several possible paths through the sequence of steps (frames), with 'remedial loops' being included in order to correct misconceptions identified from student responses to individual steps, which did not necessarily have to be small. Thus, the topic to be studied was taught in a number of alternative ways in such a branching programme, depending on the performance of the learner. Figure 1.7 shows a simple example of a possible structure for a branching programme of this type.

Figure 1.7 **A simple branching programmed learning sequence**

The type of branching structure shown in Figure 1.7, only very much more complex, is the basis of many of the self-instructional programmes that have been designed for use with the computer since the 1970s. Use of the computer allowed the students to have fast and effective access to what was basically a branching programmed learning sequence. A review of the present role of computers in education is given in Chapter 10.

Later developments in individualized instruction have involved a much more flexible approach to programme design than that which was used in the relatively strict early programmed learning procedures. As we shall see in later chapters, much of the present use of individualized learning has evolved and been adapted in order to meet the specific requirements of particular educational or training establishments or in order to satisfy the special needs of particular students (eg students studying on their own at a distance from the parent institution).

The main emphasis of developmental work in individualized instruction has always been on the production of suitably structured learning materials, or, in other words, software. Early programmed learning developments were largely based on the use of 'teaching machines' as the 'hardware' medium of instruction, but practically all these machines have now become museum pieces. The construction of modern individualized learning materials is now quite flexible, and may involve the use of printed materials, audiotapes, slides, filmstrips, models, overlays, computer programs etc, either on their own or in various combinations. The modern designer of individualized learning materials selects, from the wide range of types of software available, those which he thinks will most effectively achieve the objectives of the learning sequence. Developing the optimum format, structure, and content of this software is thus the main task of such designers.

The Group Learning Phase

While it can be argued that the individualized learning phase probably had a greater impact on current education and training than the mass communication phase which preceded it, there are, in fact, definite limitations to the approach. One of the most obvious limitations is that it is, by definition, *individual*, and, as such, cannot enable students to interact with one another and develop group skills such as discussion skills and interpersonal skills. This has heralded the realization that group learning skills are an important area of concern to educational technologists in their own right.

The theoretical basis for modern developments in group learning is the humanistic psychology that was developed by people such as Carl Rogers during the 1960s — a totally different type of psychology from the behavioural psychology which formed the basis of early individualized learning developments. Humanistic psychology is concerned with how people react with and learn from one another in small-group situations.

A number of methods have recently been developed in an attempt to facilitate various kinds of learning in groups. These generally involve the techniques of *group dynamics*, which allow people to interact with one another in different ways, and most require no specialized hardware and often very little in the way of software. The emphasis is very much upon the approach or technique rather than a reliance on specific types of hardware or software.

At the time of writing, group learning has only recently approached the end of its research phase, and several of the methods and techniques that have been evolved in an attempt to facilitate this type of learning (games, simulations and interactive case studies, for example) are currently under active development. Techniques of this type will be discussed in detail in Chapter 6.

Summary of the Main Features of Mass, Individualized and Group Learning

A summary of the main features of the three aspects of educational technology that are included in the Elton model is given in Figure 1.8. As has already been stated, the results of each of these three phases are still very much with us, and will probably continue to develop and evolve as time goes on. Most of the problems associated with their use are now educational rather than technological. The associated equipment will, in all probability, tend to become as cheap, simple and reliable as possible, while the considerations that determine their use in education and training will depend upon the particular criteria that are considered to be most important in a given situation.

	Mass learning	Individualized learning	Group learning
Theoretical basis	Industrial technology	Behavioural psychology	Humanistic psychology
Model	Economy of scale	Stimulus-response	Group dynamics
Emphasis of methods	Hardware	Software	Techniques
Results	CCTV; broadcasting	Programmed learning plus derivatives; computer assisted learning	Interpersonal skill sessions; games and simulations

Figure 1.8 **Summary of main features of the three phases of educational technology**

The evolution of emphasis in educational technology from mass instruction through individualized learning to group learning mirrors the progression from a hardware approach through a software approach to a technology *of* education approach that was discussed earlier in the chapter. One notable example which Professor Elton believes reflects these changes is the development of the Open University in the UK. This institution, originally conceived during the early 1960s as the 'University of the Air', started offering courses in 1971 using the media of television and radio broadcasts, and there was an extensive period of software development (mainly textual) in order to support students studying on an individualized basis. More recently, there has been a much greater concern with providing situations for closer contact with other students and with tutors, and there has generally been a more human, or group, approach to learning, although such developments have been somewhat restricted owing to financial considerations. Although the Open University has always used all three teaching methods (mass communication, individualized learning and group learning) in its courses, there is no doubt that there has been a gradual change of emphasis over the years, and that first individualized learning, and then, more recently, group learning, gradually came to play much more important roles than were originally envisaged. In its evolution, the Open University thus represents a microcosm of educational technology itself.

Other Areas in which Education Technology has Developed

Useful as Elton's model is, there are those who correctly criticize it as being incomplete, and taking insufficient account of the evolving social and technological contexts over the timespan charted. For example, it makes no recognition of the development of other important concerns of educational technology such as the management of innovation and the development of student study skills, both of which will now be examined.

The Management of Innovation

Most of the work of the educational technologist is, by definition, innovative. Whether the innovation in question is on a small scale (for example, the development of a tape-slide programme) or much more ambitious (eg the planning of a distance learning course), the success in establishing the innovation as part of the overall educational framework depends on a wide variety of factors (the quality of the innovation, the nature of the potential users, political factors, administrative arrangements etc). Indeed, many highly promising educational innovations have foundered and died because the implementation of the innovation was mismanaged.

As a consequence, the effective management and implementation of innovation has recently been of increasing concern to educational technologists, most of whom have experienced the frustration of seeing many hours of painstaking work failing to realize its potential because of such mismanagement. Indeed, it is not unusual to find educational innovators now spending as much or even more time on fostering an environment in which an innovation can flourish as in developing the actual innovation. This concern is reflected in the literature by a rapidly expanding body of publications on managing educational innovation.

The topic is vast and extremely complex, and, in this book, we do not intend to do more than to underline its undoubted importance in educational technology. For those who want to pursue the subject further, Bolam's article in *Management in Education* (1975) is a useful starting point.

Study Skills Techniques

Another area which has attracted the attention of many educational technologists in recent years is the development of student study skills. Obviously, one way of improving the effectiveness of the teaching/ learning process is to increase the efficiency of learners in assimilating the subject matter covered. For this reason, educational technologists and teachers have used the results of educational and psychological research to devise programmes of activities that are specifically designed to assist students in their study technique. Apart from over 100 'how to study' guides that have been written for students, a number have been written for teachers in order to assist them in devising appropriate activities for students. One of the best of these is by Graham Gibbs, entitled *Teaching Students to Learn: A Student Centred Approach* (1981) and interested readers are referred to this.

The sort of areas covered by study skills include organization of time, effective use of time, reading skills, essay — writing and report — writing skills, note-taking, examination technique, and even job-hunting skills. Also, students in distance learning schemes may have special study difficulties which have to be coped with.

The growing interest in study skills development is further evidence that educational technology is concerned not only with hardware and software, but also with the less tangible aspects of the teaching/learning process.

CHAPTER 2

Basic Educational Strategies

Introduction

In Chapter 1, we discussed, in general terms, the nature of educational technology, and gave a brief historical account of the development of the field to date. In this chapter, we will take a look at two broad, contrasting approaches to education and training, within the context of which virtually all important educational technology-related developments have taken place, namely, the traditional *teacher/institution-centred approach* and the more recent *student-centred approach*. In each case, we will first examine the structure of the system that underlies the approach, then discuss its strengths and weaknesses, and finally identify the main teaching/learning methods that it employs.

The Teacher/Institution-Centred Approach

In the conventional teaching/learning situation, the teacher imparts, to a class of students, subject matter which is laid down in some form of syllabus (or, more often than not, imparts his personal interpretation of the syllabus). The classes normally take place at set times and last for a predetermined period, as indicated by a timetable, while the teaching methods are almost invariably of the 'face-to-face' type. The whole system is geared towards the smooth operation of the teaching institution, with little or no attempt being made to cater for the different learning styles and particular difficulties of individual students.

The Underlying Structure

A schematic representation of the traditional teacher/institution-centred approach to education and training is given in Figure 2.1.

In such a system, virtually all the decisions as to how a course is to be organized and taught are made either by the institution mounting the course or by the teacher nominated to take the class. The institution decides where and when the class is to meet and how long each session is to last, these arrangements being tailored to fit in with those

Figure 2.1 **The structure of the system underlying
the teacher/institution-centred approach**

for all the other courses run by the institution. The institution also decides which particular member (or members) of staff will be responsible for actually teaching the class.

The teacher or instructor makes most of the 'tactical' decisions relating to how the syllabus (which is often laid down by an external body of some sort) should be interpreted, in terms of both the specific subject matter to be covered and the level of sophistication at which this is to be treated. Decisions regarding the structuring, sequencing and presentation of the material are also made by the teacher, as are decisions concerning the teaching methods to be used and the pace of the course.

The student normally has little or no say in any of these decisions, and must try to adapt his learning style to the organizational constraints laid down by the institution and to the educational decisions made by the teacher. Finally, the student's ultimate achievement on the course is normally assessed by an examination of some sort, sometimes set externally, with the individual student again having no say regarding how this is done.

Such an approach has its advantages and disadvantages, and these may be viewed from radically different perspectives depending on the level and nature of the course being taught. Let us now examine them in detail.

Advantages

Many of the advantages associated with a teacher/institution-centred strategy stem from the very fact that this represents the traditional approach to teaching and training. Schools, colleges and training establishments are all normally geared to operate via such an approach, and the administrative systems of these institutions are designed to support it. While this administrative convenience is more a reason for the predominance and perpetuation of the teacher/institution-centred approach than an educational advantage *per se*, it is certainly a very important factor. Indeed, any attempt to adopt a radically different approach will almost certainly fail if it is alien to the teaching staff or administratively awkward for the host institution to implement. Most educational and training establishments have decades of experience in operating this traditional system, and students as well as teachers and administrators have become used to it. Also, the 'certification' of learning is strongly geared to existing teacher/institution-centred learning schemes.

Another important advantage of teacher/institution-centred strategies is that they enable institutions to make relatively efficient use of their accommodation and equipment resources and (in terms of time-tabling arrangements) fair and effective use of staff time. A set time-table allows a teacher to tackle a course or syllabus in such a way that the teaching programme fits into the time available, thus making sure that all the material is at least 'covered' — a particularly important consideration when students are being prepared for an externally-set examination.

Within this type of strategy, a teacher can attempt to provide a range of different learning situations for the students, all designed to match the type of material being covered and the level and sophistication of the learners. Remedial and/or revision exercises can be provided, and a teacher may well know from experience, and from his personal knowledge of the class, what will be the most appropriate teaching method to use in given circumstances. This advantage is particularly relevant when one is dealing with young or inexperienced learners (for example, at primary level) where strong leadership is required in order to provide effective pupil learning opportunities. Many learning activities may certainly involve a considerable proportion of individual or small group work, but the teacher remains firmly at the centre, and his experience with such learners is vitally important.

Disadvantages

While sound educational cases can often be made for the use of teacher-centred strategies in particular circumstances, there are many cases, particularly at higher levels of education and training, where strong central control of the teaching/learning situation is hard to defend other than in terms of administrative convenience and teacher/student acceptance. While the traditional system can certainly point to many outstanding successes, cynics and critics of the system might argue that these successes have been achieved despite the system and not because of it. A number of strong criticisms have been made of the traditional teacher/institution-centred approach to education and training, particularly in circumstances where it is difficult to argue a strong *educational* (as opposed to an *administrative*) case in favour of it. These include many of the situations encountered in further and higher education, industrial and commercial training, and, to a lesser extent, secondary school education.

One of the most obvious limitations of teacher-centred learning is that it is, by its very nature, extremely dependent upon the skill and ability of the teacher. While this can be a distinct advantage if the teacher is talented and experienced, it can also lead to severe problems for the students if this is not the case. The control exercised by the teacher is such that, amongst other things, he interprets the syllabus, structures the content, selects the teaching methods, dictates the pace of coverage, and makes decisions regarding the amount of reinforcement material and remedial work to incorporate. Problems may arise in connection with any or all of these factors, and, in many cases, a teacher has only his own experience and intuition for guidance.

Many syllabuses are written in very vague terms, and a teacher must frequently decide upon the level and content of, say, 10 hours of teaching on the basis of a syllabus entry which may only consist of a few words. If the syllabus is written by an external or central organization, some guidance may be obtained from advisers or past exam papers, but the onus and responsibility is still firmly with the teacher. If the syllabus is written in terms of 'behavioural objectives' (see Chapter 3), this particular problem is normally not so serious, since this type of syllabus is generally much more detailed and explicit, requiring less interpretation on the part of the teacher.

Structuring the content is again a task for the teacher, and is usually based on a combination of theory, practical experience, and consultation with colleagues. Even with a small class, the structure adopted is unlikely to be exactly suited to the different levels of pre-knowledge and different learning styles of all the individual students, and the problem obviously becomes even greater with large classes; it is, after all, simply not practicable for a teacher to present the same material in all the different ways that would be needed to match students' individual entry skills and learning styles.

Similar problems are likely to arise with regard to the pace adopted by the teacher, since the students in a class (especially a large one) are likely to differ considerably in the degree to which they have mastered earlier work and in the rate at which they can learn new material. The pace dictated by the teacher will (at best) only be appropriate for part of the class, and, even if he manages to match the pace to the needs of the middle-ability majority, it will almost certainly be too fast for the slow learners (who may, incidentally, have high ability) and will probably be too slow for the high fliers, who are liable to become bored or 'switch off' as a consequence.

Another possible drawback of the teacher-centred approach is that the actual teaching methods that are employed may be inappropriate for teaching towards the desired skills and attitudes. At school level, there is scope for a wide range of teaching methods, but school teachers all too often limit themselves to those methods with which they feel comfortable and to which they are accustomed. Teachers at further and higher education levels are generally even more limited in their approaches, and it is still fair to say that the lecture continues to dominate teaching practice at these levels, often at the expense of alternative methods which may be more appropriate in certain situations.

The amount of reinforcement and revision to be provided is yet another decision that is left to the teacher. It is well established (from psychological research) that the level of skill in executing a given task, or the amount of recall associated with a subject, is very strongly related to the amount of reinforcement or back-up teaching and learning that is carried out. Once again, a good, experienced teacher will almost certainly try to incorporate a reasonable amount of reinforcement into the teaching scheme, but others may either deliberately leave this to the student to do for himself or may be under such tight time constraints to 'finish' a course that the reinforcement aspect has to be neglected.

Problems can also arise from the very factors that make the teacher-centred approach administratively convenient from an institution's point of view. Classes, for example, are almost invariably timetabled to fit into standard time slots — normally one hour in length in the case of the lectures that form the 'staple diet' of most students undergoing further and higher education. It has, however, been established that the attention levels of both teacher and student fall off rapidly with time, and that the optimum time for a straight lecture is between 20 and 30 minutes — well below the standard length. While it is true that a good teacher or lecturer will probably take steps to counteract this tendency for attention to decrease by (for example) introducing periodic interactive sessions into a lecture or using a variety of methods within a given teaching period, in many cases the problem is either not recognized or simply ignored.

A further weakness of systems that rely on rigid timetables, at all levels of education and training, is that insufficient attention tends to be given to the problems or difficulties that are faced by individual learners. Even when practice sessions or tutorials are arranged, these cannot hope to deal efficiently with all such problems, particularly if they originated in a class talk or lecture given some time previously and are not related to the topic that is scheduled for revision at the time. The scale of this problem is again obviously greater with large classes in further or higher education, but it does also exist at secondary school level and in training courses.

Teacher/institution-centred systems have also been criticized on the grounds that they tend to encourage spoonfeeding of students, and give little scope for individual investigation and choice of appropriate topics of study related to a student's own interests. While the spoonfeeding practice can be defended in the case of many school courses, and also in the case of core courses in colleges, universities and training establishments, it is less easy to defend if one accepts the view that one of the primary functions of education is to foster the development of an inquiring mind. It is generally true that teacher-centred strategies at most levels of education encourage neither intellectual curiosity nor an individual student's responsibility for organizing and planning his learning.

It must be emphasized that many of the above criticisms of the teacher/institution-centred approach can be of greater or lesser importance depending on the level of education involved, the particular institution, and (most important of all) the individual teacher. However, while it is not suggested that any educational or training system could (or should) be 'teacher proof', it must be pointed out that the success or otherwise of the teacher-centred approach is strongly dependent, in a number of important ways, on the teacher(s) involved. In this lies both its strength and its weakness.

Teaching Methods/Used

Within the context of the teacher/institution-centred approach, a wide range of different teaching methods can be used. These range from purely expository methods such as the lecture or talk to methods which involve a much greater degree of individualized learning or group work. The important point is that all these various activities occur within an educational or training structure which is organized or run by the teacher, operating within the fairly rigid constraints of the institution in which he works.

As mentioned earlier, the almost complete emphasis on the teacher-centred approach at primary school level entails the teacher organizing and controlling virtually all pupil learning opportunities; this may involve, amongst other things, short expositions to the class as a whole, individual work and group work.

At secondary school level, expository methods of one form or another are probably the most widely used teaching technique, with set exercises, group discussions, practical work and a certain amount of individualized learning being used to back these up.

At tertiary level, expositions in the form of lectures, films, broadcasts etc are by far the most common teaching methods, together with private reading and other individual work, tutorials, seminars and practical work. Tutorials are meant to allow students to discuss individual problems arising from lecture work or private reading, but, if not handled properly, they often tend to become 'mini-lectures'. Seminars that allow discussion of topics within a group and other group learning methods are becoming progressively more popular (see Chapter 6). Practical work commonly takes the form of laboratory work in the case of most science and engineering courses, but may involve anything from the use of television equipment by students to produce programmes, to first aid, depending on the course.

The Student-Centred Approach

While conventional teaching strategies are strongly dominated by the teacher and by institutional constraints, student-centred strategies are designed to provide the student with a highly flexible system of learning which is geared to individual life and learning styles. In such strategies, the teacher and the institution play supportive, rather than central roles.

A wide range of approaches has been developed and used at different levels of education. These vary from systems designed to individualize learning within an existing educational or training environment by extensive use of resource-based learning, to systems where practically all of the conventional barriers to educational opportunity have been removed, so that a potential student can be of any age or background, and can study in places, and at times, which suit the individual rather than the institution. Such systems are called *open learning systems,* and are at present engendering a great deal of interest within the further and higher education and training sectors in the UK.

The Underlying Structure

The basic structure of the system that underlies the student-centred approach can be represented diagrammatically by Figure 2.2, although not all of the factors shown are applicable in every case. In such a structure, the individual student's requirements are the most important considerations, with all the other components of the system being geared to assist the student to achieve his particular learning objectives as effectively as possible.

The relationship between the student and his host institution can vary considerably within the context of the student-centred approach, but we can identify at least three basic organizational systems, namely, *institution-based systems*, *'local' systems* and *distance learning systems*. Let us examine these in turn.

Figure 2.2 **The structure of the system
underlying the student-centred approach**

1. *Institution-based systems*. Here, the students work at a particular institution, with learning facilities and tutor help being provided by the institution on an 'open-access' basis, and the students attending the institution for study at times and at a pace which suits them. A popular system of this type is the *Keller Plan*, which will be described in more detail towards the end of this chapter.

2. *Local systems*. Here, the host institution sets out to offer the student the facilities normally associated with a correspondence course and to back this up with on-the-spot institutional support. Such systems are aimed specifically at members of the local population whose personal situations render it difficult or impossible for them to conform to the rigid constraints of the formal education system. The student does not have to attend the college on a regular timetabled basis, and may use a range of individualized learning facilities, both in and out of college. As in institution-based systems, college learning facilities are made available on an open access basis. An example of this type of system is *Flexistudy*, which is becoming increasingly popular in the UK, especially in the field of further education.

3. *Distance learning systems*. Here, most of the learning takes place

away from the host institution. Individualized learning materials are provided for the student, and tutorial help may be made available through correspondence with the institution or via a local tutor (or both). Self-help groups organized by students in a particular geographical area may also spring up. The best known example of a distance learning system is the *Open University* in the UK.

In each of the above systems, the student has a high responsibility for virtually all aspects of his learning, including (in most cases) choosing the time and place, so motivation must, of necessity, be high. Course material is usually broken up into a number of discrete units, which allow the student to master one section before progressing to the next. As students are permitted to learn at their own rate in such systems, the administrative and tutorial support must be flexible enough to cope with this.

In student-centred courses, the individual course units are often described in detail in the student's study guide. This document may also list the behavioural objectives of each unit, thus enabling the student to have a clear idea of exactly what is expected of him (see Chapter 3). Guidance may also be given on how these objectives may be achieved, and this may (ideally) allow the student to select, from a range of alternative methods, those particular methods which best suit his personal characteristics.

The learning material that is available in such courses may take several forms. It may be mainly textual, in the form of set books (or sections of books), 'custom-designed' material produced by the host institution, or a combination of the two. Easy access to a library (either an institutional library, or, if this is not possible, a good public library) is thus more or less essential for students undertaking a course of this type. Individualized material which has an audiovisual content (for example, tape-slide programmes, videocassettes etc) may also be made available, and so the student must also have access to suitable replay equipment, either at home or through a local college, school or multi-media resources centre. Practical facilities may also be an important component of the course, and these must be made available either in the host institution (or some other local establishment) or in home-based 'kit' form.

An obvious potential weakness of any highly individualized study system is that of student isolation, and, in order to prevent this, some mechanism for providing tutorial guidance and remedial help must be built in. In most systems of this type, each student is allocated at least one tutor who can easily be contacted as and when required. Such tutor help may take the form of face-to-face guidance, telephone tutorials or correspondence, depending on the distance between tutor and student and the circumstances of the latter. The role of the tutor is, of course, vital in any student-centred strategy, especially in the early stages, where the student is trying to adapt to a new style of learning. The tutor is in a key position to monitor an individual's progress and to provide strong support in terms of encouragement and counselling. Valuable support for individual students can also be provided through the formation of small local student self-help groups, where common problems can be tackled on a group-discussion basis.

In any student-centred system, the administrative support of the host institution must be geared towards its smooth operation, otherwise the resulting frustration may prove disastrous. This vital area includes making arrangements for recording and monitoring student progress, distributing learning materials, assignments, tutor feedback etc, handling finance, supporting and training teaching staff in materials production, counselling etc, and handling publicity. In addition, the institution's student services staff may provide vocational guidance, as well as ensuring that the examination systems (if applicable) are available and familiar to the student.

As with the teacher/institution-centred approach, there are obvious advantages and disadvantages of such strategies. The relative importance of these is again very dependent upon the level of education or training involved, the type of learner, and the specific constraints associated with the institution mounting or hosting the course.

Advantages

In most student-centred learning systems, the material to be learned is much more readily available than in a teacher/institution-centred course. The individual units of study can be learned one at a time, and often in a place which suits the individual. In addition, students normally have access to well-prepared, well-tested learning materials; hence the quality of the learning material available is less dependent on particular teachers. As the rate of learning is self-paced, the student is not rushed past parts of a course he finds difficult, nor is he held back on the parts that are easier to master. This aspect makes student-centred learning particularly appropriate for groups that have mixed abilities and/or mixed backgrounds.

Since the course units are normally accompanied by a set of behavioural objectives which spell out precisely what the student will be expected to do at the end of each unit, both student and tutor know exactly what has to be achieved. Such objectives also help the student to focus his work towards any subsequent test or examination.

Within most individualized learning units, a variety of different media (such as slides, audiotapes, models, videocassettes, practical exercises, computer-based materials and textual material) can readily be incorporated. The characteristics of different media can thus be exploited to the full, and students tend to find such a multi-media approach both stimulating and motivating. Much of the material produced for individualized use is interactive in the sense that it involves the student in active participation and in responding to the learning material rather than simply reading, listening or watching in a purely passive manner. This structured interaction facilitates learning and maintains concentration.

The course units are themselves designed to be student-centred, and, in many cases, there are several ways in which the same course material may be approached. Ideally, students can select, from a range of options, those methods which best suit their individual needs, interests and personal learning styles. Units may be produced in a number of formats, from which the student chooses the most appropriate 'package' in order to achieve the required objectives. Depending on the subject matter, students may be able to select the order in which they study the units of a course, although the sequence will obviously be partly fixed in that some units will depend and build on more basic units. Also, although some 'core' material is generally compulsory, students may usually select from a range of optional, remedial and enrichment units, depending on their individual needs and progress.

With most student-centred learning strategies, tutor help, counselling and guidance are generally more readily available and relevant than in more traditional courses. The role of the tutor is absolutely vital in supporting the individual students as they progress through a course. The advice and academic assistance given can in this case be geared to *individual* worries and problems rather than to more generalized group needs. Also, in such a system, the weaker students have the opportunity of receiving more attention than stronger or more independent students. Indeed, one of the most useful secondary outcomes of such courses is that students learn to study effectively on their own, rather than being spoonfed, as is often the case in more traditional systems. It is one of the roles of the tutor/counsellor to help students new to this style of learning to adjust in order to get the most out of the system.

Owing to this close relationship between tutor and student, together with the results of tests on each unit, both tutor and student receive regular feedback on the student's progress. Also, as each unit is successfully completed, both the student and the tutor are assured that something definite has been achieved. This provides regular encouragement and motivation for the student.

On a broader base, student-centred learning systems can provide greater educational and training opportunities for those who cannot attend institutions during 'normal' hours. This applies particularly to those in regular day-time employment and those whose personal situations (for example, dependent relatives, physical disability or problems related to distance) make it difficult or impossible for them to attend regular timetabled classes. Thus, at the levels of further, higher and adult education, a completely new market of potential students has been identified, the exploitation of which may even have implications for the long-term viability of some colleges in these sectors of education. There is vast scope for student-centred courses for training, re-training and career updating. Such courses need be neither long nor certificated, yet can still play a vital role in on-going and community education.

Disadvantages

Since student-centred learning places much more reliance on the active role of the student than does traditional teaching, where the student has a relatively passive role, student commitment and motivation must of necessity be very high. Thus, it may be less appropriate for use with young or inexperienced learners than with older, more mature learners, who have a definite goal to aim for and who enter a student-centred system knowing that they are going to have to work hard and expend effort, not least in organizing their study strategies. Even with a highly motivated group of students, some students may, indeed, never adapt to this style of learning.

There may also be difficulties in setting up a student-centred learning system in terms of the preparation of new materials. Teachers need to learn new skills for the production of good learning materials, and the (often considerable) time required to do this effectively must be found. The difficult and time-consuming nature of this task must not be underestimated. Also, it must never be forgotten that student-centred courses are just as much dependent on good instructional materials as institution-centred courses are on good teachers.

As well as being the producer of learning materials, the teacher has another new role in a student-centred learning system. He is no longer the primary conveyor of information, but adopts a more supportive counselling and tutorial role. This function may be difficult for some teachers to fulfil effectively (or even to accept), and, in many cases, it may be necessary to organize in-service courses and other staff development activities in order to train teachers to carry out their new role effectively.

A further disadvantage of student-centred learning is the rather limited range and type of courses to which the strategy is applicable. Because of the generally prescriptive nature of course units (due to the specification of precise objectives), some may consider that this limits breadth and choice of study. Indeed, most applications of the approach to date have been in introductory courses requiring mastery of basic 'core' knowledge, mainly in subjects with a strong factual content and structure such as the sciences, engineering, mathematics and medicine, and also in short training courses. There have, however, also been some developments in arts-based courses. In subjects with a high practical component, it is often extremely difficult to build in suitable laboratory work, practical demonstrations and skills-related work into essentially self-paced courses. Also, the student-centred approach is not particularly suitable for any type of learning that makes heavy use of discussion groups.

A student-centred course must obviously have the support of the administrative system of the host institution in terms of funding arrangements and day-to-day operation of the course in matters such as secretarial support, correspondence, telephone calls, access to special facilities — library facilities, computer facilities, laboratories, etc — and providing a suitable examination system.

All of these can cause severe administrative problems, especially if the host institution is not geared up to cope with learners in student-centred schemes. All too often, such learners simply do not fit into the system, and, as a result, are not given the same priority as 'conventional' students when it comes to allocating resources and facilities. A further potential drawback of student-centred learning schemes is that any qualification gained as a result may be regarded as second-rate or inferior to similar qualifications gained by traditional means. While this may have no foundation in reality, potential students may fear that society, employers or the academic community at large may perceive this to be the case, and so they may be deterred from joining such schemes.

Finally, teachers must realize that student-centred learning is not a soft-option on their part, and that it requires a tremendous amount of effort in writing and revising suitable units, together with tutorial and counselling duties, marking tests and assignments, and providing student feedback.

Teaching Methods Used

The main teaching methods used in the great majority of student-centred courses are individualized methods of one form or another. Many of the materials associated with individualized learning are highly structured and interactive, although this is not necessarily the case. The materials may or may not have an audiovisual element, depending on the topic being covered and the specific design objectives. A review of individualized learning methods and techniques is given in Chapter 5.

As we have seen, tutorial support is a vital feature of all student-centred learning systems, with the precise nature of this support being strongly dependent upon the situation and location of the individual learner. Some courses may require practical work to be incorporated, but this has to be made as accessible as possible for the student, and may involve the development of individualized kits for use at home, or the provision of more organized facilities within the host institution or some other centre.

Expository methods such as lectures normally have little place in such strategies. However, some student-centred courses have included a certain number of lectures, often on an optional basis, in order to provide an introductory review of a topic or for 'enrichment' purposes.

The Keller Plan Approach

As many readers may have had little or no experience of student-centred strategies, we will now describe the operation of one of the most popular personalized systems of instruction (or PSI). This system, known as the *Keller Plan*, was developed in the late 1960s by Professor F S Keller of Columbia University in the USA, and is an example of the way in which student-centred learning can be used within a college or similar institution.

In the Keller Plan, the course material is divided into a number of units, each with specified learning objectives, and the students receive a study guide which suggests a number of means of achieving these objectives. Armed with this information, students work largely on their own, using a range of self-instructional materials. The study guide leads students through set text books, and contains supplementary notes, worked exercises, assignments, etc. Some units may also incorporate learning aids such as loop films, slides, models and other structured learning materials specially prepared for use in the course. Typically, each unit represents roughly one week's work for an 'average' student, but, as students work at their own pace, this is variable. The student is free to discuss problems associated with the unit with his tutor at any time. For this reason, tutors have to be available on a fairly regular basis. Tutors are normally members of the teaching staff, but they may, in certain circumstances, be students who have previously completed the unit successfully. Thus, the possibility of *peer teaching* can be incorporated into a Keller Plan approach.

When a student feels that he has mastered a given unit, that is, he feels that he has achieved all the objectives set, he presents himself for a test (which may be oral or written) and this test must be passed at a predetermined level before going on to the next unit. With the Keller Plan, a high degree of mastery is often required, and pass marks on tests may be of the order of 80 or 90 per cent. There is, however, no penalty for failing, and students may attempt tests on a given unit as many times as is necessary. After each test, the student and tutor discuss any problems which may have arisen during work on the unit, or during the test itself.

In the Keller Plan, lectures, although not a main element of the teaching, are sometimes used to provide an overview of the course material or to illuminate certain aspects of the topics studied.

Laboratory work (if required) is normally carried out under the direct supervision of a laboratory assistant.

The basic Keller Plan approach has been modified and adapted to meet a wide variety of needs. Peer teaching is not always used; tests on groups of units (rather than on single units) may be included; a high level of mastery is not always required; and the final grades can be decided using different methods. Whatever the variations, however, the essential elements of the Keller Plan are individualized learning, independent study and self-pacing. Although the Keller Plan has been used with a wide range of subjects, the most common applications to date have been with medical and science subjects, usually at college or university level.

The distinctive features of other well-known examples of student-centred systems of learning (eg 'local' systems such as Flexistudy, and distance learning schemes such as the Open University) are described in Chapter 5.

CHAPTER 3

Educational Objectives

Introduction

In the two preceding chapters, we mentioned the key part played by *objectives* in any systems approach to course and curriculum design. In this chapter, we will try to explain why they are so important.

We will begin by looking at the role of objectives in a systematic course design process and distinguishing them from their 'close relatives' *aims*. We will then give guidelines on how objectives can be written, and outline the different categories of educational objectives that have been identified. Finally, we will discuss some of the advantages and disadvantages of an objectives-based approach to course design, and suggest how to set about establishing criteria for choosing valid objectives in a given educational or training situation.

An Objectives-Based Approach to Course Design

The formulation of precise educational objectives is usually considered to be one of the first crucial steps in the process of systematic course or curriculum planning that was described in Chapter 1 and represented schematically in Figure 1.4. As we showed, this is essentially a cyclical process, and we can see this even more clearly if we rearrange the various elements of the system in the way shown in Figure 3.1.

Within such a system, the original objectives on which a course is based serve three basic functions. First, they help to define the general direction of the course and indicate the material that should be covered. Second, they give some guidance as to what teaching/learning methods should be employed. Third, they are of considerable assistance in planning assessment procedures. The objectives can, of course, subsequently be modified in the light of experience gained during the operation of the course; indeed, on-going modification of all aspects of a course is one of the key features of the system. Objectives should always be formulated taking due cognisance of the relevant existing skills and knowledge of the target population, together with its level of maturity and the nature of the topic area in question.

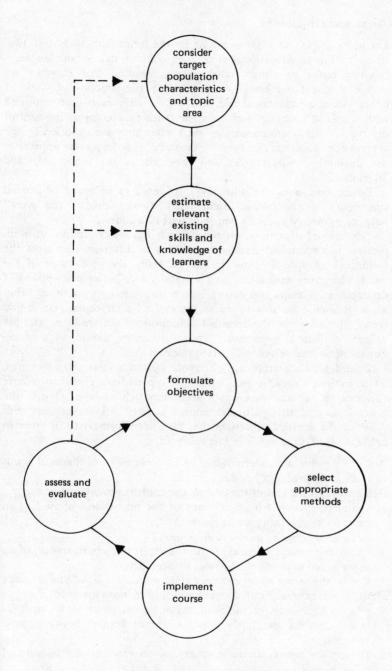

Figure 3.1 A simplified systems approach to course design

Aims and Objectives

Let us now look at what is meant by the terms 'aim' and 'objective' when used in an educational or training context. In common language, the two terms are almost synonymous, meaning 'that at which we decide to direct our energies'. However, in the jargon-filled world of education and educational technology they have each been endowed with a special meaning, and, to some, with an accompanying aura of mystique. This is unnecessary — even when they are qualified by the adjective 'educational', or even 'behavioural' — as long as we appreciate the distinctly separate roles and functions of the terms 'aim' and 'objective'.

Educational *aims* are normally considered to be broad or general statements of educational intent. They usually indicate the overall purpose or desired goal of a course or part of a course.

Educational *objectives*, on the other hand, are collections of more precise, more detailed statements relating to different aspects of the fulfilment of specific aims. In the generally accepted usage of the word, objectives have taken on the status of definitive descriptions of desirable educational outcomes, often expressed in terms of what students should be able to *do* at the end of their course. (In jargon terms, they express the *terminal behaviour* of the students, and are called *behavioural objectives*.) Thus, objectives should, as a consequence, lend themselves to accurate assessment.

In order to illustrate the difference between aims and objectives, let us look at a specific case, namely, a typical basic chemistry course designed to be taught at upper secondary school level. One of the general aims of this particular course is given below, together with some of the detailed objectives that have been formulated in order to help ensure that the aim is in fact achieved.

Aim: to develop an understanding of the properties of chemical bonds and of the principles of bonding.

Objectives: At the end of the course, the student should be able to:

1. Define the term *orbital* in terms of the probability of finding an electron in a given region of space;
2. Define the terms s-, p- and d- *electrons*;
3. Given the atomic number, write the electronic configuration of an atom or ion in terms of s-, p- and d- electrons;
4. Define the terms *ionic*, *covalent* and *co-ordinate bond* and describe these bonds in terms of the electronic interactions involved;
5. From a knowledge of the positions of two elements in the periodic table, describe the likely types of bond formed between these elements;
6. Define the terms *electronegativity* of an element and *polarity* of a bond;
7. List *five* of the important properties of bonds, namely (i) strength,

(ii) length, (iii) orientation in space, (iv) polarity, and (v) vibration, and, by suitable choice of examples, describe each of these properties;

and so on.

Thus, we see that *objectives* can be considered to be specific sets of well-defined activities that a student must exhibit in order to demonstrate achievement of more loosely-defined *aims*.

Writing Objectives

All too often, teachers, lecturers and trainers state or write objectives for a course which are extremely vague, and are, in fact, more like aims than true objectives. Compiling a list of objectives involves carrying out a thorough analysis of the content subsumed under a general aim and listing the chosen objectives in as unambiguous and explicit a manner as possible, so that both student and teacher have a clear idea of what has to be achieved. The precise form of the objectives will, of course, vary considerably, depending on the nature of the people or bodies for whom they are primarily intended (students, staff, potential recruits, internal committees, course validating bodies, etc) but their function should always be that of defining the behaviour expected at the end of the course.

Because of this, the key part of each objective is the *verb*, which should be carefully chosen so as to describe as unequivocally as possible exactly what the student should be able to do on completing the particular learning activity (or group of activities) that the objective covers.

In order to achieve this clarity of statement, expressions such as 'to know', 'to understand', 'to *really* understand', 'to appreciate', etc should be avoided, since they are far too vague to convey the exact nature of the behaviour being sought. Objectives such as:

'the student should *know* the plays of Shakespeare'
'the student must *develop an appreciation* of thermodynamics'or
'the student should *really understand* Ohm's Law'

tell us little or nothing about what the student will actually be expected to do in order to demonstrate his achievement.

Rather, more active, more explicit verbs such as 'state', 'explain', 'define', 'describe', 'predict', 'summarize', 'recognize' and 'criticize' should be used wherever possible, since these can form the basis of much tighter, more clearly-defined objectives. Three examples of objectives that make use of such verbs are given below.

'the student should be able *to name* and *identify* the bones of the human leg'
'the student should be able *to derive* Ohm's Law from first principles'

'the student should be able *to summarize* a 1,000-word article in 50-100 words'

Each of the above examples uses verbs which attempt to define an activity or behaviour in terms of what the student should be able to do at the end of the relevant section of the course. As a result, their similarity to examination questions is obvious. Indeed, in courses that are designed using an approach similar to that shown in Figure 3.1, the performance of students in examinations and other forms of assessment provides important information about the suitability of the objectives chosen — information that can be used as a starting point in the next cycle of the course development process. It is no coincidence that, in courses where detailed objectives are *not* clearly stated and made available to the students, the latter place great reliance on past exam papers in order to try to identify the behaviour that is expected of them, that is, in order to determine the 'objectives' of the course.

The Magerian Approach to Writing Objectives

The case for writing very tightly constructed behavioural objectives as an integral part of course, curriculum and lesson design has been strongly influenced by the leading proponent of such objectives — the American psychologist Robert F Mager. His definitive work on the subject, *Preparing Instructional Objectives* (1962), triggered off a 'bandwagon' movement during the late 1960s and early 1970s, a movement that led to the widespread adoption of a rigorous objectives-based approach to the design of courses and teaching materials. Although Mager's stringent rules for formulating objectives are not so strictly adhered to nowadays, his influence still remains strong in many areas of education and training.

According to Mager and his followers, an objective should be written in clear, unambiguous terms that any teacher or student can understand without the need for further explanation, and should include the following three basic elements:

1. It should state what the student should be able to *do* at the end of the learning experience (ie should specify the required *terminal behaviour*).
2. It should state the *conditions* or *constraints* under which this behaviour is to be exhibited.
3. It should give a clear indication of the minimum *standard of performance* that is considered acceptable.

Two examples of objectives that have been written in this fashion are given below, and, in each case, we have identified each of the three elements that are required by Mager 'purists'.

(a) 'The student should be able to weigh an object (*element 1*) of less than 100 grams using a single-pan balance (*element 2*) and obtain the correct answer to four decimal places at least nine times out of 10 (*element 3*)'.

(b) 'The recruit must be able to fire five shots from a standard-issue rifle (*element 1*) in 20 seconds at a standard circular target 50 metres away (*element 2*) scoring at least four bullseyes (*element 3*)'.

Formulating objectives in clear, unambiguous behavioural terms can be deceptively difficult, requiring a considerable amount of skill and practice. Clearly, if Mager's criteria were rigidly adhered to, drawing up a full list of objectives for a teaching or training course would be an onerous and time-consuming task, and the resulting list would probably be highly cumbersome and off-putting. Partly for this reason, there has been a move away from the strict Magerian position in recent years, and, although writers of objectives still try to define the required terminal behaviour as explicitly as possible, they often omit the specifications of the conditons under which the behaviour should be achieved and the minimum satisfactory performance.

This relaxation of Mager's criteria has been particularly pronounced in the case of institution-centred courses in the higher education sector. Here, it is often felt that the wide range and complexity of the subject matter make the writing of highly-specific Mager objectives impracticable, quite apart from the fact that they impose (in many people's opinion) unacceptable constraints on academic freedom.

On the other hand, in the case of teaching/learning situations which are more task-oriented or more student-centred in the sense that the student works largely alone, there is no doubt that Mager-type objectives do help to provide the student with a clear idea of *what* has to be achieved, *how* this has to be achieved, and the *level of performance* that is required to demonstrate satisfactory achievement of the objective. As Mager himself put it: 'If you don't know where you're heading, you'll probably end up someplace else, and not even know it'.

Skills Analysis

During the 1950s and 1960s, the 'skills analysis' or 'task analysis' approach, which was originally championed by W D Seymour, became very popular as a means of breaking down a complex task into a sequence of its component parts. Such a breakdown is intended to enable a systematic training system to be devised by re-assembling the various identified sub-skills, and it can also allow for the precise specification of objectives for each stage, as well as for the identification of any necessary pre-knowledge.

Once the separate sub-skills related to a specific overall task have been identified, they can be described, in sequence, on a chart of the type shown in Figure 3.2. This gives a skills analysis for the task of

Figure 3.2 **Skills analysis for the operation of a micrometer**

training a person to use a micrometer, a mechanical instrument that is used for measuring the size of small objects with a high degree of precision. The figure clearly illustrates the hierarchical nature of the various skills identified.

These sub-skills can be translated into objectives for the training system, and careful analysis of such a range of skills can usually be used to identify an optimal sequence for instruction. This approach also identifies skills down to, and below, the prerequisite level, so that appropriate pre-knowledge and existing skills on the part of the learners can be taken into account when designing the training programme.

The skills analysis approach has been particularly widely used in industrial and manipulative skills training contexts, and, indeed, is well-suited to many training situations in these areas. However, many other educational and training aims are much less well suited to a skills analysis approach, and instructional designers should be fully aware that there are definite limitations to its use and potential dangers in its mis-use. Indeed, in a wide range of circumstances it is by no means the best, or easiest, or most valid way of determining course design objectives.

Types of Objectives

With the general acceptance of objectives as a key component of the systems approach to course and curriculum design, it has become fashionable to think in terms of broad types of objectives. Here, another American, Benjamin Bloom, has been extremely influential in clarifying and organizing educational thought regarding the classification of objectives. Bloom and his co-workers contend that objectives are attainable in three distinct areas, or domains, to which they have assigned suitably impressive jargon names: the *cognitive domain*, *affective domain* and *psychomotor domain*. At the risk of over-simplification, these can be thought of as being respectively concerned with *knowledge-related objectives*, *attitude-related objectives* and *motor skills-related objectives*. Let us now examine them in more detail.

1. *The cognitive domain.* This contains objectives which are related to the acquisition and application of knowledge and understanding, and probably includes the great majority of educational and training objectives. As we will show later, Bloom has further categorized this area into six sub-areas, which he claims form an ascending hierarchy, with each sub-area dealing with a progressively higher level of sophistication at which knowledge and understanding can be displayed. An example of a simple cognitive objective might be: 'The student should be able to calculate all the dimensions of a triangle given the lengths of two sides and the size of the angle between them'.

2. *The affective domain.* This contains objectives that are concerned with attitudes and feelings which are brought about as a result of some educational process. Bloom has again further divided this domain into sub-areas, in this case five in number, which he again believes to form an ascending educational hierarchy. In general, affective objectives are much less easy to formulate than cognitive objectives, since the behaviour expected is often difficult to identify and virtually impossible to quantify. Also, although they are often just as important as cognitive objectives (more so, in some cases), they can be extremely difficult to teach towards in a formal educational situation. An example of an affective objective might be: 'The trainee lecturer should learn to exercise empathy when counselling students'.

3. *The psychomotor domain.* This contains objectives that deal with the development of manipulative or physical skills — such as measuring, setting up and using equipment, using tools, drawing graphs, and so on. An example might be: 'The student should be able to assemble and use the distillation apparatus provided'.

Although these three areas might, at first sight, seem to constitute neat and distinct packages, real life does not allow things to be quite so simple, and the domains do, in fact, interact to a considerable extent. For example, working in a science laboratory or driving a car both involve a broad spectrum of objectives drawn from all three domains, namely, the acquisition and application of knowledge (cognitive domain), the development of appropriate attitudes to safety, together with responsibility and confidence (affective domain), and, of course, the development of manipulative ability and motor skills (psychomotor domain). Also, it is normally virtually impossible to bring about desirable attitude changes without an associated increase in knowledge, while, conversely, the development of a positive attitude to work or study will almost invariably exert a favourable influence on the uptake of knowledge. Thus, the cognitive and affective domains are, in fact, intimately linked, and cannot really be considered in isolation. Similarly, the psychomotor domain has links with each of the other domains — albeit not quite such strong ones.

Bloom's Taxonomies of Educational Objectives

Let us now take a closer look at the two highly-influential *Taxonomies of Educational Objectives* that have been published by Bloom and his co-workers. The first, which dealt with the cognitive domain, was published in 1956, while the second, which covered the affective domain, appeared in 1964 (see the Bibliography for further details).

Of the two books, the one dealing with the alleged hierarchical structure of the cognitive domain has been by far the more influential, having had a considerable effect on both curriculum planning and assessment. Bloom's six sub-divisions of the cognitive domain are listed below, in order of increasing sophistication of the mental processes involved.

1. *Knowledge.* The lowest level of cognitive objective. To demonstrate the attainment of objectives at this level, students would be expected to perform such tasks as name the parts of an object, point out a certain object, state a definition, recognize a phenomenon when it is seen, etc.
2. *Comprehension.* The lowest level of understanding. Activities demonstrating comprehension include selecting an example of a particular phenomenon, giving reasons for a phenomenon, classifying objects into categories, extrapolating trends, translating verbal material into symbolic statements, etc.
3. *Application.* The application of theoretical statements in real situations. Examples would be for the student to calculate a mathematical result, perform a standard task, use a particular set of rules and procedures, predict the result of a proposed course of action, etc.
4. *Analysis.* This involves the breakdown of material into its constituent parts, including the ability to analyse elements and relationships of elements, compare and contrast alternatives, justify the adoption of certain procedures, etc.
5. *Synthesis.* This involves the combination of elements or components to form new structured wholes. Skills involved include the ability to write an original essay, propose ways of testing hypotheses, derive mathematical generalizations, etc.
6. *Evaluation.* According to Bloom, the highest level of cognitive objective, involving making judgements (quantitative and qualitative) about the extent to which material satisfies evidence or criteria. This includes the abilities to indicate logical fallacies in arguments, argue for or against a proposal, compare a work with others of recognized excellence, etc.

What Bloom is suggesting is the existence of a continuum in the development of cognitive attainment from the simple and concrete to the complex and abstract. The six levels should be thought of as milestones on the way to perfect accomplishment rather than watertight categories with specific and exclusive characteristics. By writing objectives at these different levels, a course designer should be able to generate appropriate types of task or assessment questions. The taxonomy does not, incidentally, make any attempt to formulate general rules about how one should teach in order to achieve particular objectives.

Attempts to validate Bloom's taxonomy have, in general, proved inconclusive. However, the results of much of the research which has been done tends to cast doubt on the validity of some of the basic assumptions that were made by Bloom in compiling the taxonomy.

A case in point is the assumption that the categories are hierarchically arranged, which is acceptable only if the hierarchy is viewed as progressing unevenly from low cognitive levels to higher cognitive levels. For example, the mental processes that are involved in moving from comprehension to application appear to be different in character and more sharply defined than those that are involved in moving from knowledge to comprehension or from application to analysis. Indeed, many educationalists now describe cognitive skills as either *lower cognitive* or *higher cognitive*, rather than referring specifically to one of Bloom's six sub-areas.

Bloom's classification for the affective domain is given below, again in ascending, hierarchical order.

1. *Receiving.* Developing an awareness of, and willingness to receive, certain stimuli such as the aesthetic factors of a subject.
2. *Responding.* Showing active attention at a low level, ie taking an interest.
3. *Valuing.* Perceiving phenomena as having worth, and revealing behaviour consistent with this attitude.
4. *Organization.* Conceptualization of values and ordered relationships between values.
5. *Characterization.* Organization of values into a total and consistent philosophy.

To date, very little research designed to test the validity of this proposed hierarchy has been carried out, largely because of the intrinsic difficulties associated with carrying out quantitative measurements of affective changes.

Despite the above reservations regarding their validity, Bloom's taxonomies have been of great value (particularly in the cognitive domain) in that they have provided a useful formalized classification of objectives in an area where formalization is difficult. Their main use has been in analysing objectives and as diagnostic tools rather than as prescriptive tools for setting objectives. Two areas where the taxonomies have had a particularly important impact are *curriculum design* and *assessment*.

In curriculum design, for example, pre-written course objectives often tend to be concentrated in the higher cognitive sub-areas of application, evaluation, synthesis and evaluation, while the main teaching instruments (lectures and/or individualized study) are perhaps best suited to developing the lower cognitive skills of knowledge and comprehension. Careful analysis of course objectives can point to the need for adopting a much broader range of teaching methods designed to help students achieve objectives that lie in these highly important higher cognitive areas.

In the field of assessment, it is possible, by matching test questions with predetermined objectives at various levels, to devise a test to precise specifications, for example, 40 per cent recall (knowledge), 20 per cent comprehension, 20 per cent application, 10 per cent analysis, 5 per cent synthesis and 5 per cent evaluation. Such a breakdown not only helps teachers and lecturers to clarify their thinking regarding the selection of assessment questions, but also helps them to avoid mistakes like basing a supposedly high-level examination mainly on the simple recall of learned material or attempting to test knowledge of factual material by setting a question based almost entirely on reasoning. A well-stocked bank of suitably graded objective test questions can be extremely useful in pre-specified tests of this nature (see Chapter 7).

Some Advantages of Using Objectives

Detailed, well-written objectives allow both teaching staff *and* students to have a clear picture of the behaviour that is expected of the latter at the end of a course. This can help to provide direction and stability in the course, and can also help to guard against over-reliance on a particular staff member or idiosyncratic interpretation of syllabuses. It is, of course, strongly recommended that the students should always be included in this pre-knowledge of objectives. All too often, their only clue to course objectives comes from a study of previous exam papers — a situation that is difficult to defend, since students have quite enough problems to face without being involved in academic guessing games.

Nor is this mutual awareness of objectives limited to the more academic aspects of a course, since it is also possible to employ an objectives-based approach when planning laboratory and other practical work. Here, it should, in principle, be possible to provide the students with a clear indication of the desired outcomes of such work before the start of each practical session. The need for such a procedure was emphasized by the results of a recent research project that was carried out in one of the science departments of a large Scottish university. This compared the tutors' intended (but unwritten) objectives with the students' perceptions of the educational objectives of various laboratory experiments, and it was found that any resemblance between the two was purely coincidental!

Another advantage that clear behavioural objectives can provide is in adjusting teaching methods to facilitate the achievement of the stated objectives. If a teacher has made a serious attempt to analyse the objectives of the course he is teaching, and compares his teaching methods with these, some anomalies will probably become apparent. If he is honest, he may well conclude that the methods adopted have only a remote chance of enabling students to attain some of the stated objectives and take appropriate action. However, objectives need not be restrictive, and, within the framework which they provide, there may be many possible routes to the stated goals.

A further benefit which can arise from a clear statement of objectives is that a teacher who is in possession of such objectives should be in a much better position to decide how they may be assessed, since he should know exactly what behaviour he is supposed to be assessing. Different types of behaviour require different forms of assessment, and methods that may be highly appropriate for assessing lower cognitive skills such as knowledge and understanding may well be far less suitable for assessing higher-level skills such as reasoning, creative thinking and logical presentation. This topic will be discussed in detail in Chapter 7.

It is not, of course, being suggested that *all* the objectives of a course can be assessed in a quantitative manner; indeed, in some cases, it is difficult to assess them at all, particularly in the case of those that lie in the affective rather than the cognitive domain. Nevertheless, it is becoming increasingly widely accepted that non-assessable affective objectives of this type are an extremely important component of most courses, and may, in some cases, be the longest-lasting and most beneficial outcomes of the course. Thus, it is highly desirable that such objectives be included in the list of course objectives; even though they cannot all be formally assessed, they do at least help give direction to the course, as well as focusing attention on the need to use teaching methods that are capable of achieving them.

Finally, the very act of sitting down to write a list of course objectives can be an extremely useful staff development exercise in its own right. It not only forces a teacher to think deeply about what he is trying to achieve, but, in many cases, also makes him take the first step towards a systematic approach to course design and course monitoring.

Some Weaknesses of the Objectives-Based Approach

One danger of adopting an objectives-based approach to course design is that the objectives may be given greater status than they deserve. Despite their name, objectives are anything but 'objective' in the manner in which they are selected and written, since both processes are usually highly subjective in character. Thus, objectives should never be treated as if they are in any way sacrosanct; they are, after all, merely the end result of a value judgement on someone's part.

Another danger inherent in a thorough-going objectives-based approach is that teaching and learning may become so prescribed that spontaneity withers and initiative is stifled. Also, a total concentration on the achievement of clearly-defined objectives may lead to the production of students who are certainly well-trained in specific areas, but who lack the broad spectrum of abilities, skills and desirable attitudinal traits that are normally associated with a balanced, 'rounded' education. When a student is being trained in a skill where straight-forward mastery is required, for example, learning the rules for naming chemical compounds or learning how to operate complex machinery, a rigid set of behavioural objectives is usually very much in order. Also, when a piece of individualized instruction involving, say, written or tape-slide material is being designed and evaluated, a clear set of objectives is always extremely valuable to both learner and designer. However, when a teacher is concerned with the outcomes of education in its broadest sense, there are many aspects which defy circumscription in the form of set objectives. Indeed, we would argue that it is sheer nonsense to suggest that a teacher should only teach towards that which can be formulated in terms of Mager-type objectives or that which can be rigidly assessed. If we accept the definition of education as 'what is left after the facts have been forgotten', this argument becomes even more compelling. It is obviously the case that some subjects (eg mathematics and science) lend themselves more readily to a 'straight' objectives approach than others (eg art appreciation and debating); nevertheless, even in these subjects, it is important that the teaching/learning process should have a *direction*.

A less fundamental, but very practical, weakness of the objectives-based approach is that objectives can be difficult and time-consuming to construct. Many teachers may feel that they simply do not have the time to develop well-written objectives, and, if insufficient time and skill are devoted to the task, the net result may well be anything but beneficial to the course. For example, it is usually the simplest and perhaps the most trivial objectives that are the easiest to write in standard format; this may lead to low-grade objectives of this type dominating a course at the expense of potentially more valuable goals which are not included simply because they are less easy to encapsulate in unambiguous statements.

Choosing Valid Objectives

We have indicated above that the precise choice of objectives for a course is essentially a subjective decision based on a series of value judgements. The factors and requirements involved in the compilation of a set of course objectives have their roots in a number of sources, listed below.

1. *Vocational needs.* There may be a need for certain specific skills and knowledge, dictated by a student's possible future job, profession or social role.
2. *The cultural view.* The concept of 'the subject for its own sake', which views education as passing on a body of accepted knowledge.
3. *Social factors.* The knowledge, skills and attitudes held to be desirable by the society in which the student lives.

4. *Student factors.* The individual student may be interested in attaining certain knowledge or skills.
5. *Teacher factors.* The individual teacher may have personal interests and preferences which he feels should be built into the course.

Faced with these often conflicting factors, we see how vital it is to carry out a careful and critical analysis of each in order to establish their relative importance — both during the formulation of objectives for a course and throughout the subsequent process of course design and development. The level and function of the course itself will also exert a considerable influence on these matters, as will the nature of the institution or environment in which it is to be operated. Finally, we should always remember that course development is a cyclical process, and that all objectives should themselves be reappraised at regular intervals — not only to determine whether they are being achieved in the course, but also to establish whether they continue to reflect a valid interpretation of the course's direction and emphasis; if they do not, then it is time to change them.

CHAPTER 4

Mass Instruction Techniques

Introduction

Let us suppose that a teacher, lecturer or trainer is involved in the development of a new course or curriculum, and, as a first step, has produced a clear set of objectives. The next step is to choose the most appropriate methods for achieving these objectives, and just how he might go about this task will be the topic of the next three chapters of this book. The particular methods that are eventually chosen will depend on a large number of factors, including the detailed nature of the objectives in question, institutional constraints, student characteristics and his own preferences. They will, however, be of three broad types, namely, those associated with *mass instruction*, *individualized learning* and *group learning*, so we will look at these three types of instructional methods in turn.

In this chapter, we will examine some of the more common methods that are used in mass instruction, that is, in the teaching or training of relatively large groups or classes, usually within the context of a teacher/institution-centred course of some sort. First, we will look at the methods themselves, identifying their main characteristics and discussing their respective strengths and weaknesses. Then, we will turn our attention to the various audiovisual media that can be used to support these different methods, dealing in turn with non-projected visual aids, projected visual aids and audio aids.

The Main Mass Instruction Methods

In this section, we will discuss four of the most common methods that are used in mass instructional situations, namely lectures and talks, practical activities, film and video presentations, and educational broadcasts. Within each of these categories, there are a wide variety of different approaches and tactics that may be adopted, but, as we will see, a number of generalizations can be made, and it is on these that we will concentrate. It should be emphasized at this point that the techniques of 'mass instruction' may well be received by small numbers of students (or even by individual students) as well as by large audiences. Thus, the term 'mass' is used more in a qualitative than a strictly quantitative sense.

Lectures and Talks

Although the term 'lecture' is normally used in the context of tertiary education and training, we will take it to cover any situation in which a teacher or instructor talks to (or at) a class of pupils, students or trainees. Despite a plethora of other teaching methods being available, the face-to-face talk or 'lecture' still holds a central position at many levels of education, and will undoubtedly continue to do so for some considerable time to come. It is therefore rather surprising that comparatively little is known about the educational effectiveness of the lecture. Also, what little information has been established as a result of controlled, empirical research is not particularly widely known, especially among practising teachers, lecturers and trainers. Thus, the strength with which opinions on the usefulness of lectures are held is frequently greater than the strength of the grounds upon which these opinions are based! In addition, the problem of defining what constitutes a 'good lecture' is exceeedingly difficult, since several research studies have indicated that individual students appreciate not only different, but sometimes conflicting things in a lecture.

SOME ADVANTAGES OF THE LECTURE METHOD

Undoubtedly, one of the reasons why the lecture has retained its dominant place in the educational and training scene is that the method appears to be highly cost-effective, since it enables high student/staff ratios to be achieved; 100 students can, for example, be taught just as effectively as 10 in a lecture situation.

Another point in the lecture's favour is that it appears to be just as effective as other teaching methods at conveying information *when well done*. The majority of studies which have compared the lecture method with other methods designed for developing lower cognitive skills have not been able to detect any difference that is statistically significant, and those studies which have shown a measurable difference have been approximately equally distributed either way. (It is worth pointing out, however, that most teaching methods are not particularly efficient at imparting information; a common figure quoted is approximately 40 per cent recall of information by students immediately after a lecture —and, unless reinforcement takes place, even this ability to recall material falls off rapidly with time.)

Many teachers feel more comfortable using the lecture method than they do using other, perhaps more participative, methods. Also, the lecture method appears to be popular with students, although this may be largely due to familiarity and to a lack of appreciation of the possible advantages of alternative methods of teaching.

SOME WEAKNESSES OF THE LECTURE METHOD

One aspect of the lecture method which causes some concern is that its effectiveness is inevitably very dependent on the skills of the individual lecturer. The ability to organize and explain a topic does not come naturally except to a fortunate few individuals, while fewer still are able to capitalize on their personal charisma in order to 'capture' their audiences. George Brown's book *Lecturing and Explaining* (1978) gives many useful guidelines on the art of structuring and presenting a lecture, and is heartily commended to all who lack these skills.

In addition, the resultant effectiveness of a lecture relies heavily on the ability of the students to learn from it. Here, the range of study skills mentioned in Chapter 1 are extremely important, and it may well be necessary to make a conscious effort to inculcate good study techniques before the full educational potential of the lecture method is realized.

Research studies, which are specified and explained in detail in McLeish's book *The Lecture Method* (1968), aimed at comparing the lecture with other teaching methods have shown that it is not particularly effective in developing high-level thought amongst students (Bloom's higher cognitive areas), nor at teaching towards desirable attitudes (Bloom's affective domain) compared with methods of learning such as group discussions or participative simulations which involve more student activity. Thus, the lecture may not be quite as economical as it is generally believed to be in terms of achieving the entire range of course objectives, especially if a teacher does not appreciate the limitations of lectures and fails to combine their use with other, more active, methods.

Many of the disadvantages of the lecture method stem from the fact that students are normally completely passive in lectures, spending most of their time either listening or writing down notes. The method is usually non-interactive, although some teachers attempt to get round this deficiency by building in, for example, 'buzz' sessions (short problem-solving or discussion sessions in which the students work on their own or in small groups and then feed back information to the teacher and to the rest of the class based on the task set).

In a lecture, all students are forced to proceed at one pace, namely, that dictated by the teacher, with usually very little opportunity for feedback from the students. This inevitably produces a wide variation in understanding throughout a lecture class, making the method useless for achieving universal mastery of topics. Also, within a lecture structure, individual problems and difficulties cannot normally be dealt with in a satisfactory manner. A related difficulty is that the teacher's perception of a subject is not necessarily the same as that of the students in all cases.

Another problem caused by the passive nature of lectures is that student attention tends to fall off fairly rapidly with time. This fall-off takes the form of an increasing frequency of attention breaks (sometimes called *microsleeps*) in which the student 'switches off' concentration for a short time. The length of time for which a student can maintain full attention to the task of listening and writing is called the *attention span*. In a typical 50-minute 'straight' lecture, student attention span decreases steadily as the lecture progresses. Typically, it falls from about 12 to 15 minutes at the start of the lecture to around 3 to 5 minutes towards the end. Attention breaks usually last for about two minutes, although their pattern of occurrence is affected by a number of factors. It is found, for example, that, if the lecturer includes deliberate breaks in the lecture (practical demonstrations, 'buzz' sessions, visual stimuli and so on), the net effect is that the progressive decline in student attention is temporarily halted. Skilled timing of these variations can improve the attention span pattern considerably, and it is likely that any lecture time that is lost in providing these 'mental breathers' for students is more than recouped in terms of effective student learning.

Thus, for a straightforward, fact-giving lecture, the optimum time for the most effective transfer of knowledge is probably no longer than about 20 minutes, even with comparatively bright students; with young, immature or less able students, it is even shorter. Despite this, virtually all institutions continue to timetable lecture-type classes for much longer periods — anything from 40 minutes to two hours and more.

Thus, if they are to be used to optimum effect, the limitations of lectures *must* be recognized, both by course and curriculum planners and also by the teachers, lecturers and trainers who actually work at the 'coal face'. The latter, in particular, should realize that lectures are much more effective if they are used in conjunction with a suitable combination of supportive and complementary teaching methods rather than entirely on their own.

Practical Activities

Within most teacher/institution-centred instructional systems, laboratory-type classes are a common way of demonstrating the practical elements of a subject and of 'using the theory'. On the face of it, the use of practical sessions in this context would appear to be capable of doing nothing but good; nevertheless, careful analysis of their use is often necessary if the fullest potential of such exercises is to be realized.

SOME ADVANTAGES OF PRACTICAL EXERCISES
For subjects in which the development of manipulative (psychomotor) skills is important, a certain amount of practical experience is obviously necessary. Indeed, in many cases, there is no suitable alternative to

'hands-on' practice. However, it should be emphasized that such manipulative skills must be consciously taught for, and not just allowed to develop (it is to be hoped) of their own accord.

Another strength of practical sessions is that students generally enjoy their participative nature, which may also provide a stark contrast to other, more lecture-oriented classes. Also, such sessions may give students an idea of some of the real-life applications of topics which have only been treated theoretically in lectures, thus helping to demonstrate the relevance of the course as a whole.

SOME DISADVANTAGES OF PRACTICAL EXERCISES
Practical and laboratory exercises tend to be very expensive in terms of time, manpower, equipment and materials. Hence, the reasons for using practical sessions should be well thought out, and they should not merely be used to fill allocated timetable slots, as is so often the case.

As mentioned in the previous chapter, it is highly desirable that the objectives of each practical session should be stated in advance, so that both staff and students know what should be gained from the work. If this is not done, the results may simply be 'recipe following', with little or no understanding of what is going on, or appreciation of the purpose of the exercise.

The design of practical or laboratory work is all too often completely unrelated to situations and problems which exist in real life. Thus, the perceived relevance of such sessions is often much lower than might be possible with a little more thought and ingenuity on the part of the designers.

Although we have stated that practical sessions have the advantage of illustrating practical applications of more theoretical work, it must be pointed out that student-based laboratory sessions may not be the most economical or efficient means of showing these. In some cases, a simple lecture/demonstration may be much more effective. Thus, while basic psychomotor skills may well be taught extremely effectively in the laboratory, question marks hang over the efficiency of the method in achieving other, higher level objectives that are commonly associated with 'practical work'.

Film and Video Presentations

For many years, films have been widely used in education (and, even more commonly, in training situations) as a mass-instructional teaching method in their own right. With the arrival of the videocassette recorder, which makes it even easier to show film-type programmes in the classroom, this practice has become even more prevalent. Thus, an ever-increasing range of films and videocassette programmes are now being made for all sectors of education and training. As well as being a teaching method in their own right, short films and video clips can also be incorporated into lecture-type presentations in order to provide illustrative visual stimulation and variety of approach.

SOME ADVANTAGES OF FILM AND VIDEO PRESENTATIONS
Film and video presentations can be used in education and training as an effective lecture-substitute. They are particularly useful if the content has a high visual impact, where a variety of techniques such as animation, time-lapse photography and close-up work can be used to good effect.

Film and video programmes can provide an impression of life outside the classroom which would otherwise be inconvenient or perhaps impossible to achieve. They can, for example, show lifestyles in other countries, scientific processes at the microscopic level, complicated industrial processes, theatrical productions, and so on.

A professionally-scripted and produced film or video programme may well be better structured than its lecture-type equivalent, and is almost certain to be more visually relevant and more stimulating than a lecture, even if the latter is supported by slides and other visual aids. Further advantages are that appropriate films or videos can help to add variety to lecture-dominated courses, and can be used to stimulate discussion and debate.

SOME DISADVANTAGES OF FILM AND VIDEO PRESENTATIONS
The most common mis-use of films and videos occurs when the media are used purely for convenience rather than for sound educational reasons. The use of a film or video should not be thought of as an easy option, or 'something to keep a class quiet'. Indeed, it is important that a teacher or instructor should carry out a critical preview of the programme in order to check on its quality and assess its relevance to the course. This will enable the teacher or instructor to introduce the programme properly, to explain its context and to prepare for class discussion after it has been shown.

Another possible educational disadvantage of using film and video presentations is that the teacher or trainer effectively relinquishes control over his class for the duration of the presentation, handing over control to the maker of the film or video. This makes it doubly important that such presentations should only be used where they offer some distinct advantage over other, more conventional, methods of teaching in achieving a particular set of objectives.

One practical disadvantage of film and video is that neither can be shown without the appropriate hardware. Also, there is often a financial implication associated with using a programme; indeed, in many cases, hiring or buying a film or video can be quite expensive, particularly if it is to be used in a commercial or industrial training context rather than in an educational situation.

An additional problem associated with the use of videocassette machines to record broadcast television programmes off-air is that there may well be copyright difficulties associated with showing the programmes in an educational or training situation. Although certain programmes are officially classified as 'educational', and can therefore be used with classes, the main television output (parts of which — documentaries, popular science programmes, etc — may in fact have a high degree of educational relevance) cannot legally be recorded on a videocassette recorder for subsequent use with a class. Some of these programmes are, however, available for purchase or hire from the appropriate broadcasting authorities.

Educational Broadcasting

Broadcast radio and television have a long history of use in education and training, with programmes designed specifically for class use in schools and colleges being transmitted by a large number of broadcasting organizations in many parts of the world. In most cases, however, the role of such programmes has been limited to that of general interest, 'optional extra' or 'back-up' material, and it is only since the mid-1960s that such broadcasts have been used as front-line teaching tools. As we saw in Chapter 1, this development was pioneered in the UK by the Open University; since then, it has been used as a key part of similar distance learning schemes that have been set up in several other countries, including Israel, Canada and Norway.

Strictly speaking, the use of broadcast radio and television programmes in a distance learning as opposed to a classroom situation should be classed as an 'individualized learning' technique rather than a 'mass instruction' technique in the sense in which we are interpreting the latter term in this chapter. Such programmes are designed to be received by *individuals*, and, in many cases, incorporate features (such as active participation on the part of the lecturer or viewer) that are more generally associated with individualized instruction than with mass instruction. Thus, they are only 'mass instruction' techniques in the sense that they are capable of being received simultaneously by large numbers of people.

SOME ADVANTAGES OF EDUCATIONAL BROADCASTS

Educational radio and television broadcasts have the same basic educational advantages as film and video presentations in that they constitute high-quality material that can be used as an effective substitute for, or supplement to, a conventional taught lesson as and when appropriate, thus enabling a teacher, lecturer or trainer to introduce variety into a course. They have a further important advantage in that the material is made available free of charge.

SOME DISADVANTAGES OF EDUCATIONAL BROADCASTS

They also share some of the disadvantages of film and video in that they are always liable to be used in the wrong way (eg for keeping classes quiet or filling slots in timetables) and again entail handing over control of one's class to someone else. A further disadvantage is that the timing of such broadcasts is fixed, so that they may be difficult (or even impossible) to fit into the timetable and cannot usually be previewed before showing to a class. Both of these problems can be overcome by recording the programmes.

Audiovisual Media used in Mass Instruction

Within the context of the various teaching methods that can be employed as vehicles for mass instruction, it is possible to make use of a wide range of *audiovisual media*, both hardware and software. In some cases, these are used to increase the effectiveness of the teaching method (for example, using visual aids to back up a lecture), while, in others, they constitute a vital part of the method itself (for example, film or video presentations or off-air broadcasts). As the name implies, an audiovisual medium can be thought of as a vehicle through which a message can be conveyed to learners; the medium, in other words, *mediates* between the teacher and the learner, as shown in Figure 4.1

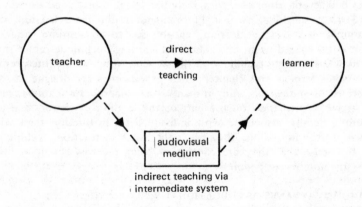

Figure 4.1 **The intermediary role of audiovisual media in teaching**

Thus, it is important that audiovisual media should be carefully chosen for use in particular teaching or training situations because of their suitability and not merely because they 'happen to be available'.

In the remainder of this chapter, we will look at the hardware and software that are associated with mass-instructional teaching methods under three broad headings, namely *non-projected visual aids*, *projected visual and audiovisual aids*, and *audio aids*. In each case, we will discuss the medium in fairly general terms, outlining its main features and identifying its educational strengths and weaknesses rather than giving detailed instructions on its use. Readers requiring the latter type of information are referred to the many excellent books that deal specifically with the use of audiovisual media — Romiszowski's *The Selection and Use of Instructional Media* (1974), for example. (See the Bibliography for full details of this and other books on audiovisual media.)

Non-Projected Visual Aids

As their name suggests, non-projected visual aids are those that do not involve the use of an optical or electronic projector. They include *chalkboards, whiteboards, feltboards, magnetic boards, wallcharts, flipcharts, models* and *handouts*, all of which will now be examined.

CHALKBOARDS

These are often referred to as 'blackboards', although many are in fact coloured — usually blue, brown or green. This is because coloured boards produce less glare and reflection, give less 'ghosting' (marks left when the chalk is rubbed out), and generally produce greater legibility than the traditional 'blackboard'.

Chalkboards are widely used in all sectors of education and training, and are most suitable for displaying impromptu notes and diagrams during a lesson and for working through calculations or similar exercises in front of a class.

A disadvantage of using chalkboards is that they tend to be difficult to write on and read from; practice in writing and drawing on them is thus often necessary. Chalkboards are also relatively messy to use, and even 'dustless' chalk tends to impregnate one's hair, fingernails and clothes. A further minor disadvantage is that the range of colours of chalk which can be used is often limited.

A major drawback of extensive use of the chalkboard in a classroom is that the teacher has, of necessity, to face away from the class for long periods. This not only means that the teacher is speaking 'into the board' for most of the time, but he also loses the advantage of eye-contact with the class — something that can help to convey meaning and provide useful feedback (by enabling the teacher to spot puzzled looks, loss of interest, etc).

WHITEBOARDS

These are used in much the same way as chalkboards, but have a number of advantages over the latter. For example, there is no mess from dust, the range and strength of colours which can be used is much greater, and, in an emergency, the whiteboard can double as a projection screen. Against this, care is necessary to ensure that the correct, recommended markers and cleaning materials are used with a given board; use of the wrong markers may result in acute and even permanent 'ghosting' problems.

FELTBOARDS

As its name implies, the feltboard is simply a board covered with felt or some similar material. Shapes cut out of felt will adhere to the board if pressed on to its surface, and paper or cardboard cut-outs may also be used by backing them with felt, thus allowing the user to write or draw on the shapes being displayed. To save time, felt-embossed wallpaper is a useful, relatively cheap substitute. Heavier materials can similarly be fixed on to feltboards by backing them with special material (such as velcro) that incorporates large numbers of tiny hooks on its surface. Commercially-produced shapes and charts are available for some purposes, although these tend to have limited application.

Feltboards can be used for permanent or semi-permanent displays, but their main application is in situations requiring the movement or rearrangement of pieces, for example, demonstrating table settings, showing traffic movements, carrying out sports coaching, etc. They are also highly portable and comparatively inexpensive.

MAGNETIC BOARDS

These are ferromagnetic boards to which magnetic symbols or shapes (commercially-available or 'home-made') can be stuck. They have the same type of applications as feltboards, although they can also be used in conjunction with appropriate felt-tipped markers, and, at a push, as small portable projection screens.

WALLCHARTS

Large numbers of professionally-produced wallcharts, covering a wide range of topics and often incorporating eye-catching features such as photographs, maps, diagrams, graphs and cartoons, are generally available to the educational and training community. In many cases, such wallcharts are available free of charge from commercial organizations as 'goodwill' gestures, while others can be purchased at relatively low cost. Even if such a 'ready-made' wallchart is not available for a particular purpose, it is fairly easy to produce one's own, simply by using a little ingenuity and applying basic graphic and design skills.

In an educational or training situation, wallcharts can play a variety of different roles. They can, for example, be used:

☐ to stimulate interest and provide motivation;
☐ to act as a source of ideas or topics for discussion;

☐ to be referred to at random in order to produce gradual familiariz-
ation with their content;
☐ to act as an information store and memory substitute.

The prominent display of a chart of the periodic table of the elements
in virtually every chemistry classroom and laboratory illustrates most
of the above uses.

FLIPCHARTS

Flipcharts are best used to present visual information which supple-
ments a verbal explanation. They can be used on an impromptu basis
to jot down key points or to note down replies from class members
to a given question. It is also possible to prepare them before use, and
to 'reveal' key points during a lesson. Normally, the verbiage on flipcharts is kept to a minimum in order to increase its impact.

MODELS

These are often used in cases where movement has to be illustrated
(for example, the motion of the planets round the sun, wave motion
etc) or when a three-dimensional representation is necessary (eg crystal
structures, animal skeletons etc). However, it should always be remem-
bered that, to a large audience in a lecture situation, even the best
three-dimensional model invariably appears two-dimensional except to
those who are very close.

HANDOUTS

Pre-prepared notes, diagrams and tables can be given to students in the
form of handouts. This can save the student from tedious and perhaps
inefficient note-taking, thus allowing him to concentrate better on what
is being said. However, the use of very complete handout notes may
encourage laziness or absenteeism, and, for these reasons, some teachers
prefer to use partial handouts which list the main points but allow the
students to add their own notes in the spaces provided. Thus, the
student has some involvement in the process, and interacts better with
the handout.

Projected Visual and Audiovisual Aids

These include all visual or audiovisual aids that involve the use of an
optical or electronic projector, whether of the front-projection or back-
projection variety. For our purpose, we will divide them into six broad
groups, namely *filmstrips and filmstrip projectors, slides and slide projectors, overhead projectors, opaque projectors, films and film projectors* and *videocassette and videodisc machines*. Let us now look
at these in turn.

FILMSTRIPS AND FILMSTRIP PROJECTORS

Filmstrips come in two formats — *full frame* (as produced by a standard

35mm camera) and *half frame* (which gives smaller pictures, but twice as many of them on the same length of film). It is thus obviously necessary to have appropriate viewing equipment to accommodate the particular type of filmstrip being used. With large classes, a specially-designed filmstrip projector plus a standard projection screen will probably be necessary; most of these projectors can be adjusted to take both formats of filmstrip. With smaller classes or small groups, it may be possible to achieve satisfactory viewing conditions using a *filmstrip viewer* of the type that projects the image being viewed on to the back of a small translucent screen. Most viewers of this type can only be used with half-frame filmstrips, however. Filmstrips covering a wide range of topics are available from a large number of commercial and other organizations, many of these being accompanied by audiocassettes carrying a synchronized commentary. It is also possible to make one's own filmstrip using a 35mm camera.

The main advantage that filmstrips have over slides is that they are cheaper to mass produce, so that a commercially-available filmstrip tends to be considerably less expensive than a corresponding set of slides. They have, however, a number of disadvantages compared with slides, being less hardwearing, and, because the sequence of frames cannot be altered, less flexible from a user's point of view. A further disadvantage is that a filmstrip can become out of date because of a single frame. For these reasons, filmstrips are sometimes cut up into their individual frames, which are then mounted as slides.

SLIDES AND SLIDE PROJECTORS
Ever since the days of the 'magic lantern', slides have been one of the simplest and most popular methods of introducing supportive visual material into a lecture or taught lesson. The original 'lantern slides' (which were roughly 3¼" square) are very rarely used nowadays, having been almost entirely superseded by 'compact' 2" x 2" (or 35mm) slides. These consist of single frames of 35mm or similar film mounted in cardboard, metal or plastic binders, often between twin sheets of glass for added protection, and are considerably easier to make, handle, use and store than their more cumbersome predecessors.

Slides are normally shown to a class with the aid of a suitable slide projector. Nowadays, these are usually fully automatic, having either linear (straight-through) or circular 'carousel'-type slide magazines. Such projectors can also be linked to a tape-recorder in order to enable synchronized tape-slide presentations to be shown.

If properly designed, slides can be of great assistance to a teacher or lecturer in providing visual reinforcement for what he is saying, and are particularly useful for showing photographs, diagrams, and other graphic material. However, they are also one of the most mis-used of all audiovisual media, largely because of the all-too-common practice of including far too much information on a slide. To be effective, a slide should be clear, simple, and capable of being seen and understood from all parts of the room in which it is being projected. If you are in any doubt about the clarity or legibility of a slide, go to the back of the room in which it is to be shown and see whether you have any difficulty in making it out; if you do, throw it away, for it is almost certainly worse than useless.

OVERHEAD PROJECTORS

The overhead projector (or OHP) is probably the most versatile visual aid that can be used to support mass instruction methods, with the result that its use has become extremely widespread and popular over the last 20 years. Indeed, the OHP has now replaced the traditional chalkboard as the most commonly-used visual aid in many schools, colleges and training establishments.

The OHP has a number of definite advantages over other methods of presenting visual information. A teacher or trainer can, for example, use it in exactly the same way as a chalkboard or whiteboard (for writing up notes, showing diagrams, working through calculations, and so on) but with the great advantage of always facing the class. Another important advantage over the chalkboard or whiteboard is that the OHP can also be used to show pre-prepared material, thus enabling teachers and trainers to build up banks of notes, diagrams, etc that can be used over and over again. Such material can be prepared using a variety of production methods (free-hand writing or drawing, transfer lettering, thermographic or photographic copying, and so on) and can incorporate a wide range of presentation techniques (progressive 'build-ups' and disclosures, animation, movement and re-arrangement of items, etc). Overhead transparencies are also extremely compact, and are therefore easy to store in suitable boxes, large envelopes, folders or files. Compared with other projected aids, the OHP also has the great advantage that it does not require the room to be blacked out, thus allowing students to take notes; indeed it can be used in all but the very brightest light (for example, direct sunlight). The OHP is also clean, quiet and 'user friendly', requiring no technical skill or knowledge on the part of the operator.

Disadvantages of the OHP include the fact that it requires a power supply, and needs a suitable flat (preferably white) surface on which to project its image. Also, unless this surface is inclined forward at the correct angle, the image will probably suffer from 'keystoning' (being wider at the top than the bottom due to the fact that the surface is not at right angles to the axis of projection). Unlike chalkboards, OHPs require a certain amount of routine maintenance, and are also liable to break down (generally at extremely inconvenient times), so it is always advisable to have a spare bulb close at hand; some modern machines do in fact have a built-in spare bulb that can be brought into use at the turn of a knob. A further disadvantage is that some users find the glare from the OHP troublesome, although this can generally be overcome by attaching a suitably-positioned shade to the machine.

Apart from these possible 'hardware' difficulties, the main problems associated with the overhead projector stem from the fact that many users do not give sufficient thought to the production of their display material. In many cases, writing is too small or too untidy to be read easily (both, in some cases), quite apart from the fact that it frequently extends beyond the visible area of the transparency (teachers often forget that the illuminated projection area in most overhead projectors is slightly smaller than the standard square acetate sheet, and is some-times cut away at the corners). As in the case of slides, there is also a tendency to include too much information on a single frame. Finally, teachers tend, if anything, to over-use the overhead projector just because it is so convenient, employing it in situations where other forms of visual aid might, on occasions, be more effective.

OPAQUE PROJECTORS (EPISCOPES)
The opaque projector, or episcope, can be used to project an image of a small diagram or page of a book directly on to a screen. This has obvious advantages when, for example, the time or technical equipment needed to make an adequate slide is not available, or when the material is only to be used once. The main disadvantages are that complete blackout is usually required, making student note-taking difficult, and that the projection equipment is usually both bulky and noisy. Although modern opaque projectors have been greatly improved in these respects, few schools and colleges have invested in new machines recently. A further disadvantage of projecting pages of books directly is that the material is often difficult to read, and often contains superfluous information; this unnecessary detail may be both confusing and offputting.

FILMS AND FILM PROJECTORS
Films can be used to fill a number of instructional roles, ranging from front-line teaching to their use for illustrative or motivational purposes. They can, however, be expensive to hire or buy, and, for this reason, custom-built programmes developed 'in house' by schools, colleges or training organizations are now achieving much wider use — usually in video rather than film format.

Most of the standard films that are used for educational or training purposes are 16mm wide, and must be shown using a 16mm projector capable of reproducing the soundtrack, if there is one. Some films are only 8mm wide, however, and this produces further problems since 8mm films come in two formats — *standard 8* and *super 8*. Both formats have the same overall width, but the super 8 film has smaller sprocket holes, allowing a greater area of the film to be used for the pictures. Thus, a compatible projector is necessary for each type of 8mm film, although some 8mm projectors can in fact accommodate both types.

Short, single concept loop films, which can be 'slotted' into lectures or practical demonstrations in order to illustrate or demonstrate specific topics, are also produced on 8mm film, the resulting loop being mounted in a special cartridge. Such films can normally only be shown using a specially-designed loop film projector.

VIDEOCASSETTE AND VIDEODISC MACHINES

The videocassette recorder (VCR) is essentially a television receiver minus a display tube, having facilities for recording television and other video inputs and playing back programmes recorded on videocassette. Nowadays, such machines are found in most schools and colleges, as well as in many homes. A large number of different videocassette formats are now in common use, and since each of these is generally incompatible with all the others, care must be takento ensure that any tapes purchased or hired will match the available equipment. Many machines have the ability to 'freeze' the picture at a given frame, or to show frames in 'slow motion' — features that have obvious advantages in educational and training situations. However, as mentioned previously, there are stringent copyright restrictions on the type of television programme that can legally be recorded off-air for use with a class.

Although nothing like as widely used as the videocassette at the moment, the videodisc seems almost certain to play an important part in future education and training. At the time of writing, most videodisc machines cannot be used to record programmes, but it is expected that the cost of pre-recorded videodisc programmes will, in the long run, be considerably cheaper than the videocassette equivalent. Also, the range of features available on videodisc machines (eg fast search and slow motion reverse) is likely to exceed the capability of even the best videocassette machines.

Audio Aids

Apart from off-air radio broadcasts (which have already been discussed), the basic types of audio aid that are most widely used in mass instructional situations are the *taperecorder* and the *record player*. Let us therefore conclude this chapter by taking a brief look at each.

TAPERECORDERS

These can be employed in a variety of roles, the most important being their use to play back pre-recorded audio lectures or talks to a class or to provide illustrative or supportive audio material in the context of a 'live' lecture or lesson. Audio programmes covering a wide range of subjects can be purchased from a variety of commercial and other organizations, and programmes can also be recorded off-air (having regard to copyright restrictions) and prepared 'in house'. Audiotapes can also be 'pulsed' to allow them to be used in tape-slide presentations.

There are two basic types of taperecorder, namely *reel-to-reel* and *cassette* machines. The former are generally used for making original recordings, and also for editing and mixing work. In most cases, monaural sound is all that is required, but, for certain special purposes (eg music appreciation) stereo obviously has advantages. Recordings made on open-reel machines are generally subsequently 'dubbed off' on to compact cassettes, because these are much easier and more convenient to use in a classroom situation. This also has the advantage of keeping the master tape in reserve, so that a new 'using copy' can be run off in the event of damage or loss.

RECORD PLAYERS

Although they have now been largely superseded by cassette tape-recorders in many schools, colleges and training establishments, record players still provide a convenient method of playing audio material (particularly music and dramatic and literary performances) to a class. Their other main use is as a source of sound effects during the production of audio and video programmes.

The main disadvantage of the record player compared with the taperecorder is the fact that it can only be used to play back material that is commercially available on records. Also, both the machine itself and the records that are played on it are much more liable to damage as a result of careless use or handling. (This is not true of the new *compact discs*, on which the signal is recorded in digital form, but such discs seem unlikely to achieve widespread use in schools and colleges — at least in the foreseeable future — because of the high cost of the equipment needed to play them.)

CHAPTER 5

Individualized Instructional Techniques

Introduction

In Chapter 1, we looked at the historical development of educational technology, and saw how the subject entered an 'individualized learning' phase during the mid-1950s. We showed how this had its roots in the behavioural psychology-based learning theories of B F Skinner, and how it led to the development of programmed learning and to an associated concern with the design of individualized learning materials.

In Chapter 2, we compared the radically different approaches to the instructional process that are adopted in teacher/institution-based learning systems and in student-centred learning systems, showing how the latter are designed with the needs of the individual student in mind. In particular, we showed how they are made more flexible and open by reducing institutional constraints and giving the student greater control over how, when, where and at what pace he learns.

In this chapter, we will take a more detailed look at the range of approaches that can be used when developing individualized learning methods and discuss their respective characteristics. (The comparative advantages and disadvantages of the student-centred and teacher/institution-centred approaches have already been discussed in general terms in Chapter 2.) We will then take a brief look at the different types of hardware and software that can be used to support individualized methods of instruction.

Three Different Approaches to Individualized Instruction

In Chapter 2, we identified three basic organizational systems in the context of which some form of individualized student-centred approach can take place, namely *institution-based systems*, *'local' systems* and *distance-learning systems*. We will now examine these three systems more clearly, and, in particular, will discuss the range of individualized methods that can be adopted within each. However, it should be emphasized at this point that the system of classification that we have adopted below is used purely for convenience. There can, in fact, be a considerable amount of overlap between the approaches and methods that come under the general umbrella of 'individualized learning', so these should be thought of as a continuous spectrum of flexible learning systems, in which the 'sections' that we have identified have no clearly-defined boundaries.

Institution-Based Systems

In most schools, colleges, universities and training establishments, it is generally possible to accommodate some individualization of learning within the context of an overall teacher/institution-centred system. The amount of individualization in the system can vary considerably, from largely traditional courses which provide the option of a limited amount of individualized learning for remedial or back-up work, to highly-flexible personalized systems of instruction, which, although based in an institution, are nevertheless very strongly student-centred. In between, there is a continuous spectrum of emphases, both on the amount and on the type of individualization used.

The simplest, and possibly the most common method, is *unstructured reading* by the student, either at home, in the classroom, or in the library. This type of reading may be actively encouraged by the teaching staff, or may be left entirely to the discretion and motivation of the individual student, but, in both cases, the method is self-paced and fairly flexible. Unstructured reading may prove very useful in reading 'around' a subject and in broadening a student's perspectives. However, unless the student has well-defined objectives in mind, the method may be inefficient in terms of time, effort and results.

In this respect, *directed reading* has a distinct advantage, in that the student's attention can be focused more sharply on those aspects of a subject which are deemed to be relevant and important. Directed reading may be used as a front-line teaching method in its own right, or as a back up to traditional expository methods, and may also serve as a foundation for future class discussion or practical work, or for a 'problem-solving' session of some sort.

More formalized attempts can be made to provide individualized learning material for *remedial* or *back-up* purposes, generally through the facilities offered in an institution's library or resources centre (see Chapter 9). For example, students who have been found to have problems in grasping subject matter taught by traditional methods in the classroom can be directed to a range of structured remedial learning packages; these may approach a given topic in a different way from the original teacher, and will probably also allow the student to progress through difficult areas at a more suitable pace. The format of the packages may be textual, audiovisual or even computer-based, but, in this particular context, they are almost always used to complement and support traditional teaching methods, and not to replace them. Other students, apart from those in real difficulties, are generally also free to use the packages on an optional basis. Indeed, research into student use of the remedial/back-up approach to individualized learning has tended to reveal that the middle ability-to-better students make more use of the available materials than the weaker students for whom the materials were mainly devised. The learning packages used in such systems may either be purchased from a commercial organization or from another institution, or may be custom-made by teachers to support a particular course.

The main advantages of such a system are that students are given access to subject matter that is taught in alternative ways, and that weaker students have a 'safety net' in the form of well-structured learning materials. In addition, students are introduced to individualized study packages as a legitimate learning method.

On the disadvantage side, it is very rare that there are enough suitable packages available to cover all aspects of a course, so the approach may well be piecemeal. A more serious problem is that those students who would probably benefit most from individualized learning material being available for back-up purposes are the ones who are least likely to use it in practice.

Another approach to individualized learning within an institution is to accommodate it within the four walls of a conventional classroom. Such *individualized classroom work* is most common in primary schools, although a number of secondary school classrooms are now also operated in this mode. In such classrooms, the teacher is basically a manager of resources and learning opportunities for the students, who may be learning at different levels and also at different rates. The learning materials may be of a wide variety of types, but, as a general rule, the more content-based they are, the more highly they are structured. In such a system, the demands placed upon the teacher are much greater than when the teacher is in the traditional 'dispenser of knowledge' role, and it is perhaps only a minority of teachers who would feel comfortable in this alternative role. However, in the case of mixed-ability classes in particular, it is a flexible and appropriate method for allowing each student to work and develop to the limit of his capabilities, without either being left behind by the 'high fliers' or held back by the less able. As the teacher is always present, this system also allows each pupil to be given immediate personal assistance if he encounters a problem, a problem that may be specific to the individual rather than to the class as a whole.

One extremely common student-centred method, employed at all levels of education from the primary school to postgraduate university research, is the *project*. Projects are relatively lengthy activities (ranging in duration from an afternoon to three or four years) in which the student works either independently or within a small group. They involve the investigation of a problem of some sort, the precise area of investigation generally being chosen by the student himself, either on his own or, more usually, in consultation with a teacher or supervisor. Throughout the project, the role of the teaching staff is advisory rather than didactic, and it is the student who is largely responsible for making decisions which affect its progress.

Projects constitute an active learning method which allows students an opportunity to exercise initiative, to see practical applications of a subject, to cross subject area barriers, to probe deeply into a particular area of study, and to become responsible for organizing and structuring their activities. One drawback of this method is the difficulty of carrying out a fair and objective assessment of the student's work. This is often done by grading a tangible product of the project (a report, a thesis, a computer program, a model etc), but this may not accurately reflect the total amount of work that has been carried out. It may well be, for many students, that the actual 'planning and doing' aspects are more important educational outcomes than the end product itself.

As mentioned earlier, a number of courses use individualized learning materials mainly for remedial or back-up purposes, in support of more traditional 'front line' teaching methods. A natural progression is for some courses or parts of courses to use such materials as a front line teaching method in their own right. *Individualized guided study* methods involve the student studying out of class (for example, in the library, in the institution's resources centre, or at home) using a range of carefully-prepared learning materials (textual, audiovisual, or computer-based) to achieve stated objectives. Students are normally provided with a structured study guide which can direct them towards appropriate learning materials and provide assignments and other exercises.

The use of individualized guided study for parts of some courses allows teaching staff to use their timetabled student-contact time in a different way. Instead of being almost entirely devoted to information-giving sessions, as is so often the case in traditional courses, class contact time can be used to rectify individuals' difficulties and to provide appropriate remedial work. The time can also be used to investigate the wider implications of the topic under study, and hence, through discussion, attempt to achieve objectives in Bloom's 'higher cognitive' areas, allowing the individualized study methods to cover the more content-related objectives in the 'lower cognitive' areas.

In some institution-based courses, self-instructional learning methods have almost completely replaced more traditional approaches. Learning schemes of this type have been termed *personalized systems of instruction (PSI)*, the most popular paradigm of the approach being the *Keller Plan* that was discussed in some detail in Chapter 2. Although a number of variations are possible, personalized systems of instruction generally involve individualized learning materials, independent study, self-pacing and tutor support.

Local Systems

Two important areas in which student-centred flexible course developments are currently taking place on an increasingly wider scale are *community adult education* and *further education and training*. In both these sectors, local systems of flexible or open learning are being used to accommodate the special needs and particular situations of potential students who reside in the catchment area of a given college. In many cases, such potential students cannot or will not attend formal, time-tabled institution-based courses, for reasons such as distance, employers' attitudes and policies, age, and family commitments. The need to provide flexible educational, training and re-training opportunities for persons who are constrained in various ways has recently been heightened in the United Kingdom by the inauguration of the Manpower Services Commission's 'Open Tech' Programme. This has the following aims:

☐ to open up education and training opportunities for adults (most of them already in employment);
☐ to secure more and better provision for updating technicians and supervisors;
☐ to help employers and employees face up to the challenge of new technology;
☐ to help education and training make use of new technology to provide new skills where they are needed.

The Programme consists of a series of sponsored projects, each involving an industrial firm, a college or group of colleges in developing open learning materials in that particular area. The projects are supervised by a central 'Open Tech Unit', which ensures that there is no unnecessary overlap between them, and that they are properly integrated and evaluated.

Local systems of student-centred learning usually involve a host college or institution in providing (i) a source of learning materials, (ii) a tutorial system, (iii) an administrative system and (iv) a study support system (that is, counselling). The development of suitable learning materials can be one of the most exacting tasks, and is normally achieved via one of three paths: (i) adapting existing material, (ii) providing a study guide to 'conventional' resources, or (iii) developing custom-designed self-contained material. Mechanisms for practical work, student feedback and tutorials have to be carefully thought out; indeed, tutorials are often held over the telephone.

One well-known example of a local student-centred system is *Flexistudy*, which sets out to offer students all the resources of a conventional correspondence course plus local college support. It is targeted specifically at people whose lifestyle renders it impossible for them to conform to the rigid constraints inherent in conventional adult education and training courses. In Flexistudy courses, the student does not have to attend the host institution regularly, does not have to conform to conventional academic terms or years, is able to use a range of individualized learning materials, and has access to tutorial guidance as and when required. In such courses, a whole range of the resources of the host institution are made available in order to complement the correspondence and tutor support. These normally include the library, any multi-media, self-instructional resources centre or language laboratory facilities that are available, counselling and career help, and the institution's administrative and examinations machinery. Although the majority of Flexistudy-type developments have, to date, been at the lower end of the adult and further education spectrum, this is not necessarily an intrinsic limiting feature of the system.

In effect, use of Flexistudy allows institutions to offer courses which students (and employers) want, when students want them, by means which suit their circumstances, and from which they can learn effectively. It is one extremely promising method of meeting the demands of recurrent and continuous education and training, and may even have implications for the long-term viability of some colleges. Against this, the development, organization and operation of a Flexistudy-type course is by no means an easy option, requiring tremendous efforts from both teaching and administrative staff, not to mention a considerable amount of self-motivation from the students.

Other examples of flexible local methods include *learning-by-appointment* and *open access* systems. In learning-by-appointment, potential students in the local community can 'sign up' for a given course and make appointments to attend the institution at mutually-suitable times. Normally, a range of individualized learning materials (textual, audiovisual and computer-based) are made available to the student in the institution's library or learning resources centre. Tutor help can also be 'booked'. Open access methods are less formalized in that the student can have access to the institution at any time. Both methods have proved particularly useful in the field of community education.

Distance Learning Systems

In *distance learning schemes*, all (or nearly all) student learning takes place *away* from the host institution. In some cases, the 'distant student' may be on the other side of the globe from the host institution, and, as a consequence, the student is very dependent on the quality of learning materials available. However, even in such extreme cases, tutor support and feedback on assignments is an integral part of almost every distance learning scheme.

The first distance learning developments came in the form of *correspondence courses*, which still have a place in the distance learning market today. In such courses, the material is almost totally textual, the student being provided with structured course units which direct his learning activities and provide assignments. Students normally receive regular feedback on their performance, and may be required to reach a certain standard before being allowed to progress to the next course unit.

In recent years, distance learning schemes have tended to make use of a much wider range of educational techniques, with *multi-media distance learning schemes* of the type pioneered by the British Open University being developed in many parts of the world. Such schemes can combine a printed student study guide with broadcast material (radio and television), videocassettes, audiovisual learning materials, computer packages, practical 'do-it-yourself' kits, models, books and other textual material. These materials, combined with tutor support (local and distant), student 'self-help' groups and occasional centrally-organized group learning sessions, allow the student to achieve a much wider range of educational objectives than is possible with purely 'correspondence' courses. As well as being educationally desirable, the use of a variety of methods also helps to reduce the strain and boredom of working in isolation.

Media Used in Individualized Learning

In all three of the individualized approaches to learning described above, we have seen that self-instructional teaching materials play a 'front line' role in the learning process, with the actual teacher usually having a managerial and/or counselling role, as shown in Figure 5.1.

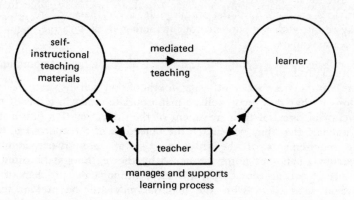

Figure 5.1 **The front-line role of teaching materials in individualized learning**

As with the exposition-based teaching methods that were discussed in the previous chapter, a wide range of hardware and software of varying technological complexity is now available to cater for individualized student learning methods.

We will consider the materials used in individualized learning under three broad headings: textual materials, audiovisual materials, and computer-based materials. Although this distinction has been made for convenience, it is often the case that a combination of media under all of these headings is used to achieve a particular range of objectives in an individualized learning situation. All the media to be described enable students to progress at their own speed and make provision for review and revision; many also provide the student with an on-going check on his progress.

Textual Materials

BOOKS

Conventional textbooks can often be used in self-instructional situations, although, by themselves, they may not necessarily be suitable for enabling mastery of desired material to be achieved. Their relevance can generally be increased by the use of a suitable *study guide* which directs students to the appropriate chapters (or parts thereof) in a range of different books; such a study guide may also include supplementary notes and assignments. Textbooks can also be used in conjunction with custom-made audiovisual materials.

In the case of certain core subject areas, the course material may be adequately covered in normal textbooks, and, if so, such books represent one of the cheapest and most convenient forms of self-instructional materials. Against this, unless participative student activities are built into the study guide, a very passive form of study may result, with the student not interacting at all with the main body of learning material.

STRUCTURED NOTES

One of the drawbacks of using textbooks in self-instructional situations is that they may well be inappropriate either in terms of their level or in terms of their treatment of the subject matter, thus making it unlikely that they will match the objectives of the course and meet the requirements of the students. Use of carefully-prepared and structured hand-out notes, produced by the teaching staff, offer one means of getting round this difficulty, although the problem of low student interaction with the material may still be present unless deliberate steps are taken to counteract it.

TEXTUAL PROGRAMMED MATERIALS

One way of making the students on an individualized learning course interact more actively with textual learning materials is to adopt a 'programmed learning' type of approach, as described in Chapter 1.

Such an approach involves continuous student interaction with the learning material, which is broken down into a number of discrete, carefully-sequenced steps. This approach is especially useful for developing lower cognitive skills, particularly by mastery teaching, since the students receive constant reinforcement of the learning material by self-checking procedures.

One problem associated with the programmed learning approach is that it can be difficult and time-consuming to produce suitable materials, although, for some subjects, a number of 'programmed' textbooks are now available. Also, it can be very boring for students to attempt to cover large sections of a syllabus using only textual programmed material. Because of this, programmed learning materials now often incorporate audiovisual or computer-based material in order to help maintain student interest.

Audiovisual Self-Instructional Materials

AUDIOVISUAL LEARNING PROGRAMMES

Although print-based, self-instructional material still has an important place in most individualized learning systems, many self-instructional learning packages now utilize a whole range of audio and visual media to increase their impact and effectiveness. Such packages may include audio and video tapes, filmstrips, loop films, slides, transparencies, models and practical kits as well as conventional printed material, the particular 'media mix' being carefully chosen with the objectives of the topic being covered in mind. For example, in a number of individualized learning packages that have been developed at Glasgow University to teach three-dimensional structures and relationships, printed material, audiotapes and slides have been used in conjunction with custom-built, three-dimensional models and construction kits; using the latter, students can build and examine their own models as directed by the programme. The precise choice of media is therefore very dependent on the objectives that the package is designed to achieve.

Audiovisual programmes can involve a high degree of student activity, and are, in many cases, used to save tedious tutor repetition. Such programmes can be used to achieve a wide range of educational and training objectives: they can, for example, be used very effectively for helping to achieve mastery of factual (cognitive) material, in psychomotor skills training, and also in the attitudinal (affective) area, eg in anti-smoking campaigns.

A range of hardware of varying degrees of sophistication is available for use with the different types of software mentioned above. A wide variety of expensive automatic playback machines can be purchased for use in institutional libraries and resources centres. However, for students working on their own at home, suitable combinations of relatively inexpensive items of equipment (cassette players, simple slide viewers, etc) are generally just as effective from an educational point of view.

LANGUAGE LABORATORIES
These involve a specialist application of the taperecorder which allows students to interact individually with audio material. Although the original use of such equipment was for language teaching, language laboratories are now also used to present audio programmes in other subjects, and are therefore of more general interest. Basically, a language laboratory allows each student to listen to a master tape and to record and listen to his own responses. The teacher can 'listen in' to any one student, and can communicate directly both with individual students and with groups of any size.

Language laboratories are an extremely expensive teaching resource, and, for this reason, are largely limited to individualized learning within groups in an institutional setting. The main advantage over the use of individual taperecorders is that, within a group, a teacher may 'listen in' unnoticed, and can therefore monitor each individual's progress and identify those who need remedial work.

BROADCASTING MEDIA
Through the media of radio and television, broadcast material is readily accessible to individuals in their own homes. The associated hardware can be used to receive programmes transmitted either through an 'open' national or regional network or through a more local network such as a cable distribution or closed-circuit system. Also, by using the appropriate recording equipment, programmes that are broadcast at unsociable times can be stored on tape and used at the convenience of the learner. Until recently, such off-air recording by individuals was largely restricted to radio broadcasts, but, with the increasingly widespread domestic use of videocassette machines, recording educational television programmes may soon be just as common.

Through the use of suitably-adapted television sets, recent developments in the field of information technology (such as the British interactive videotex system, PRESTEL) may soon play an important role in individualized learning. In such systems, the viewer can interact with the information shown on the screen via a small keyboard, and the learning sequence can be made appropriate to his individual needs. Developments within this area are progressing rapidly.

Computer-Based Self-Instructional Materials
COMPUTER-ASSISTED LEARNING (CAL)
The computer can play a number of different roles in individualized

learning schemes, including front-line teaching, assessment, managing resources and maintaining administrative records. The potential of the computer in each of these areas will be discussed in more detail in Chapter 10.

In an individualized CAL situation, a student may have access to a computer terminal linked to a large 'mainframe' computer, or to a small microcomputer with its own screen or video display unit (VDU). Whatever the hardware used, the computer acts in one of two basic roles in all CAL systems, namely, in a *tutorial* mode or in a *laboratory* mode (although it is sometimes used in a combination of both).

In the tutorial mode, the student interacts directly with the computer, which is programmed to understand and react to student responses. This is basically a sophisticated style of the branching programmed learning that was mentioned in Chapter 1.

In the laboratory mode, the computer is essentially a learning resource rather than an instructional device. The computer can be used to simulate a laboratory situation, to model experiments, to provide data-bases, to set problem-solving exercises, and so on. For example, a student can investigate mathematical models of physical systems, and see how specific factors vary under different conditions which he himself can control.

Computer-assisted individualized learning can be a highly interactive and stimulating teaching method, although problems related to cost, accessibility and appropriate software may inhibit its use to a certain extent. Nevertheless, computers are almost certain to play an important part in many future individualized learning schemes.

INTERACTIVE VIDEO

Interactive video systems are very much in their infancy, but basically they attempt to utilize two relatively well-established teaching media — *videorecorders* and *computers* — in an integrated teaching resource. In marrying the two, the aim is to combine a flexible, interactive and accessible teaching programme (through the computer) with good visual and sound characteristics (through the videorecorder).

A large amount of development work is currently being carried out on interactive video systems, since their tremendous potential for providing high-quality learning materials to suit individual needs is obvious. However, it seems likely that the most important developments will be made by combining microcomputers with videodisc players rather than with videocassette machines. This is because it is very much easier to obtain access to specific sequences or frames of a programme using a videodisc system, since there is no need to wind a tape forward or backwards in order to do so.

As with interactive videotex, the widespread use of individualized learning materials that rely on interactive video for their presentation is still in the future, although perhaps not too far away.

CHAPTER 6

Group Learning Techniques

Introduction

As we saw in Chapter 1, educational technology is currently very much concerned with the development of techniques that can be used to promote learning in group situations. Such methods normally involve very little use of technical hardware or sophisticated audiovisual software. Rather, they reflect a 'technology *of* education' approach, their main concern being associated with directing the process of interactive group dynamics towards desirable educational or training goals. As a result, less tangible factors, such as room conditions, seating arrangements, group size and the role of the teacher, may play an important role in determining the success (or otherwise) of such methods. This chapter will begin with a discussion of group learning in fairly general terms, after which a number of specific group learning techniques will be considered.

General Features of Group Learning Methods

The relevance of group learning techniques in an educational or training situation can often be assessed by carrying out a critical analysis of the aims and objectives of the course or programme in question. If the desired outcomes include the development of, for example, oral communication skills, interpersonal skills, problem-solving skills, decision-making skills, critical thinking skills, and certain attitudinal traits deemed to be appropriate, then group learning techniques may be more suitable for teaching towards such outcomes than the various mass-instructional and individualized learning methods that have just been described. Indeed, one of the major strengths of a systematic approach to education and training is that when objectives are clearly specified, appropriate teaching methods can be matched with them. The types of outcome which can be achieved through the use of group learning techniques will be discussed in detail later on in this section, after we have looked at some basic organizational considerations.

Organizational Considerations

Because of the fact that group learning techniques normally aim to stimulate effective interactive group discussions, it is obviously necessary to use a group of an appropriate size in each particular situation. The optimum group size depends on a variety of factors, including the purpose and nature of the exercise and any constraints that may be laid down by the logistics of the latter; many educational games and simulations, for example, specify the number of participants, particularly if they are highly structured. As a general rule, however, a group should be no larger than about 10 if it is to act as an effective vehicle for promoting group interaction and developing group skills, and, ideally, it should be somewhere between four and six.

In his book *Educational Technology in Curriculum Development* (1982) Derek Rowntree represents the 'group dynamics' that occur in two somewhat different small group situations in the way shown in Figure 6.1.

(a) *teacher-controlled*

(b) *group-controlled*

T teacher or tutor S student

Figure 6.1 **Patterns of communication in two different group learning situations**

In situation (a), the teacher/tutor controls the discussion, the basic pattern being a succession of dialogues between the teacher and the various individual students. This is the somewhat limited pattern of communication that often takes place within a tutorial-type group environment. In situation (b), we see the multi-way communication pattern that takes place in a group-controlled discussion or seminar, in which the students can interact freely with one another, thus allowing ideas to be built upon from within the student group. Indeed, in such a group environment, it may not even be necessary for the teacher to become actively involved in the discussion provided that it is 'set off' in the right direction.

The role of the teacher in group learning situations is, however, very important, and calls for skills and adaptability which may, for some, be difficult to achieve. First, the teacher must exhibit good organizational skills in planning and structuring the learning experience. Thereafter, his role may be more adaptive and less authoritarian or autocratic than in exposition-based situations. Depending on the form, content and structure of the group technique adopted, and upon its particular educational aims and objectives, the teacher's role may include acting as *group leader* (giving strong direction to the discussion), *group facilitator* (generating self-expression and interaction within the group), *neutral chairman* (controlling the procedure, but not contributing substantially to the discussion), *consultant* (providing assistance and/or information as and when needed) or simply *observer*. In some group exercises, another important aspect of the role of the teacher is in *debriefing* the session. This involves going over with the participants the events that occurred during the group session and 'pulling out' any important points that arose, either in connection with the nature and content of the discussions or regarding the processes and inter-actions within the group itself. Obviously, the points that are high-lighted in such a debriefing should be closely related to the main teaching objectives of the exercise.

Group learning activities can range from being highly structured and pre-planned to being essentially free or open discussions. If a structured approach is to be used, the group may be organized in a prearranged way, and directed to discuss specific subject matter in a manner that is dictated by the teacher or predetermined by the format of the exercise. On the other hand, if a free or non-directed approach is to be adopted, the group processes are far more 'student-controlled' and flexible, and consequently the learning outcomes are much more difficult to predict. In between these two extremes are a whole range of techniques and approaches which involve the use of groups in a wide variety of different ways.

Some Strengths of Group Learning Techniques

In matching the desired outcomes, or objectives, of a course with the teaching methods likely to achieve them, it soon becomes obvious that no single method is suitable in all circumstances, and that an appropriate 'blend' of teaching methods (exposition-based, individualized and group) may be required. As mentioned above, there are a number of types of objectives for which group learning techniques are particularly useful as a means of teaching. Let us now examine these in turn.

HIGHER COGNITIVE OBJECTIVES

Within the general area of knowledge and understanding (Bloom's cognitive domain — see Chapter 3), we have already seen that mass instruction techniques (for example, lectures) and individualized learning methods are well suited for teaching towards the lower cognitive areas of 'knowledge' and 'comprehension'. However, the understanding of factual material and its applications in a number of areas can often be much more effectively investigated in small group situations such as tutorial sessions. Indeed, in most colleges and universities, lectures and tutorials are generally closely linked and complementary.

Cognitive skills that lie further up Bloom's hierarchy (such as those involving the analysis or evaluation of given material) are often most effectively developed by using a group discussion technique of some sort. Here, students can discuss problems and opinions with their peers in a relatively open environment.

Group methods have also proved to be useful in problem-solving sessions, with the students either working individually and interacting with the teacher, or working as a co-operative group in tackling a project of some sort. In such activities, the subject matter is often very specific to the student's course of study. However, exercises that foster the development of decision-making skills through the use of small-group methods need not necessarily be so content-related. Many management-training courses, for example, make use of exercises which enable the participants to improve their decision-making ability through activities in which the processes by which the decisions are reached are much more important than the actual content of the exercise.

CREATIVE THINKING SKILLS

In courses that contain objectives which involve the development of creative thinking skills (for example, the ability to perceive new relationships within a topic, or the ability to produce imaginative solutions to given problem situations), group methods have often been found to be extremely useful. In situations where wide-ranging and/or lateral thinking are required, for example, ideas can be 'bounced around' within the group for comment and criticism, with the result that individual group members benefit from the perceptions of others and from the subsequent interactions and discussions.

COMMUNICATION SKILLS

A number of group learning techniques are ideal vehicles for the development of (or creation of an awareness of the importance of) the various skills that are associated with *oral communication, non-verbal communication,* and *written* communication.

Students are frequently criticized for their inability to express themselves coherently. Group techniques are particularly well suited to helping them to overcome these deficiencies, and, in recent years, a number of exercises have been designed for this purpose. These provide situations in which students can develop oral communication skills (such as presenting and defending arguments and making a meaningful contribution to discussions) and through which they can generally build up their confidence. Ideally, a planned series of such exercises is desirable if significant and long-lasting improvements are to be achieved.

A more traditional use of group methods is to provide a forum in which written work such as essays, laboratory reports, assignments and project reports can be discussed. The purpose of such discussions can be twofold: first, to discuss the content of the written work for the mutual benefit of the group; second, to discuss the form of the written work in terms of, for instance, structure, sequence and clarity of expression. In many cases, open discussion of the latter may well encourage and catalyze improved future efforts.

Finally, group exercises may help the participants to develop an appreciation of the importance of non-verbal communication and to cultivate useful skills in this often-neglected area. This can be achieved through observation of the activities of the group by the teacher, by the actual group members, by independent observers, or via a videotape recording made for later analysis and discussion. Such techniques can be used for a variety of purposes: eg for demonstrating the nature of non-verbal communication to psychology students, or for helping trainee managers to recognize and develop the various non-verbal skills that play such an important part in interviews, meetings etc.

INTERPERSONAL SKILLS

The various skills that are required in order to operate effectively within a group or social situation are often best developed by group learning methods. In many instances, students leaving school or college enter jobs which require them to work in close co-operation with other people. For some, this may involve skills of leadership, administration and delegation, for others, the ability to work as part of a team, while for others it may involve social skills such as those needed in order to deal with the general public. Again, group methods are ideal for putting theory into practice, and a whole range of simulation and role play activities can be used with small groups in order to help develop interpersonal skills of this type.

DESIRABLE ATTITUDINAL TRAITS

Research has shown that exposition-based and individualized methods are not particularly effective in the area of attitude (affective) development. It seems that active participation by students and exposure to views different from their own and to criticism by their peers are necessary if attitudes are to be changed, together with a less dominant teacher role than is found in most conventional learning situations. In other words, it appears that student interaction is the key to the achievement of such attitude changes.

The vital role that can be played by group methods in this area is self-evident. Such methods can provide an environment in which free discussion can break down prejudices and misconceptions and increase awareness of the range of factors that are involved in any given situation. An example might be the use of group methods to increase empathy towards a minority section of the community, or towards trade unions or representatives of management.

Group activities can also be an extremely powerful means of integrating an individual's cognitive and affective development within the context of a meaningful and relevant learning experience.

Some Disadvantages of Group Learning

Group learning also has a number of disadvantages, some of the more important of which will now be examined.

ORGANIZATIONAL DIFFICULTIES

Running group learning exercises can pose a number of organizational problems, not the least of which is the fact that it is often difficult to fit them into the normal teaching curriculum — particularly if the exercise is a long one or requires a large number of participants, extra teaching staff, special accommodation, etc. This is particularly true of many exercises of the game/simulation/case study type. Also, the fact that such exercises often require the participants to attend briefing or debriefing sessions or to carry out preliminary work can cause complications. Finally, it is often extremely difficult to assess student performance or evaluate the effectiveness of group learning exercises other than on a subjective basis.

PROBLEMS OF ATTITUDE

One potential weakness of all group learning methods is that they require the active co-operation of the participants if they are to succeed. In some cases, however, this co-operation may not be forthcoming. Students may, for example, simply not turn up for the exercise because they feel that it will be a waste of time or are afraid of taking part. In other cases, they may be reluctant to make the very real personal commitment that many group learning exercises require, because they do not feel that they have the necessary skills and do not want to 'show themselves up' in front of their peers.

Nor are these attitude-related problems necessarily limited to students. As we saw earlier, running a group learning exercise can make heavy demands on the staff involved, often requiring them to take on a number of unfamiliar roles which may not fit in with their conception of what their job should entail. This is particularly true of many older, or more traditional, teachers, who as a result make little or no use of group learning techniques.

Review of a Range of Group Learning Techniques

The type of group technique that is used in a particular teaching or training situation depends on a whole range of factors, including the objectives that it wishes to achieve, the relationship of the exercise with other teaching methods, the maturity of the students, the personality and experience of the teacher, and so on. The techniques described below by no means constitute an exhaustive list of those which can be used in small group situations; they do, however, illustrate a broad cross-section of approaches which vary in their degree of structure, teacher involvement and dependence on subject matter content. Some techniques can in fact be used within other group techniques, while others can be incorporated into exposition-based methods in order to generate student activity, discussion and feedback. An attempt has also been made to list the techniques in order of decreasing teacher control and increasing student control. However, these factors may vary considerably according to particular circumstances, and there may, indeed, be a large degree of overlap between several of the approaches. More detailed descriptions of these and other group techniques can be found in Abercrombie's book *Aims and Techniques of Group Teaching* (1979).

Controlled Discussions

This type of approach is often used with fairly large groups, and can be used to obtain some degree of student feedback after the completion of an exposition-based teaching session. Another common use is in schools, where a teacher strongly controls the direction of the learning by asking specific questions designed to move the class step by step towards a desired goal. Yet another use is in revision sessions.

Although students may feel freer to ask questions or add comments than they do in a lecture-type situation, the teacher is,. nevertheless, firmly at the centre of the system. For this reason, controlled discussions are generally used to reinforce the basic subject matter of a course rather than to develop broader objectives of the type described in the previous section.

Buzz Sessions

Buzz sessions are often deliberately built into a lecture or a larger group exercise in order to stimulate discussion and provide feedback. In this technique, small sub-groups of two to four persons spend a short period (generally no more than five minutes) discussing a topic or topics suggested by the teacher. Each sub-group then reports back on its deliberations to the group as a whole, or sometimes combines with another sub-group in order to share their findings and discuss the implications. In formal class situations, buzz sessions can be an extremely useful way of actively involving the students. The normal mental processes that are involved in passive sitting and listening are (for a time) forced to undergo a radical change, and the technique can also be used to foster creative thinking.

Tutorials

In group tutorials, the topic(s) to be investigated or problem(s) to be solved are chosen by the teacher, who also usually decides how to organize the session. However, what actually happens during the tutorial depends to a large extent on the performance and concerns of the individual students in the group.

Tutorials are useful vehicles for providing practice in the application, analysis and evaluation of knowledge. Very often, they take the basic factual content of a subject and treat it at Bloom's 'higher cognitive' levels. Thus, the tutorial can be used for developing skills in areas such as problem solving and critical appraisal.

In many cases, the work done by students for tutorials is pre-prepared in the form of an essay, a project, or answers to a series of problems. In such a tutorial situation, a teacher can use the fruits of the students' labours to focus upon areas of common (and individual) difficulty, and can also use the session to discuss essay writing or problem-solving techniques in more general terms.

One major drawback of such subject-based tutorials is that there is often a tendency for the teacher to become over-dominant, and, in some cases, to use the tutorial as a 'mini-lecture'. If this happens, the opportunity to develop the various critical appraisal and problem-solving skills mentioned above may well be lost.

Seminars

The seminar technique covers a wide range of general group discussion approaches to learning. Indeed, the term can have widely different connotations for people working in different subject areas and at different levels of education and training.

One common method of running a seminar is to base it on an essay or prepared talk presented by one of the students in the group. The group then discuss the content of the presentation, together with the assumptions on which it is based and its broader implications. The role of the teacher is usually less dominant than in a tutorial, with group interaction being very important. In general, the initial presentation is viewed not so much in terms of its factual correctness as in terms of its degree of perception and its analysis and/or evaluation of the topic or situation being examined.

However, a seminar discussion need not necessarily have a presentation as its focal point, since it can be run equally well on the basis of free group discussion of a particular topic. Also, the teacher's involvement in the process may vary considerably, depending on his aims or style of teaching.

An interesting variation of the seminar is the 'fishbowl' technique, in which roughly half the members of the group sit in an inner circle and conduct a discussion, while the rest of the group (who sit in an outer circle) act as non-participating observers of the proceedings. Both sections of the group then combine for a general discussion of what occurred, and views are exchanged on the basis of both the internal and the external assessments of the discussion. Such a technique can be useful for highlighting such aspects of group dynamics as, for instance, the role of the leader and non-verbal communication.

Yet another of the many techniques which have been developed for use within the context of the seminar method is 'brainstorming'. This involves group members in spontaneously noting down or suggesting a range of possible solutions to a problem or question posed by the teacher, eg: 'What items would be absolutely essential if you were marooned on a desert island?' Initially, the suggestions are compiled without comment. Following this, the group as a whole evaluates the various suggestions, and modifies or rejects them in the light of the ensuing discussion. 'Brainstorming' is very useful not only for stimulating discussion, but also for acting as an icebreaker at the start of a seminar by actively involving every participant right at the beginning. Once the ice has broken, the group's discussion will probably be a good deal more free and involve more students than might otherwise be the case.

Team Projects

A co-operative group approach to projects can be a valuable technique for developing collaborative and interpersonal skills. In this way, the advantages of individual projects that were discussed in Chapter 5 can be reinforced by the support of an organized group. Each group member must, however, pull his weight, otherwise the efficiency of the group as a whole can be seriously affected. Interdisciplinary projects are especially suitable for such a team approach, since they enable people with different subject area backgrounds to combine their various skills in order to attain a common goal.

Games, Simulations and Interactive Case Studies

During the last decade, the use of games, simulations and interactive case studies as a group learning technique has increased dramatically. Such exercises were originally largely confined to the military and business management training sectors, but they have now spread to virtually all sectors of education, where they are used in a wide range of subject areas to teach towards a wide variety of educational objectives.

The scope and range of applications of the techniques are much too wide to allow them to be discussed in any great depth here, and interested readers are referred to the various books that have been written on the subject. (Ellington, Addinall and Percival, for example, have written a number of books on the design and educational uses of games and simulations, and other useful books have been written by Tansey and Unwin, Boocock and Schild, and Taylor and Walford, to name but a few — see the Bibliography for details.)

THE DIFFERENT TYPES OF EXERCISE

In an educational or training context, *games* are exercises which involve competition and have set rules. The term covers an extremely wide range of exercises — everything from simple card and board games to large-scale management games and sophisticated competitions. When playing a game in a group learning situation, the participants, acting either individually or in co-operation with others, use their skills and knowledge to compete with one another in order to 'win'.

Simulations, on the other hand, are exercises that involve an on-going representation of some aspect(s) of a real situation of some sort. In many cases, they involve the members of a group in taking part in *role-play*, during which each member acts out the part of another person such as a lawyer, local councillor, trade union representative or conservationist.

Finally, *interactive case studies* are exercises in which the members of a group have to carry out an in-depth study of a process, situation, event, document, etc in order to examine its special characteristics, characteristics that may either be limited to the particular case under examination or may be general features of the broad set or class to which it belongs. Obvious examples are the group discussions of specific cases that are carried out in the context of medical or legal training, but the case study technique can also be used in a wide range of other areas.

There are also various types of 'hybrid' exercises in the game/simulation/case study field, exercises which have characteristics that are drawn from two or even all three of the basic areas that have just been described.

Simulation games, for example, have a competitive element and also involve a simulated situation, a well-known example being MONOPOLY. Other variations might involve using the actual process of playing a game as a case study in itself (in the study of probability theory, for example) or basing a case study on a simulated rather than a real situation (as in the simulated patient technique developed at McMaster University in Canada for use in the training of medical staff). Such hybrid exercises are described in detail by Ellington, Addinall and Percival in *A Handbook of Game Design* (1982).

SOME ADVANTAGES OF GAMES, SIMULATIONS AND CASE STUDIES
Let us now examine some of the reasons why games, simulations and interactive case studies are useful in a group learning situation.

(a) The techniques constitute a highly versatile and flexible medium whereby a wide variety of educational aims and objectives can be achieved. In a group situation, they can be used to achieve objectives in all parts of Bloom's cognitive and affective domains. Although the methods are no more effective than any other method when used to teach the basic facts of a subject, they have been found to be particularly valuable in teaching towards high-level cognitive objectives relating to such things as analysis, synthesis and evaluation, and also for achieving a variety of affective (attitudinal) objectives. Thus, their use is often as a complement to, and a support for, more traditional teaching methods, and they can be also used for reinforcement purposes or to demonstrate applications or relevance.

(b) The use of a simulated as opposed to a real situation as the basis of a group exercise allows the situation and learning experiences to be tailored to meet the needs of the group, rather than requiring the exercise to be designed within the constraints imposed by the situation. Only very rarely does a real-life situation have all the features that the designer of a case study-type exercise wishes to bring out, whereas a simulated situation can have all such features built in. Also, real-life situations are often much too complicated to be used as the basis of an educational or training group exercise as they stand; the simplification that the use of simulation allows can often overcome this difficulty by reducing the complexity to manageable proportions.

(c) Work by Paul Twelker (see the Bibliography) has indicated that well-designed games, simulations and interactive case studies can achieve *positive transfer of learning*, that is, they can produce in participants the ability to apply skills acquired during the exercise in other situations. It would, in fact, be difficult to justify the use of many exercises of this type if no such transfer of learning occurred.

(d) In many cases, exercises in the game/simulation/case study field constitute a vehicle whereby students can use and develop their initiative and powers of creative thought. This feature may prove increasingly important in the future if the educational system continues to place progressively greater emphasis on the cultivation of divergent thought processes.

(e) Apart from their specifically content-related outcomes, many exercises of the type under discussion help to foster a wide range of useful skills (such as decision-making, communication and inter-personal skills) and desirable attitudinal traits (such as willingness to listen to other people's points of view, or to appreciate that most problems can be viewed in a number of different ways). Indeed, many people believe that it is in these areas that games, simulations and case studies can make their most valuable contribution to education. Exercises which have been designed to involve a high degree of interaction in the group are found to be particularly effective in this regard.

(f) In cases where a competitive element is involved (not necessarily at the expense of co-operation), this can provide strong motivation for the participants to commit themselves wholeheartedly to the work of the exercise. This competitive element may be overt (when sub-groups or individuals are in open competition with one another) or it may be latent (as, for example, when sub-groups or individuals have to perform parallel activities and report their findings to the group as a whole).

(g) Many exercises in this field have a basis in more than one academic discipline, a feature that can help the participants to integrate concepts from otherwise widely-related areas into a cohesive and balanced 'world picture'. Exercises which require the students to formulate value judgements (for example, weighing economic benefits against social costs) or examine problems from a number of different perspectives are particularly valuable in this respect.

(h) Multi-disciplinary exercises have an additional advantage in that they can provide a situation in which participants with expertise in different subject areas have to work together effectively in order to achieve a common end. Interpersonal skills of this type are very important in a student's later life, and constitute an area of education and training in which the multi-disciplinary simulation and simulation game may be the only means of providing practical experience in a school or college environment.

(i) Finally, one universally-observed advantage of game/simulation/ case study techniques is that student involvement and motivation are normally very high — features that are particularly beneficial when using these techniques with the less able. In addition, most participants find the approach extremely enjoyable.

SOME DISADVANTAGES OF GAMES AND SIMULATIONS

Apart from the various organizational and attitude-related disadvantages which they share with other group learning techniques (see p 91), there are two main disadvantages that are specifically associated with games and simulations.

1. There is always a danger of using such exercises for the wrong reasons, for example using them as 'diversions' or 'time fillers' rather than for some specific educational purpose. Also, with some 'educational games', it is possible for students to play them purely as games, without deriving any worthwhile educational benefit, because the 'educational' and 'gaming' elements are not fully integrated. (A number of commercially-available card games tend to have this weakness to some extent, as do many board games.)

2. If a game or simulation is to be of any real use in a given educational situation, it must not only be capable of achieving the desired educational outcomes but must also be properly matched to the target population with which it is to be used; in other words it must be pitched at a suitable level. It is, however, very unusual to find an exercise that is ideally suited to the purpose which the teacher/tutor has in mind, so it may be necessary to carry out a certain amount of adaptation or modification, or even to 'start from scratch' and design a completely new exercise. Obviously, this requires a certain amount of expertise and (preferably) some previous experience.

THE ROLE OF THE TEACHER

In most exercises of the game/simulation/case study-type, the role of the teacher is mainly organizational, with the actual activities that take place within the exercise being largely under the control of the students. The extent to which an exercise is pre-structured (and hence the degree of student freedom) can, however, vary considerably.

One of the most important roles of the teacher is in *debriefing* the participants after the completion of the exercise, such debriefing being absolutely vital if the full educational value is to be derived from their experience. The form of the debriefing will depend on the nature and function of the exercise concerned, but should generally include the following four elements:

1. review of the actual work of the exercise, and discussion of any important points raised by the students;
2. discussion of the relationship between the exercise and the subject matter on which it is based (for example, discussion of the degree of realism in the case of a simulation);
3. discussion of the group processes which occurred during the exercise;
4. discussion of any broader issues raised.

The debriefing session is particularly important in the case of exercises that involve role play, or which place the intrinsic subject matter in a social, political, economic or environmental context; indeed in such cases, it is often the most important part of the whole experience.

Microteaching

This is an example of a video-replay method that is used mainly in the training of teachers. In microteaching, attention is focused on specific teaching skills, which the trainee teacher practices for short periods (from five to twenty minutes) with a small group of pupils (usually four to seven). The session is recorded, usually on videotape, and is then played back to the trainee teacher (usually in the presence of other trainees) in order to obtain immediate feedback and to catalyze discussion of various aspects of the performance.

The resulting group feedback (together with the supervisor's comments and any observations made by the actual pupils) helps the student teacher to analyse his performance, and thus enables him to restructure the lesson in order to teach it to a second group of pupils. Again, this is followed by immediate video replay, so that further analysis and evaluation can take place in order to identify any areas where further improvement could be made. By employing this 'teach-reteach' cycle, it is possible to give the student teacher the opportunity to put into immediate practice what he has learned from the video replay and from the peer group and other feedback on the previous attempt.

There are many variations of microteaching and, indeed, such video-replay methods for analysing performance are now used in many areas of skills training other than teaching practice. Readers wishing to know more about microteaching are directed to the books that have been written on the subject by Brown and by Hargie and Maidment (see the Bibliography).

Self-Help Groups

These arise when students meet on their own (that is, with no teacher or tutor present) in order to discuss common problems, share ideas and generally help one another by a process of *peer teaching.*

In many cases, such groups form spontaneously; in others, some encouragement from the teacher or institution may provide the necessary catalyst. Students obviously need to be motivated to participate in such groups, but the peer teaching aspect can be extremely valuable in helping them to cope with difficulties. In many distance learning courses, such as those offered by the Open University, the formation of self-help groups is actively encouraged, and, in such circumstances, can often do a great deal to help offset the isolation of independent study.

CHAPTER 7

Student Assessment

Introduction

In Chapter 1, we discussed the main features of a systematic approach to course design, and in Chapter 3, we argued a case for the formulation of clear, unambiguous objectives as the first stage of such an approach. One important advantage of defining objectives in this way is that it puts a teacher in a much better position to know how to assess the attainment of each objective, since he should (as a result of writing the objective) have a relatively clear idea of the behaviour to be measured. Conversely, the feedback obtained from the results of properly designed procedures almost invariably helps to shed light on the efficiency of the teaching system, and may well demonstrate the need for changes in the original objectives, in the teaching methods employed, or, indeed, in the assessment procedures themselves.

In the latter situation, the results of the assessment are being used not only to assess the students, but also to help *evaluate* the teaching system itself. It is important at this stage to draw a clear distinction between the processes of assessment and evaluation, because, although the terms are often considered to be virtually synonymous when used in common parlance, they have in fact radically different connotations when used in an educational or training context.

By assessment we mean those activities that are designed to measure learner achievement brought about as a result of an instructional programme of some sort. Evaluation, on the other hand, refers to a series of activities that are designed to measure the effectiveness of an instructional system as a whole. Clearly, the results of student assessments may be just one of the areas of evidence that are taken into account in such a process. The role of evaluation and the different types of evaluation procedures will be discussed in detail in the following chapter, while a much fuller discussion of the relationship between assessment and evaluation can be found in a book by Derek Rowntree – *Assessing Students: How Shall We Know Them?* (1977).

In this chapter we will first discuss the general principles that underlie effective student assessment procedures, and will then describe a number of approaches to student assessment and test construction. We will conclude the chapter by giving a review of a range of common student assessment methods, discussing them in terms of their design characteristics, their functions and their respective strengths and weaknesses.

Desirable Characteristics of Student Assessment Procedures

Ideally, any student assessment procedure should be valid, reliable, practicable, and fair and useful to students.

Validity

A valid assessment procedure is one which actually tests what it sets out to test, ie one which accurately measures the behaviour described by the objective(s) under scrutiny. Obviously, no one would *deliberately* construct an assessment item to test trivia or irrelevant material, but it is surprising just how often non-valid test items are in fact used — eg questions that are intended to test recall of factual material but which actually test the candidate's powers of reasoning, or questions which assume a level of pre-knowledge that the candidates do not possess.

As we will see later in the review of assessment methods, validity-related problems are a common weakness of many of the more widely-used methods. For example, a simple science question given to 14-year-old schoolchildren ('Name the products of the combustion of carbon in an adequate supply of oxygen') produced a much higher number of correct answers when the word 'combustion' was replaced by 'burning'. This showed that the original question had problems of validity in that it was, to some extent, testing language and vocabulary skills rather than the basic science involved.

Reliability

The reliability of an assessment procedure is a measure of the consistency with which the question, test or examination produces the same results under different but comparable conditions. A reliable assessment item gives reproducible scores with similar populations of students, and is therefore as independent of the characteristics and vagaries of individual markers as possible; this is often difficult to achieve in practice.

It is obviously important to have reasonably reliable assessment procedures when a large number of individual markers assess the same question (eg in national school examinations). A student answer which receives a score of 75 per cent from one marker and 35 per cent from another, for example, reveals a patently unreliable assessment procedure.

To help produce reliability, the questions which comprise a student assessment should (ideally) test only one thing at a time and give the candidates no choice. The assessment should also adequately reflect the objectives of the teaching unit. Note that the reliability and validity factors in an assessment are in no way directly linked — a test or examination, for example, may be totally reliable and yet have very low validity, and vice versa.

Practicability

For most purposes, assessment procedures should be realistically practical in terms of their cost, time taken, and ease of application. For example, with a large class of technicians being trained in electrical circuitry, it may only be convenient to use a paper-and-pencil test rather than set up numerous practical testing situations. It should be noted, however, that such compromises can, in some cases, greatly reduce the validity of the assessment.

Fairness and Usefulness

To be fair to all students, an assessment must accurately reflect the range of expected behaviours as described by the course objectives. It is also highly desirable that students should know exactly *how* they are to be assessed. Indeed, it could be argued that students have a right to information such as the nature of the materials on which they are to be examined (ie content and objectives), the form and structure of the examination, the length of the examination, and the value (in terms of marks) of each component of the course.

Also, students should (ideally!) find assessments useful. Feedback from assessment can give a student a much better indication of his current strengths and weaknesses than he might otherwise have. In this respect, the non-return of assessment work to students greatly reduces its utility.

Criterion-Referenced and Norm-Referenced Assessment

Two contrasting general approaches to student assessment are *criterion-referenced* and *norm-referenced assessment*.

Criterion-referenced assessment involves testing students in order to measure their performance in tasks described by a particular objective or set of objectives (the criterion). In any systems approach to education or training (which is invariably geared towards the achievement of clearly-specified objectives), it is normal to use some kind of criterion-referenced test for student assessment. In such a test, the relative performances of the various individuals in the class are of little consequence — indeed in the unlikely event of the whole class demonstrating complete mastery of the objectives, this would simply indicate that a highly-successful teaching/learning system had been developed.

A good example of a criterion-referenced test is the driving test, in which the learner driver has to demonstrate a certain level of competence before being allowed to pass. His performance relative to other learner drivers should (in principle) be of no consequence.

This approach contrasts sharply with *norm-referenced assessment*, which is altogether more competitive. Norm-referenced assessment involves tests of ability or attainment which are intended to probe differences between individual students, and hence to determine the extent to which each individual's performance differs from the performance of others of similar age and background.

In cases where there is a choice of questions in a norm-referenced test, a need is highlighted for *standardization* of scores for comparison purposes. A typical norm-referenced test may have a fixed pass rate (say 55 per cent) which is strictly adhered to, no matter how high or how low is the general level of attainment. This is, on the face of it, a much less fair approach to assessment than criterion-referenced assessment, since only relative attainment, not absolute attainment, is recognized. However, the approach is widely used — in many national school examinations and professional examinations, for example.

Basically, criterion-referenced assessment and norm-referenced assessment differ in the purpose for which the assessment is carried out, the style in which the component tests are constructed, and, finally, in the use to which the information derived from the results of the assessment is put.

In the remainder of this chapter, we will attempt to demonstrate the role of assessment techniques in a general systems approach to course design. Thus, our main concern will be with criterion-referenced assessment related to the attainment of pre-specified objectives and identifiable behaviours.

Test Construction

As mentioned earlier in this chapter, a student assessment should be directly geared towards the stated course objectives (while remembering that not all objectives are formally assessable, yet may nevertheless be very important). The attainment of assessable objectives may be measured in a relatively sporadic programme of *set examinations*, or, more consistently (and possibly less stressfully for students), by some form of *continuous assessment* procedure. However it is done, it is likely that a combination of assessment techniques will be necessary in order to assess the range of objectives under investigation validly and comprehensively.

In order to ensure that particular sets of skills are being assessed, some individuals and organizations have drawn up 'tables of specifications' for tests to ensure that due weight is given to all skills and content areas. For example, Figure 7.1 is a typical specification of the cognitive skills to be assessed in the UK Ordinary National Certificate (ONC) in chemistry. The course syllabus is written in the form of behavioural objectives, and the specification is given in terms of Bloom's classification of educational objectives (which was discussed in Chapter 3) and the various areas of course content. Tables of this sort, while perhaps a little rigid, do enable exam setters to design assessments to cover the full range of skills (in this case, cognitive skills) that are under scrutiny, and to promote good syllabus coverage. They also ensure that certain skills (eg factual recall) are not over-emphasized, and that due attention is paid to higher cognitive skills.

The type and range of techniques used within a given assessment strategy will depend upon a number of factors — the most important (at least from an educational point of view) being the student behaviours that are specified in the objectives being tested. The basic characteristics of a range of assessment methods will now be discussed, together with their respective advantages and limitations.

A Review of Student Assessment Methods

Student assessment methods can have a wide variety of forms. The most common general approach is via some form of written response, ie the 'paper-and-pencil' approach. This approach encompasses a whole range of 'traditional' assessment methods such as essays, 'short notes' questions and problems.

Another form of 'paper-and-pencil' approach involves the use of 'objective tests', although such tests seldom involve the student in writing very much; in most cases, a mark made beside one of a range of possible options, or a single word answer, is all that is required. Also, the word 'objective', when used in the 'objective test' context, can be somewhat confusing, since it neither means that the questions are necessarily related to the course objectives, nor implies that the questions are objectively chosen. The term simply indicates that the answers to such questions can be marked totally reliable by anybody, including non-subject specialists, and, in some cases, even by a computer. The most common type of objective question is the *multiple choice question* (or, more correctly, *multiple choice item*), together with its range of variations. Other types of objective questions include *completion items, unique answer questions*, and *structural communication tests.*

Practical tests are often used to assess psychomotor objectives, and include such techniques as *project assessment, laboratory examinations*, and other *skill-tests* designed to assess specific manipulative skills. Also in this category are *situational assessment* techniques, which involve students using non-cognitive skills (such as decision-making

Subject and topic \ Ability	Recall	Comprehension	Non-routine application	Analysis/ evaluation	Totals
Inorganic chemistry					
Revision and extension	7	6	4	6	23
Chemical reactions	8	10	2	0	20
Group I and II elements	5	10	2	2	19
Group VII elements	5	10	2	2	19
Group V elements	5	10	2	2	19
Totals	**30**	**46**	**12**	**12**	**100**
Organic chemistry					
Nomenclature	3	2	0	0	5
Stereochemistry	1	6	2	0	9
Hydrocarbons	5	7	4	2	18
Halogen derivatives	1	6	3	0	10
Hydroxyl compounds	2	8	3	2	15
Carbonyl compounds	3	10	3	3	19
Acids and derivatives	3	6	2	1	12
Bases	2	6	2	2	12
Totals	**20**	**51**	**19**	**10**	**100**
Physical chemistry					
Gases	4	5	3	1	13
Solutions	8	9	6	3	26
Thermodynamics	3	4	2	1	10
Chemical equilibrium	3	3	2	2	10
Electrochemistry	6	7	4	2	19
Ionic equilibria	6	7	6	3	22
Totals	**30**	**35**	**23**	**12**	**100**

Figure 7.1 **Typical tables of specifications for the UK
Ordinary National Certificate (ONC) examinations in chemistry**

skills) in a real, or (more likely) in a simulated environment.

Finally, there are a range of unobtrusive and observational techniques which can take place without the student necessarily being aware that he is in fact being assessed.

Let us now look at each of these techniques in turn.

Long-Essay Questions

Long-essay questions are often considered to be one of the bluntest instruments of assessment, having very low reliability and, in many cases, low validity. Often, in a single question, the setter attempts to test knowledge, reasoning, written communication skills (including English language skills, and, perhaps, graphical skills and mathematical skills), creative thinking abilities, and interpretation (not only of the question itself, but often of the implied objectives of the setter). All these factors and skills are interwoven in an extremely complicated matrix, and much is left to the judgement (or caprice!) of the marker. Even with the best of intentions, it is almost impossible to tease these skills out and mark them independently. Even when an assessment grid is used, thus enabling the various components of the essay to be marked independently, research has shown that reliability is still very poor, with markers varying widely in their scoring of this kind of question.

ADVANTAGES OF LONG-ESSAY QUESTIONS

(a) They give students an opportunity to organize their ideas and express them in their own words. Also, scope is provided for the demonstration of written communication skills and for the expression of unconventional and creative thinking. (These opportunities are, however, often lost when essays consist simply of regurgitated class notes).

(b) They allow students to display a detailed knowledge of related aspects of the course being assessed, as well as a knowledge of relevant topics outside the course proper.

(c) The questions are relatively easy to set.

(d) Many teachers and users of the results of assessments (eg employers) hold the opinion that student tests and examinations should contain at least an element of essay writing (except, perhaps, in mathematical subjects).

DISADVANTAGES OF LONG-ESSAY QUESTIONS

(a) Essay questions are exceedingly difficult to mark reliably and, with only one marker, the subjective element can be considerable. The correlation between the scores of two markers for the same set of answers on different occasions is seldom sufficiently high to justify confidence.

(b) Essays are very time-consuming to mark, especially if the marker adds comments and criticisms in order to provide feedback for the student.

(c) Only a small number of long essays can be answered in a given time, thus effectively restricting the assessment to a few (often student-selected) areas of the course content. Other equally-important areas may be completely neglected, and the total mark may therefore be an unreliable index of the student's grasp of the course as a whole. Also, in an examination which consists of a limited number of essays, luck in 'spotting' questions beforehand is often a significant factor.

(d) Where there is a choice of questions, this enables different students to answer, in effect, different papers, so the same total mark may not represent comparable performances. This will almost certainly be the case when the questions vary in difficulty, in content, in the types of skills involved, and are scored by different markers. For example, a '5 from 8' paper contains a total of no less than 56 different combinations in which the 5 questions can be selected.

(e) Occasionally, students may not appreciate the true intent of an essay question because of inadequate directions (eg 'Write an essay on proteins'). Markers then have the choice of ignoring the answer, accepting the student's interpretation as an answer to a question which was not intended, or adopting an uneasy compromise. Clearly, this adds neither to the reliability nor to the validity of the assessment.

(f) Irrelevant factors often intrude into the assessment, eg speed of handwriting (especially with restricted time), style and clarity of handwriting, and grammatical errors.

'Short Notes' Questions

In cases where short notes on a subject or topic are required, rather than an extended essay, many of the problems associated with long-essay questions are reduced, although not necessarily eradicated. 'Short notes' questions should (in principle) be more valid and reliable than essay questions, because the marker is able to concentrate more sharply on particular aspects of the answer. In addition, they allow wider coverage of course content, and are generally more specific.

However, although reliability is increased, some deviation in scores may still occur between markers. Also, course coverage may still not be adequate, and students' individual written and presentational skills may again cloud the validity of the questions.

Problems

Problem-solving questions are an excellent method of testing some of the middle-to-higher cognitive skills (such as comprehension, application and analysis), and for demonstrating extended reasoning skills. Mathematical, scientific and engineering subjects, in particular, lend themselves readily to assessments of this sort.

With such questions, validity may well be high, but problems of reliability may arise in respect of the marking of partially-solved problems.

Objective Test Items

Objective items are assessment procedures which can be marked totally reliably. Although such items are often criticized on account of assessing only at low intellectual levels, this is not necessarily the case. It is possible (although more difficult) to design items to test skills in the higher cognitive areas, and even to test logical thinking and skills related to structuring arguments.

Before looking at the characteristics of specific techniques of objective testing in more detail, we will summarize the main advantages and disadvantages of using objective tests in general.

ADVANTAGES OF OBJECTIVE TEST ITEMS

(a) The tests can be marked with complete inter-marker reliability.
(b) Large numbers of questions can be answered, thus ensuring a thorough sampling of course objectives and content.
(c) Objective items can be designed to test specific abilities in a controlled way.
(d) The difficulty of the items is often known from trial-testing. Hence, by selection of appropriate items, the difficulty level of the test can be adjusted to meet particular requirements.
(e) Items can be 'banked' and re-used.
(f) There is no need to provide a choice of questions for the students, and, indeed, this is not desirable, since it tends to reduce validity.
(g) Tests lend themselves to inexpensive and easy marking, and also to thorough statistical analysis. This allows investigation of individual difficulties, and also permits the general problem areas of the student population as a whole to be identified.

DISADVANTAGES OF OBJECTIVE TEST ITEMS

(a) They are very difficult and initially expensive to construct, and considerable preparation time is necessary. Their *apparent* ease of construction often leads to amateurish attempts, resulting in very poor, invalid items. (This, in turn, has been responsible for some of the criticisms levelled at objective tests.) Expert advice is often required in designing items, and all items should be pre-tested in order to measure their level of difficulty and the extent to which they discriminate between the better and poorer students in a given population.
(b) The teacher or marker cannot see the reasoning behind the choice of a wrong answer.
(c) It is difficult or impossible to construct tests to assess certain high-level abilities such as extended reasoning and written communication ability. Thus objective tests are probably best suited for testing lower cognitive skills, and items at these levels are certainly the easiest to write.

DIFFERENT TYPES OF OBJECTIVE TEST ITEMS THAT CAN BE USED

Multiple-Choice Items. Multiple-choice items are probably the most widely used component of objective tests. Several variations on the multiple choice theme are possible, such as when several items arise out of one situation, graph or set of figures. A number of references to sources of further information on the construction of multiple-choice items are given in the Bibliography.

The advantages and disadvantages of objective items in general (as listed above) apply fully to multiple-choice items.

An example of a multiple-choice item that is designed to test knowledge is given below:

Which city is the capital of Australia?
(a) Melbourne
(b) Brisbane
(c) Sydney
(d) Canberra

Multiple-choice objective testing has its own associated jargon, the most common terms being as follows:

Stem: the introductory part of the question out of which the alternative answers arise. Ideally, this should be a self-contained question containing all the basic information which the student needs in order to respond to the item, so that he does not need to read through the options to discover what is being asked. The stem should be concise, should use unambiguous language appropriate to the students' ability, and should avoid negatives if at all possible.

Options: the range of possible answers. The options should be parallel in content and structure, ie they should all have the same kind of relationship to the stem, and should all follow grammatically from it. Obviously, the item should not contain clues in the structure of the options (eg mixtures of plurals and singulars).

Key: the correct answer. This must be unarguably correct, hence the option 'all of these' should never be used.

Distractors: the wrong answers. These must be unarguably incorrect answers, yet should appear plausible to weaker students.

Non-functioning distractors: those distractors which attract less than 5 per cent of the responses. When an item is re-written, an attempt should be made to replace such distractors with more plausible ones.

Facility value (FV): the fraction (normally expressed as a decimal) of the candidates choosing the key in any given item. Thus, if half the students answer correctly, the facility value for that item is 0.50. In tests of achievement designed to rank students in order of merit, the facility values should lie between 0.35 and 0.85, since very difficult or very easy items do not normally contribute to the role of such a test.

Discrimination index: a figure which represents the degree to which the item separates the better students from the poorer students, since a 'good' item (particularly in an achievement test) is one which the better students should get right and the poorer students should get wrong. There are several ways in which the discrimination index can be calculated, but one of the simplest is to calculate the difference between the facility values for the top third of the population (on the test as a whole) and for the bottom third for each item under consideration.

The discrimination index can obviously never be greater than +1.0, and should always be greater than +0.2 for a 'good' item. A negative discrimination index is a sign of a very poor item that should either be discarded or revised.

When there is a choice of pre-tested items of known quality, the facility values and discrimination indices chosen will depend on whether the test is meant to be of a simple 'pass/fail' type, is meant to produce a meaningful class ranking, is meant to serve as a diagnostic instrument providing feedback on progress for students, or is designed to help evaluate the efficiency of a teaching/learning system.

Completion Items and Unique-Answer Questions. In both these types of assessment question, the student must *supply* the answer rather than select from a set of choices provided. Examples are given below:

Completion item: 'The United States equivalent to the British House of Commons is known as the ....'
Unique-answer question: 'What is the equivalent temperature in degrees Centigrade to $185°$ Fahrenheit? ....'.

In both these cases, the answer is unique, and so the test can be marked reliably; it has, however, to be marked manually. In such items, skills can be examined one at a time, eg mastery skills (recall, using formulae, simple calculations, etc), organizing skills (categorizing, etc) and interpretation skills (of graphs, tables, etc). Such items can, in fact, be set at surprisingly high cognitive levels. Again, relatively full representative coverage of course objectives and content is possible, since only very short written answers are required.

Structural Communication Testing. This is a recent development in objective testing in which an attempt is made to carry out a reliable test of a student's ability to select relevant information from irrelevant information and to present structured arguments logically.

Initially, students are presented with a grid containing statements pertaining to a particular topic, all of which are factually correct. The grid can contain any number of statements, but 16 or 20 are typical. Students are then asked questions on the topic, to which only some of the statements are pertinent. The student has to select from the grid the relevant pieces of information to answer the question(s), and then has to arrange them in a logical order, in order to present the argument.

Allowance in the scoring can be made if several logical sequences are permissible. In some cases, structural communication testing can be computer-marked.

Practical Tests

Practical tests are highly appropriate in cases when the development of psychomotor or manipulative skills is an important part of a course. Their main drawbacks are that they may be logistically difficult to arrange and administer, and may have low reliability. However, the face validity of actually performing a set task would seem to be high compared (for example) with giving a simple written description of how the task should be performed.

PROJECT ASSESSMENT

In such assessment, a student may be assessed in terms of his cumulative work over a period of time, or perhaps on only the end result of the project, such as a working model, the results of a set of experiments, or a computer program.

LABORATORY EXAMINATIONS

When manipulative laboratory skills are important (eg in science courses), assessment in the laboratory may be carried out. This usually takes the form of continuous assessment over a period of time or a one-off practical examination at the end of a course or section thereof. The latter has the disadvantage that it may be unfair to students who have an 'off-day', and also to students who react badly to exam pressure but have otherwise performed well during the course. From the marker's point of view, it can also be exceedingly difficult to monitor the progress of even a small number of students effectively during such an examination.

SKILL TESTS

Tests of specific manipulative skills may be important in some courses, eg dismantling and reassembling a car engine, cutting hair in a particular way, or repairing a piece of technical equipment. For each of these, a suitable practical test can generally be devised, depending on the circumstances. Such tests are more common in training courses than in general educational courses.

SITUATIONAL ASSESSMENT

These stem originally from management education, and involve the appraisal of complex decision-making skills. Such activities may involve the student in performing such activities as dictating letters, dealing with personnel problems, formulating agendas, and dealing with budgets or financial problems. Such activities are normally simulated, and a whole range of activities and crises can be 'built in' to arise in the same way as they might in the real world. Such an approach is often called an 'in-tray' exercise.

The validity of such a technique would appear to be high, but care must be taken in marking the performance in order to ensure reasonable reliability. To this end, a checklist containing the objectives under assessment provides a useful guide for the marker.

UNOBTRUSIVE ASSESSMENT

Unobtrusive techniques involve the students being observed and assessed without their prior knowledge. Such techniques can be important in assessing a student's commitment and attitudes to work, rather than simply his ability to perform tasks under the controlled conditions of more formal assessment. They can, therefore, be more valid than (for example) written examinations, which invariably contain a large element of artificiality. On some occasions, video techniques are used for recording student performance, and for subsequent analysis and assessment of personal skills and traits. However, there are often considerable logistical problems in operating such an approach, not to mention the obvious doubts over the ethics of unobtrusive assessment.

Summary

If one has an area of course content, a list of objectives and an exam specification of required skills, it should be possible to construct a valid programme of assessment by selecting those objectives which can be tested by objective items, those which require short written notes, those which require to be assessed in a practical setting, and those which lie in the area of attitudes and disposition. The few objectives left over (eg those involving extended reasoning or written communication skills) may then need essay-type questions. If everything else has been dealt with by more appropriate methods, the marker can concentrate comparatively single-mindedly on these few areas in the essays, thus tending to make marking more reliable.

In short, an appropriate battery of assessment techniques should be used to match specific objectives, thus producing a practicable assessment strategy that not only has a high degree of validity and reliability, but is also fair and useful to students.

CHAPTER 8

Evaluation

Introduction

In the previous chapter, we distinguished between assessment and evaluation by describing the former as those activities that are designed to measure *student learning* achieved as a result of a teaching/learning situation, and the latter as a series of activities that are designed to measure the *effectiveness of a teaching/learning system* as a whole. However, we noted that the results of student assessment may well form part of the wider evaluation process.

Within the systematic approach to instructional design which was described in Chapter 1 and which is argued for throughout this book, the role of on-going monitoring and evaluation of the system is of vital importance to its development and evolution. Because of the cyclical and interactive nature of the systems approach, each cycle can benefit from the experiences and feedback obtained from previous cycles. Evaluative feedback can be gained from a wide range of sources and via a wide range of methods, and, in many cases, a battery of evaluation techniques are used in order to gain an overall view of the effects of an instructional system.

Whether the teaching/learning system in question is a fully self-contained course, part of a course, a particular teaching session, a self-instructional programme, or a teaching aid such as a film or video, a designer (or team of designers) should never be happy with their first attempt, or even with revised versions. If one takes the view that the system can always be improved, on-going evaluation should be an integral part of the design process.

The scope and depth of the evaluation will vary in each particular situation, as, indeed, will the evaluation methods used. However, whatever the circumstances, the general importance of using evaluation procedures to monitor the instructional system and provide the basis for improvements should not be underestimated. Feedback obtained from the critical evaluation of an instructional system should shed light on the appropriateness of the teaching methods used, the structure adopted, the implementation strategy, the student assessment methods, and even the original objectives themselves. With each successive cycle of the systematic design approach, the teaching/learning situation should become progressively more finely 'tuned', and should consequently become more efficient and more effective through a continuous process of evolution.

In this chapter, we will first describe more fully the philosophy that underlies the role of evaluation in the evolution of instructional processes. In order to do this, we will adopt the basic 'error elimination' approach advocated by the philosopher Karl Popper and adapt it for use in the on-going development of instructional systems. We will then describe two contrasting paradigms (or models) of evaluation — one of which concentrates mainly on the *outcomes* of an instructional system (the *agricultural/botanical paradigm*, or *scientific approach*), and one which pays more attention to what happens during the educational process itself (the *social/anthropological paradigm*, or *illuminative approach*). Finally, we will review the range of diagnostic techniques which are commonly used as part of an evaluation strategy, and discuss the evaluation of cost-effectiveness.

Instructional Development by Error Elimination — A 'Popperian' Approach

The philosopher Karl Popper originally used the concept of 'error elimination' to explain how progress is made in developing scientific theories. We believe that the same concept can be applied to the logical development and improvement of instructional systems of all types. (See the Bibliography for details of Karl Popper's work.)

Underlying Rationale

The 'error elimination' approach to the development of instructional systems is based on two assumptions: first, that the instructional system is not an independent entity, justifying its existence *a priori*, but is part of a total system — fulfilling a specific function by helping to get from Situation A to Situation B as in the diagram below:

Situation A		Situation B
Students thought capable of achieving certain objectives, but lacking some or all of the necessary knowledge, practical skills and attitudes	Instructional system designed to supply all or part of the necessary education and/or training	Students who have achieved the specified objectives, and can proceed to the next stage of education or training (or take their place in society)

The second assumption is that the development and improvement of the instructional system can most effectively be tackled by adopting the general methodological approach proposed by Karl Popper, an approach that can be summarized by the following schema:

P₁	TS	EE	P₂
initial problem situation	*trial solution*	*error elimination*	*new problem situation*
(identification of need for the instructional system)	(development and operation of the instructional system)	(looking for ways in which the instructional system is failing to achieve its objectives)	(identification of areas in which the instructional system could be improved)

Stages in the development of an Instructional System

We can see that there are four general stages in the above approach.

THE IDENTIFICATION OF THE INITIAL 'PROBLEM SITUATION' (P₁)
This itself can be seen as having three sequential stages:

(a) Identification of the desired objectives (knowledge, skills and attitudes) — let us call these X.
(b) Identification of the relevant knowledge, skills and attitudes already possessed by the prospective students — let us call these Y.
(c) Identification of the objectives represented by X-Y, the gap to be bridged by the instructional system.

DEVELOPMENT AND OPERATION OF THE INSTRUCTIONAL SYSTEM (TS)
This falls into two stages:

(a) Designing an instructional system capable of achieving the objectives represented by X-Y (or at least a part of the difference). This involves developing the overall structure, selecting and sequencing the content, choosing appropriate teaching methods, and so on.
(b) Making appropriate administrative arrangements to put the instructional system into operation (ie implementation of the system).

THE 'ERROR ELIMINATION' PROCESS (EE)
This stage involves carrying out a *critical analysis* of the above two stages. This is the key stage in Popper's methodology, according to which a new instructional system can be regarded in the same way as a new scientific theory which has been developed in an attempt to resolve a specific problem situation, but which has not yet been subjected to rigorous experimental testing. According to Popper, such a theory should be tested not by trying to prove it *right* (an impossible task from a logical point of view) but by trying to prove it *wrong*, ie by looking for specific ways in which the theory can be shown to be

incompatible with experimental evidence. In the case of a new instructional system, the testing should be carried out not by trying to prove that it is succeeding in achieving its objectives (a very difficult task to do with any degree of rigour) but by looking for ways in which it is manifestly *not* succeeding (a much easier task). Needless to say, such an approach requires a healthy attitude towards criticism that is frequently lacking in those who develop and operate educational and training courses, who frequently try to defend their course against criticism by contrived arguments and rationalization rather than accepting valid criticism and attempting to rectify the situation through improvements to the instructional system.

IDENTIFICATION OF THE NEW 'PROBLEM SITUATION' (P_2)
If carried out correctly, Stage 3 should reveal areas in which the instructional system needs to be improved, and (it is to be hoped) point to how these improvements might be carried out. It therefore leads to a new problem situation, P_2, that can form the starting point of a further development cycle.

$$P_2 \longrightarrow TS \longrightarrow EE \longrightarrow P_3$$

Thus, Popper's methodology is seen to be both open-ended and ongoing, forming a basis for the continuous development of instructional systems of all types.

How the Error Elimination Process may be Carried Out

There are two basic questions that should be asked of an instructional system:

1. Are there any ways in which the instructional system is manifestly failing to achieve its design objectives?
2. Are there any ways in which the mechanics and operational features of the instructional system are unsatisfactory?

Finding answers to question 1 is essentially a long-term process and can be done:

(a) by surveying students who have undergone the instructional system; and
(b) by surveying people who are not directly involved in the instructional system under scrutiny, but who nevertheless may have relevant comments and observations, eg employers who subsequently take on the students, or the teachers and organizers of any subsequent courses or training situations to which the students proceed.

Finding answers to question 2 is usually easier, and can be done:

(a) by surveying the staff who are involved in implementing the instructional system; and

(b) by surveying the students who are involved in the system.

Techniques through which the above information can be obtained are reviewed later in this chapter.

Two Contrasting Paradigms of Evaluation

A major area of debate in educational evaluation is concerned with the contrasting merits of two distinctly polarized approaches. On the one hand, there is the *agricultural/botanical approach*, which reflects a 'scientific' approach to evaluation; on the other, there is the *social/anthropological approach*, which is more concerned with the hidden processes which occur during an educational experience. The latter approach has become known as *illuminative evaluation*.

The *agricultural/botanical approach* has its origins in scientific experiments set up to assess the effects of specific variables (the nature of the soil, fertilizers, etc) on the growth of crops. The experiments have tight controls, and the resulting outcomes can be relatively easily measured. When applied to education, this approach has led to the use of systematic, objectives-oriented evaluation procedures. This 'traditional' strategy sets out to measure the extent to which a given instructional system has achieved certain specific goals (or objectives) in relation to the students' pre-knowledge or existing skills. To this extent, the agricultural/botanical evaluation paradigm measures *output* against *input*, and often treats the differences statistically. Other factors in the system, such as the learning environment, teaching personnel, course content and structure, and teaching methods, normally receive only incidental examination if they are considered at all. This general approach has been used when measuring the relative efficiency of different methods in teaching towards a common end, and also to measure the effectiveness of self-instructional programmes in achieving stated objectives.

By comparison, the *social/anthropological approach* is more concerned with studying the on-going process of education, and, in general, the techniques used are far more subjective and often involve personal value judgements of the results. The arguments in favour of this type of approach are that the variables in educational developments cannot be readily identified or controlled, and that 'inputs' and 'outputs' can be varied, complex, difficult to specify with certainty, and often virtually impossible to measure. In such cases, the evaluator explores the perceptions, opinions and attitudes of staff and students, using a variety of methods, in an attempt to reveal what was otherwise hidden in the educational process. The evaluation process is generally not rigidly structured or constrained, and usually gives the evaluator scope to follow up specific areas of interest as and when they become apparent. Illuminative evaluation of this kind has often been referred to as 'attempting to open up the black box of the educational process'.

Malcolm Parlett and David Hamilton, amongst others, have been influential in presenting the case for a greater emphasis on illuminative evaluation.

These two basic paradigms of evaluation differ significantly both in their methodologies and in their treatment of results. They also differ in their focus. The agricultural/botanical approach is basically designed to find out if *specified goals* have been achieved. The social/anthopological approach, on the other hand, is more flexible, and is designed to find out *what* has been achieved and *why*.

Clearly, there must be some middle ground between what, on the one hand, purports to be a purely objective approach, and the largely subjective approach that is embodied in illuminative evaluation. Where the correct balance lies, however, depends to a large extent on what is being evaluated, and for what purpose. A useful review of how appropriate evaluation strategies can be matched with different types of educational development has been given by Tony Becher (1981) — see the Bibliography for details.

A Review of Evaluation Techniques

There is no single correct way to conduct an evaluation exercise. One may, for example, be looking for outcomes (whether intended or not) in cognitive, affective and skills areas, and also for an insight into possible problems concerning the implementation and operation of an instructional system. Much depends also on whether one is adopting an 'illuminative' strategy or a more rigid 'objectives-based' approach.

Because of the variety of information that one may be seeking during an evaluation, it is normally advisable to use an appropriate battery of evaluation techniques. Some of the possible information sources are listed below:

(a) Results from student assessment.
(b) Student questionnaires and interviews.
(c) Observations of the instructional system in progress.
(d) Feedback from teaching staff directly involved with the instructional system.
(e) Feedback from people having an indirect link with the instructional system.

Each of these approaches generally has an important part to play, regardless of whether the evaluation is of a course or unit of teaching that is still in the process of development (*formative evaluation*) or of a fully-developed instructional system that is already in use in order to assess its total range of effects (*summative evaluation*).

Let us look at each of these approaches in more detail.

Results from Student Assessment

When an instructional system has sharply-defined objectives, a critical study of the results obtained from student assessment (as described in the previous chapter) can be of great assistance in the error elimination process described above.

ANALYSIS OF IN-BUILT STUDENT ASSESSMENTS

When student assessments are an integral part of a course or other instructional system, the results of and trends indicated by these assessments can usually shed considerable light on the operation of the system as a whole. The evaluation should, as a result, be able to judge which objectives are being well achieved, and, more importantly, which objectives are not being well achieved. In education, when students do not perform as well as expected, there is a traditional tendency to conclude that it is basically the fault of the students. This may occasionally be the case, but, more often than not, there are other factors involved. A systematic approach to instructional design allows *all* aspects of the system to be analysed, and may reveal that there are a number of reasons for unsatisfactory student achievement, for example:

(a) the teaching methods were not well matched to the course objectives;
(b) there were problems in the operation of the instructional system;
(c) the assessment methods used were not suitable;
(d) the objectives themselves were not realistic.

Such critical analysis allows the instructional system to be continuously monitored and progressively 'tuned'.

ANALYSIS OF CUSTOM-MADE STUDENT ASSESSMENTS

When an instructional package is being trial tested, or when the relative effectiveness of two methods is being measured, student assessment techniques can be used to evaluate the effectiveness of the methods involved, rather than to assess the students. Such approaches are normally essentially agricultural/botanical in nature, and often involve the use of pre- and post-tests, 'control' groups, and statistical analysis of differences.

Student Questionnaires and Interviews

Feedback from students regarding their experiences and their opinions of an instructional system is one of the most common appproaches to evaluation. The information can be sought through questionnaires and interviews, and can be treated either objectively or in a more illuminative manner. Student feedback can be obtained through several 'self-reporting' techniques. Several of these have been adopted from the field of attitude measurement.

LIKERT SCALES

Essentially, a Likert rating scale is an attitude measurement instrument consisting of a list of statements, the person responding having to make a judgement on each statement, often selecting one response from a number of degrees of agreement and disagreement. An example is given below.

	Strongly agree	Agree	Disagree	Strongly disagree
1. I find the course easy				
2. There are too many lectures in the course				

etc

The number of points on the scale depends on the specific require- ments of the setter, although the use of an even number of options has the advantage of making it impossible for students to duck the issues by repeatedly taking refuge in a completely neutral category.

In practice, it is harder to produce 'good' statements than it first appears, and some trial testing of the statements may well be necessary. Indeed, there is a fair amount of skill associated with preparing state- ments which are valid and which, at the same time, provide good discrimination.

Likert scales can be used to monitor students' general opinions of an instructional system. It is also possible to use such statements for comparative purposes, eg by pre- and post-testing the students, or by comparing an 'experimental' group with a matched 'control' group.

SEMANTIC DIFFERENTIAL TECHNIQUE

This is another type of attitude scale, and it can be used to measure connotations of any given concept for an individual. Here, word pairs of antonyms such as 'valuable/worthless' are joined by a 3, 4, 5, 6 or 7 point scale. The method is based upon the premise that the word pairs are opposites, although this may not always be valid in practice, because particular words sometimes have different meanings for different students.

OBJECTIVES RATING

Student ratings of the degree of achievement of student objectives is sometimes used in a student feedback questionnaire. Here, the objectives of an instructional system are listed, and the student is asked to indicate whether each objective has been 'well achieved' through to 'not achieved at all'. The rating is generally carried out using a five-point scale, but variations are possible. This type of scale is particularly useful in cases where no other suitable technique exists for measuring the achievement of certain objectives, or as a cross-check on other evaluation techniques.

STUDENT COMMENTS

If students are allowed to respond freely on topics raised in a questionnaire, unexpected outcomes and attitudes may often emerge. Although it may be difficult to categorize free responses, these should normally be sought as a matter of principle, since they can often add a completely new dimension to an evaluation.

INTERVIEWS

Student interviews are basically a verbal form of student questionnaire. A well-run interview can, however, probe more deeply and sensitively into specific areas of interest than can normally be done in a written questionnaire. One drawback is that individual interviewing is a time-consuming procedure. Thus, the most effective role of sampled interviews may well be to check the validity of a more widely-used formal questionnaire.

Observations of Instructional Systems in Progress

An understanding of the hidden educational processes occurring within an instructional system may be developed by means of careful and sensitive observation of these processes. The observation can be direct and immediate, or may be recorded in some way (eg on videotape) for later analysis. Such techniques are particularly useful when one is evaluating exercises designed to develop communication and inter-personal skills. The ethical problems associated with 'unobtrusive assessment' that were mentioned in the last chapter are not really a problem in this case, as it is the instructional system (rather than the students themselves) which is under scrutiny.

Feedback from Teaching Staff Directly Involved with the Instructional System

Through questionnaires, interviews and solicited comments, the opinions of staff directly involved in the implementation and operation of an instructional system can be of great value in course evaluation. Their comments may be influential in evaluating all aspects of the system, including the validity of the objectives, the course structure, the teaching sequence, the assessment methods, and the day-to-day organization and management.

Feedback from People Having an Indirect Link with the Instructional System

People who do not have a direct link with the actual teaching/learning system under investigation may still be able to make an important contribution to its evaluation. Again, questionnaires, interviews and solicited comments are appropriate means of gathering information.

The advice of employers, for example, may be sought if a vocational course is being evaluated. This may occur both at a preliminary evaluation stage, before a course has been fully developed (in order to assess the skills and qualities which employers are looking for from students), and also as part of a summative evaluation process (to gather information on the relevance of the course to the actual work situation and on the general strengths and weaknesses of former students).

Similarly, the opinions of former students can be important, as they can comment on the relevance of a course or other instructional system in retrospect, and perhaps suggest improvements with the benefit of hindsight and experience.

If a course has external examiners, their comments are usually very influential in course development. This may prove even more valuable if the external examiners are given some guidance as to what aspects should be commented upon.

Finally, the opinions of teachers who subsequently take on a particular group of students for a related course are often highly relevant. Their comments on the students' strengths and weaknesses may be important when revising a particular instructional system, or part thereof.

Evaluation of Cost-Effectiveness

The perceived balance between the cost of an educational programme or innovation and its eductional effectiveness depends upon a multitude of factors. Deciding whether or not the initial costs and on-going running costs justify the end results is a value judgement, involving a wide range of educational, financial, social, and political considerations. Improvements in the effectiveness of teaching/learning can also be measured in several 'dimensions', as discussed in Chapter 1.

It is not our intention in this book to deal in any depth with the complexities of cost-effectiveness. It is, however, important to bear in mind the overall financial implications and on-going financial commitment associated with *any* educational development, and to weigh these against the expected educational benefit using whatever criteria are deemed important.

The financial costing of an educational development is a complex system in itself. Fielden and Pearson, in their book *Costing Educational Practice* (1978), describe a practical approach which they believe could be generally adopted, and give an insight into some of the associated problems, using a number of case studies for illustration. Other interesting case studies of educational costing are provided by Birch and Cuthbert (on open learning methods) and by Fielden and Pearson (on computer-assisted learning). (See the Bibliography for further details.)

Summary

Evaluation is a valuable and essential component of the process by which the on-going development of instructional systems occurs. The evaluator has a wide range of techniques at his disposal, and also has several relevant sources of feedback which may assist in compiling a 'total picture' of the system and its effects (both good and bad). No single approach is the best in all circumstances, and, as in the case of assessment, it is again probably most profitable to use a battery of techniques to ensure that the evaluation process is as valid and useful as possible.

Resources Centres

Introduction

In Chapter 5, we looked at a range of individualized learning approaches and techniques, all of which give the student greater control over such factors as how, when, where and at what pace the actual learning takes place than is the case in most traditional institution-centred courses, thus making them more flexible from the student's point of view. One of the key components of many individualized learning approaches is a *resources centre*, in which much of the learning material and many of the aids that are provided to support self-learning may be housed. In this chapter, we will first take a more detailed look at the role of resources centres in education and training, and will then examine some of the practical considerations that relate to their operation.

We will begin by distinguishing between *resources, resources centres* and *resource-based learning*, and indicating how these three concepts are linked. Then, concentrating more specifically on resource centres *per se*, we will describe how such centres are used in different educational systems and at different levels of education. Finally, we will discuss some of the factors that are involved in the planning, organization and operation of a learning resources centre.

Resources, Resources Centres and Resource-Based Learning

In essence, resources, resources centres, and resource-based learning may be thought of as progressively more highly structured systems through which flexible, student-centred learning can be achieved. Let us illustrate this thesis by examining each in turn.

Resources

Basically, a resource in education or training is a system, set of materials or situation that is deliberately created or set up in order to enable an individual student to learn. To qualify as a true learning resource, the resource must satisfy all of the following three conditions:

(a) it must be readily available;
(b) it must allow student self-pacing; and
(c) it must be individualized, ie it must cater for the needs of students working on their own.

It therefore follows that a resource must be *student-centred*. Thus, in a traditional teacher/institution-centred system involving teaching methods such as lecture-type expositions, timetabled laboratory classes, and textbooks, it is only the textbooks which normally satisfy the criteria for being resources in the sense we have described here. However, in such a course, lectures could be made more like a resource by having them packaged in some form, eg by recording them on videocassette or in some other format such as duplicated notes backed up by audiotape commentaries. Similarly, a laboratory situation could be made into a resource by allowing more flexible student access to the laboratory facilities.

Resources can come in many forms. *People* can be resources — for example, when teaching staff make themselves available on a flexible basis in order to deal with individual student difficulties as and when they arise. Similarly, *places* can be resources, as in the case of an open-access laboratory of the type mentioned above. Finally, a whole range of *instructional media* can be resources, examples including books, structured notes, videocassettes, tape-slide programmes, computers, etc. Instructional media in all their various formats are probably the most common type of learning resource, and these are often housed centrally in a resources centre.

Resources Centres

A resources centre is a place (anything from part of a room to an entire complex of buildings) that is set up specifically for the purpose of housing and using a collection of resources, usually in the form of instructional media.

Resources centres (which are sometimes given equivalent names such as *learning aids laboratories* or *self-study centres*) may serve the needs of an individual department within a school or college, an entire institution, or even a collection of institutions, as, for example, when several schools are served by a single central resources centre. In many cases, such centres are housed in libraries, which often double up as resources centres by providing for the storage and use of both book and non-book learning materials.

Student use of resources centres may, at one extreme, be very loosely structured, and, in some institutions, may not even be an integral component of their courses. On the other hand, in strongly student-centred courses, students may spend a large proportion of their time using the facilities offered by such centres.

The different uses that are made of resources centres, and the various factors that are involved in their planning, organization and operation, will be discussed later in this chapter.

Resource-Based Learning

Courses that involve resource-based learning generally provide for individual study by including some measure of self-teaching and self-pacing. Such courses invariably make wide use of learning resources in the sense described above, and *may* make use of the facilities of a resources centre. However, true resource-based learning goes far beyond the mere use of a resources centre, involving a highly structured system of individualized, student-centred learning experiences that make full use of both human and non-human resources. The class of resource-based learning systems encompasses many of the individualized learning approaches that were discussed in Chapter 5, for example, Keller Plan, Flexistudy and distance learning courses, including all correspondence courses.

Within the broad spectrum of resource-based learning, resources centres can be used as a basis for implementing and assisting developments of this type. Such centres are not, however, necessary prerequisites for *all* resource-based learning schemes.

Several texts which further explain the concepts of resources, resources centres and resource-based learning are listed in the Bibliography.

The Role of Resources Centres in Different Educational Systems

Resources centres are exploited in fundamentally different ways at different levels of education, and the way in which they are used also depends to a considerable extent on the nature of the strategic approach to instruction that is adopted.

Within flexible student-centred approaches to learning of the type discussed in Chapters 2 and 5, a resources centre may have a key role to play in providing students with a whole range of learning resources, together with any associated hardware that may be required for the use of these resources. Within such flexible learning systems, students are often given free access to a resources centre within a host institution, and are permitted to attend at times which suit *them* rather than the institution. Advice is normally given (via a 'study guide') regarding the range of resources which may be suitable to assist in the achievement of a given set of objectives within a given course unit. Teaching staff may be present in order to assist with any problems or difficulties that may arise, and, as such, constitute another resource within the centre.

In the case of courses which are based on the more conventional, more constrained *teacher/institution-centred approach* (see Chapter 2), the role of resources centres is generally completely different. Here, their role is not so much to serve as a means of providing a front-line teaching facility, but rather to provide remedial or back-up material to support other teaching methods.

In primary and secondary schools, a centralized resources centre may store and supply both book and non-book materials which individual teachers are able to borrow for use with their classes. In such cases, the resources are most often used as aids within a traditional expository approach rather than for individualized instruction.

Individualized use of resources centres by students undertaking traditional teacher/institution-centred courses is often completely voluntary (that is, an 'optional extra'), although students may sometimes be directed or recommended to use certain resources by particular teachers or lecturers. All resources are normally available at most times, but the choice of what particular resource(s) to use is often left to the student. Indeed, students may elect to use the facilities of a resources centre in order to study subjects that are not directly related to the content of their courses, for example learning foreign languages for holiday purposes, or studying computer programming out of general interest. However, the main uses of resources centres by such students include remedial study, immediate follow-up of class work, revision before exams, and extra study carried out in order to benefit from an alternative approach to specific subject matter.

Some institution-based resources centres also lay on a programme of displays and exhibitions for general motivation and background interest purposes. This practice is most common in resources centres that are based within a particular department, or which deal only with resources in specific subject areas (eg the biological sciences or health education).

The Planning, Organization and Operation of a Resources Centre

As we have seen, there are several ways in which the concept of a resources centre can be used at different levels and in different systems of education. Clearly, the method of use will have a marked effect on how the resources centre is organized and developed. There are many factors that have to be considered before embarking on the planning and operation of a resources centre, and, in the remainder of this chapter, we will take a detailed look at some of the more important of these.

Constraints

The development of a resources centre is often constrained by a number of factors, including *finance, space, staffing, attitudes,* and *general educational policy.*

FINANCE

Money is obviously required both to set up and to operate a resources centre. An initial outlay is required to buy furniture (for example, study carrels, desks, chairs and storage shelves), to purchase any necessary hardware (for example, tape-slide players, cassette players and videocassette recorders) and to purchase appropriate commercially-available resources (in both book and non-book format). As well as this 'pump-priming' money (which may be considerable), an annual operating budget is required in order to maintain and enhance the equipment and resources housed within the centre.

SPACE

Suitable space clearly has to be found in order to site the development. In some cases, it may be possible and desirable to place the resources centre within an existing library; in others, it may be better to use an independent room − particularly if the resources centre is to be departmentally rather than centrally based. The amount of space required will be directly related to the amount of use that students are expected to make of the centre. Experience shows that there are liable to be peak times of use (lunch times, free periods etc), and the size of the development should (ideally) be adequate to cater for such 'peaks', although in practice, this is often simply not possible.

In addition to providing sufficient student spaces, an appropriate amount of storage space is required, both for equipment and for resources; if possible, this should be flexible enough to cater for any planned future expansion of the resources centre.

STAFFING

Several staffing problems have to be faced. The cataloguing and administration within the centre is sometimes handled by a specialist librarian, but such a person may not be available. It may be desirable to use teaching staff within the resources centre as 'human learning resources' to which students can have access, but this may lead to timetabling problems, and also to problems related to staff willingness (or unwillingness!). Finally, some technician back-up is generally necessary in order to check and maintain any audiovisual equipment housed in the resources centre.

ATTITUDES

Positive attitudes to the resources centre from both staff and students are absolutely vital to the success of the venture. Unless a resources centre is generally considered to be capable of playing an effective and valuable part within the teaching system in which it is to be used, the development is almost certainly doomed to failure. All too often, teaching staff in particular (especially the older members) are highly sceptical regarding the value of a new development such as a resources centre. If this is the case, it may be necessary to take positive steps to convince them that all the expense and effort are worthwhile, and that a more flexible student-centred approach is capable of producing extremely worthwhile results.

POLITICS AND POLICY

Factors ranging from intra- and inter-departmental politics, through general institutional policy to local and central governmental policy, can all affect the development of learning resources centres. For example, if a college of further education is attempting to implement a policy of flexible course provision that includes community education, this will probably stimulate the development of a resources centre in the college; conversely, in the absence of any policy of this type, any attempts to establish such a centre may well be stifled. Similarly, important central government initiatives such as the setting up of the 'Open Tech' programme in the UK (designed to foster the training and re-training of adults at technician level by open learning methods) will almost certainly give an impetus to the development of resources centres in a wide range of educational institutions and training centres.

Organization and Management

Thought must also be given to a number of other factors, including the centre's management stucture, the resources themselves, the equipment, and the general administration of the centre.

MANAGEMENT STRUCTURE

Problems related to the organization, management and operation of a resources centre must be faced on a regular basis, and firm decisions must be made as a result. In some resources centres, these decisions are made by a single person or a small team, whereas in others, a committee of some sort is responsible for deciding policy. Such a committee might involve teaching staff, library staff, educational technologists, students and technicians.

RESOURCES

Basically, the instructional media which comprise the actual learning resources in a resources centre can come from two sources: those that are 'bought in' from commercial organizations or from other educational institutions, and those that are produced within an institution in order to cater for the requirements of a given set of students within a specific subject area.

'Bought in' resources have the obvious advantage of allowing a usable collection of resources to be assembled relatively quickly. However, some resources, particularly those with an audiovisual component, can be expensive, and, in most cases, their content is not entirely relevant to the objectives of the course in which they are to be used.

Resources which have been custom-made by a teacher, on the other hand, may be much more relevant to the specific needs of a course, but, at the same time, can be very time-consuming to plan, produce and evaluate. In addition, devising effective student-centred learning resources may call for new skills from the teaching staff, skills which often have to be nurtured and developed over an extended period.

The various media which might be used in resources production have been discussed in detail in Chapter 5, where it was argued that the media should (ideally) be chosen to match the objectives of the teaching plan. However, the precise choice of media may be influenced by other factors, including the range of equipment available in the resources centre. For example, if basic slide viewing facilities are the only visual equipment available, staff will clearly have to use slides rather than filmstrips or videocassettes. Also, when buying in audio-visual resources, care must be taken to ensure compatibility with any standardized equipment already installed; for example, any pre-recorded videocassettes that are purchased should be of the appropriate format to be played on the videocassette recorders that are available in the centre.

Finally, the effective production of resources within an institution also depends on having adequate production facilities available, including reprographic, photographic, graphics, audiorecording, and possibly also television services, together with adequate secretarial support. In addition, some resources centres include facilities for reproducing certain types of resources within the centre itself. For example, a student-centred course involving extensive use of a resources centre may have a relatively large number of students progressing through the course at roughly the same pace. If reproduction facilities within the centre allow rapid duplication of resources, such as textual notes and audiotapes, this may reduce the need to store multiple copies of particular resources in order to cope with peak demand, and may well result in greater overall efficiency. Where such immediate duplication facilities are not readily available, consideration should be given to the optimum number of copies which are to be held. With 'bought in' materials, copyright restrictions may preclude direct copying, and, in such cases, any additional copies required would have to be purchased.

EQUIPMENT

The range and type of equipment that needs to be installed in a resources centre depends on a number of factors, including the nature of the media to be deployed and the amount of money available. For example, if tape-slide instructional programmes are to form a significant proportion of the resources in the centre, specialist machines, through which the audio commentary is automatically linked to the slides by means of electronic 'pulses' recorded on the tape, can be provided in order to enable students to study these programmes. If finances do not permit the purchase of this type of (relatively expensive) hardware, however, simple manually-operated slide viewers and basic cassette players can be combined to provide a reasonably inexpensive alternative that is almost as effective.

The number of sets of equipment to be installed in the centre has also to be determined, and should (ideally) be sufficient to cope with the expected peak demand. If this proves to be impossible, some form of 'timetabling' or booking of student use of the resources centre may well be necessary, albeit somewhat undesirable.

The actual location of the equipment within the centre may also cause problems. If the equipment is permanently set out in the resources centre ready for use, there may be problems relating to its security. If the equipment is stored centrally, on the other hand, and has to be collected by students every time they want to use it, this inevitably reduces the 'openness' of the resources centre by erecting a (perhaps unnecessary) administrative barrier, and may well deter some students from making full use of the facilities.

As mentioned previously, regular technical maintenance of all audiovisual equipment is extremely important. If minor faults are not immediately rectified, student interest and motivation may again be lost; it is, after all, extremely frustrating for a student to go to a resources centre, get hold of the material he wants, and then find that the hardware needed to study it is not working properly.

GENERAL ADMINISTRATION

A whole series of factors have to be considered regarding the running and administration of a resources centre. One of the most important of these is the question of whether the students are to be allowed open access to the resources, or whether access is to be closed (that is, restricted to staff). In an *open access* system, the resources are usually housed in the main body of the resources centre, so that the students can select and use resources 'off the shelf'. In a *closed access* system, on the other hand, the resources are usually held in a central store, and students must request resources more formally. This factor is linked both to the staffing levels that are available to run the resources centre and also to the degree of student supervision that is thought necessary for educational, operational and security reasons.

Regardless of whether open or closed access is used, the resources of the centre must be systematically catalogued in some way in order to facilitate efficient retrieval. Where resources are in closed access, or are 'non-browsable' (eg videocassettes), it may help to annotate the catalogue entry with a fuller description of the content of the resource. The importance of a good cataloguing system becomes more crucial as the number of resources in the centre increases. Indeed, in the case of a resources centre where a large collection of materials is being built up, there is a strong case for placing the cataloguing of the resources in the hands of a specialist audiovisual librarian.

Other administrative duties which may be important include arranging the booking and borrowing of resources, since it may be desirable for students to be able to use the resources outside the premises of the resources centre. Also, someone must be made responsible for obtaining for preview and eventually purchasing resources produced elsewhere, on the basis of staff recommendations or some other criteria. A further duty may be in keeping records of usage of resources, possible for the purpose of student 'credit' assessment, or, alternatively, for more administrative reasons such as assessing relative demand for different resources or establishing the level of use made of the resources centre.

Finally, the possibility of using human resources in the centre has already been raised. Normally, these are teachers or lecturers, but some university and college centres also make use of senior students as resources, while some school-based resources centres even enlist the help of parents.

Educational Considerations

Once the idea of setting up a resources centre has been firmly established in a school or college, a number of additional factors have to be taken into account regarding the educational (as opposed to the administrative) aspects of its operation and function.

INTEGRATION WITH THE TEACHING/LEARNING SYSTEM

We have already pointed out that there are many possible ways in which resources centres can be used in educational and training systems. One key decision that has to be made is whether the resources centre is to operate in a 'front line' or in an optional 'back-up' role.

Within the context of an open student-centred learning facility such as a resources centre, the amount of direction and advice given to students in the selection and use of resources must strike an appropriate balance between constructive direction and guidance and student flexibility. This depends upon just how open and flexible the learning situations can be while still remaining relevant to the course objectives.

When a resources centre is used as an agency within a strongly student-centred, self-paced course, there is the very real problem of coping, on the one hand with students who complete work quickly, and on the other hand with those who fall far behind. Some resources centres do in fact provide 'mind-broadening' or 'enrichment' materials for the 'high-fliers'. Another approach is to use the better students to help their weaker colleagues through a process of *peer teaching*.

In many schools and colleges, there is an increasing awareness of the need to integrate the actual teaching and learning process with the entire range of available support services. This has led to many institutions combining library, computer and media resources under one 'umbrella' service in order to co-ordinate their activities, and thus (it is hoped) to best serve the needs of the institution's courses and students.

THE ROLE OF THE TEACHER

In a resources centre, the role of the teacher effectively changes from being the sole supplier of information to being a provider of counselling and assistance for those who need it. Within a student-centred resource-based learning course, the teacher is much more a 'manager' of resources than a 'provider' of information. As we saw in Chapter 5, this role is not easy for some teachers to adopt, especially if skills related to the in-house production of resources have also to be learned. These factors indicate a very real need for programmes of in-service training for teachers relating to, for example, the production of resources, the organization of resources centres, and the use of resource-based learning.

STUDENT CHARACTERISTICS

It is a well-known fact that different students learn in different ways. To cater for individual differences in learning style, it may well be desirable to present similar information in alternative resource formats. In some instances, there may even be a case for introducing small-group teaching methods for the benefit of those who find studying on their own particularly difficult.

When the role of a resources centre is that of being an 'optional extra', there is the additional problem of attracting those students who have seldom or never used the facilities on offer. It is a disturbing fact that many institutions which provide resource material of a remedial or 'back-up' nature find that it is the better students who use it voluntarily, rather than the weaker students who would, perhaps, have most to gain.

FEEDBACK AND EVALUATION

As with all learning situations, feedback obtained from both students and staff regarding their problems and experiences relating to resources centres can be of considerable value in determining where and how improvements need to be made. We saw in the previous chapter that on-going evolution based on such feedback should be a feature of *all* components of an instructional system, and it is probably true to say that this is particularly important in the case of a resources centre, especially if it plays a key role in the work of the pupils or students who use it.

Further useful information on different aspects of the planning, staffing, organization and exploitation of learning resources centres is given in a series of three books published by the Scottish Council for Educational Technology (see the Bibliography for further details).

CHAPTER 10

Computers in Education

Introduction

In Chapter 5, we made brief mention of the role which computers can play in the area of self-instructional teaching and learning. In this chapter, we will take a broader look at the different ways in which computers can be used in education and training. These uses are almost certain to become increasingly widespread if computer hardware continues to become progressively less expensive — and, at the same time, progressively more sophisticated and versatile — as a result of developments in the field of microelectronics and information technology. The resulting widespread presence of computers in schools, colleges and training establishments, as well as in the home and in many common areas of everyday experience, already means that our society has a young, computer-literate element capable of making maximum educational use of the adaptable learning facilities that can be developed through computers, and that element is becoming progressively larger every year.

For the benefit of readers who are unfamiliar with the computer field, we will begin by defining a few basic terms and explaining the functions of the different components of a computer system. Then, we will examine the different ways in which the computer can be used in education, looking at its use as a 'supercalculator', its role in computer-assisted and computer-managed learning, its use as a data-base, etc. Finally, we will look at some of the factors that affect the educational use of computers — factors that may well be instrumental in determining whether computers are allowed to play the revolutionary role of which they are potentially capable.

Basic Concepts and Terminology

A computer can be defined as a device which is able to accept information, apply some processing procedure to it, and supply the resulting new information in a form suitable to the user.

The great majority of modern electronic computers, particularly those that are used for educational purposes, are *digital computers*.

By this we mean that the information that they handle is converted into digital form (that is, into a code based on the binary number system, which only uses two symbols — 0 and 1) before processing. Computers that are designed to handle data which have not been converted into digital form are known as *analogue computers*, and are mainly used for specialized technical or scientific purposes.

Digital computers are subdivided into *mainframe computers, minicomputers* and *microcomputers. Mainframe computers* are large, highly-expensive machines (costing at least several hundred thousand pounds) which normally require a custom-built suite of rooms in which to house them and a highly-trained team of staff to operate them — the type of machines that are installed in the central computer units of large organizations such as universities. *Minicomputers* are basically simpler, cheaper versions of mainframe machines — the type of computers that might well be used by a small business or college or by a major section of a larger organization. *Microcomputers* are small, 'desktop' machines that can be purchased for as little as a few hundred pounds or less and can be used for a wide range of purposes — everything from straightforward calculations to word processing and interactive video. These are the machines that are now finding their way into our schools and colleges in increasing numbers.

All computers consist of three basic systems, as shown in schematic form in Figure 10.1.

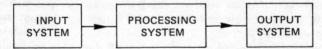

Figure 10.1 **A simple schematic diagram of a computer system**

Input System

The input system is the system whereby information is fed into the computer. This information can be of two types, namely, instructions to the computer (the *computer program*, written in a special code — known as a *program language* — whose nature depends on the nature of the computer and the specific use to which the program is to be put) and data (the material on which the computer will actually operate). Both types of information can be fed in via a wide range of systems, but the one most likely to be encountered is the *keyboard terminal*, a typewriter-like device, whereby instructions or data can be fed directly into a computer in the form of coded patterns of holes in punched cards or tape, coded patterns of magnetic pulses on magnetic tape or discs, or patterns of bars or symbols that can be 'read' using a variety of optical scanning devices. Other methods of communicating with computers (eg by speech) are currently being developed.

Central Processing Unit

The second major part of a computer system is the central processing unit (CPU), which is the part where the actual processing of the material fed into the computer takes place. This consists of three separate sub-systems, namely the *memory* system (where instructions and data are stored in coded form), the *arithmetic and logical unit* (where standard arithmetical and logical operations are applied to the coded signals that represent these instructions and data) and the *control unit* (which co-ordinates all the functions of the CPU by interpreting and executing instructions held in the computer memory).

Output System

The output of a computer can be presented in three different ways. First, it can be produced as *hard copy* — alphanumeric or graphical information that is actually printed on paper using a device such as a line printer or graphic plotter. Second, it can be produced in the form of *soft copy* — similar information that is temporarily displayed on the screen of a *video display unit* (a device similar to a television set). Third, it can be produced in the form of a coded signal of some sort, a signal that can be either used directly for some immediate purpose (for example, control of another machine or system) or passed into a storage system for future reference or use. Storage systems that are used for this purpose include punched cards and tape, magnetic tape and discs, and a variety of 'optical' devices such as videodiscs.

A much fuller, non-technical account of all the above topics can be found in *A Handbook of Computer-Based Training* (1983) by Dean and Whitlock (see the Bibliography).

The Different Roles of the Computer in Education

Over the last decade, the range of uses of the computer in education has expanded rapidly. At first, its role was largely confined to that of a 'supercalculator', but it is now also used in a wide variety of other ways, some of the more important of which are examined below.

Use of the Computer as a Supercalculator

This was the original — and, for some time, only — role of the computer in education, namely, as a tool for carrying out complicated and/or time-consuming calculations as part of academic research programmes. Digital computers are ideally suited to this form of use, since they enable calculations that would previously have taken hundreds or even thousands of man-hours to be completed in a matter of seconds. As computers became progressively more powerful, their usefulness in this role continued to increase steadily, and they have now become an indispensable research tool in a wide range of subject areas.

The use of the computer as a 'supercalculator' is not limited (as was often previously the case) to research scientists and academic staff of universities and polytechnics. In the authors' own colleges, for example, students at all levels — from first-year undergraduates to postgraduate research students — are making increasing use of the computer as a tool in their day-to-day work, and we have no doubt that the same is true in countless other establishments. As a matter of routine, students now use computers to calculate the slopes of graphs, carry out statistical tests on data, and compute the results of experiments — tasks that were, until comparatively recently, all carried out manually using such stone-age aids to calculation as slide rules or (as in the case of one of the authors of this book) logarithmic tables. The availability of computers (and their near-relatives, pocket calculators) to carry out calculations of this type has already had an impact on education, particularly at secondary and tertiary level, that can truly be described as revolutionary.

Use of the Computer to Teach about Computers and Computer Programming

Following on from their original applications in academic research, computers eventually started to be used for teaching *about* computers and computer programming. During the 1970s, this use of the computer became increasingly widespread, until, at the present time, there is hardly a secondary school or tertiary education establishment in the industrialized world that does not include at least *some* computer science or computer programming in its curriculum.

Furthermore, this teaching of basic computer literacy is no longer confined to students of mathematics or computer science or students in traditional computer-using disciplines such as science and engineering, as was (until comparatively recently) largely the case. It is now becoming increasingly widely recognized that almost all tomorrow's citizens will have to acquire computer literacy if they are to be able to cope with the technological complexities of everyday life — or, at the very least, should be given an idea of the vital role of computers in the modern world. Clearly, the use of computers as vehicles for the achievement of these various educational goals is almost certain to continue to increase.

Use of Computers as Direct Aids to the Teaching/Learning Process

A third way in which computers have been able to make a major contribution to education and training is in *computer-assisted learning* (CAL), in which the computer plays a key role in the teaching/learning process. When employed in this role, the computer is normally used in one of two distinct modes (although in some cases, it is used in a combination of the two). In the first, the computer acts as a *substitute tutor* with which the student can participate in an on-going dialogue via an interactive terminal of some sort. In the second, it acts as a *simulated laboratory*, providing facilities whereby the student can carry out 'experiments' on a model system that has been programmed into the computer. Because of the importance of these two modes of operation, we will now examine them in some detail.

THE 'SUBSTITUTE TUTOR' MODE
In the 'substitute tutor' mode, the student interacts directly with the computer, which is programmed to react to student responses to the questions which it sets. The computer may then ask supplementary questions, or provide additional learning information, before requiring the student to respond once more. This adaptive style of learning is directly descended from the programmed learning movement of the 1950s and 1960s (see Chapter 1). It is essentially similar to 'branching' programmed learning, but is capable of being much more sophisticated than the latter because of the greater flexibility and data-handling capacity of computers compared with early 'teaching machines' or typewritten programmed texts. For example, in tutor mode CAL, a student may not be directed to a remedial exercise purely on the basis of a single response; his pattern of responding over a period of time, or even over an entire lesson, may be taken into account by the computer. Such a facility is obviously very useful when basic skills such as mathematical or reading skills are being learned.

Normally, tutor-mode CAL may be just one of the several self-instructional techniques that are employed in a given student-centred educational or training situation. Such a combination of approaches obviously leaves room for flexibility, and allows a closer matching of teaching methods with the course objectives to be achieved.

When a computer is used interactively in a self-instructional capacity, the form of student responses is dependent upon the sophistication of (a) the computer, and (b) the computer program. A simple program may require a student to respond to a given question from a multiple-choice set of options by typing in the code for the selected response. More sophisticated packages may allow the student to respond freely in his own words, the computer being programmed to identify key words, phrases, or numbers, and to respond accordingly.

An example of a section of interactive dialogue between a student and a computer is given in Figure 10.2. In this, the computer is assisting the student to plan a chemistry experiment, and the student may in fact investigate various possible experimental methods by interacting several times with the computer. In the dialogue, the student responses are italicized.

You are required to investigate experimentally the chemical equilibrium of the system: Fe^{3+} + SCN− FeNCS^2 ⇌ in order to discover how the equilibrium constant varies as a function of the ionic strength.
You need a method which is both sensitive and discriminating. Which method(s) do you suggest?
I'm sorry, but I haven't a clue

You first need to consider the physical properties of the individual species, or of the system as a whole, which you might use.
What feature do all the species involved have in common?
They are all ionic

Good!
So what method or methods might you choose which makes use of this property?
Conductivity methods

Yes — a conductance method.
Is a conductance method sensitive? (Very, Fairly, Not Very, Not at All)
Very

No. A conductance method is only fairly sensitive.
Is it a discriminating method?
Yes

Conductance methods are only really discriminating when applied to H^+ ions: for all other ions, the readings are rather similar.
Do you want to consider this method further?
No

What other method(s) might be more discriminating and sensitive?
Possibly a colourimetric method

Good. Are colourimetric methods sensitive?

and so on

Figure 10.2 **Extract from a 'tutor' mode CAL dialogue**

THE 'SIMULATED LABORATORY' MODE
In the 'simulated laboratory' mode, the computer is more of a learning resource than a direct instructional device. In this mode, practical situations can be modelled on the computer, thus allowing the system to be studied as changes are made to key variables. The simulated practical situation can come from a wide variety of subjects, and developments in computer simulation have taken place in such diverse areas as medicine, engineering, geography, mathematics, the physical sciences, economics, business and management training, and military training.

Examples of situations which might point to the use of computer simulations include the following:

(a) where a conventional practical demonstration is either extremely difficult or impossible (eg in manipulating a country's national economy);
(b) where the apparatus or machinery required is either not readily available or is too complicated or expensive for general classroom use (eg in training off-shore oil drilling personnel);
(c) where a conventional, real situation would take an unacceptably long time to investigate (eg experiments in population dynamics or genetics).

Figure 10.3 gives an example of a 'laboratory mode' CAL application. In this case, a complex, highly-expensive industrial process (the production of ammonia) has been modelled on the computer. This process is impractical to carry out in the science laboratory owing to the high pressures involved, but, with the aid of the computer, students are able to discover the effects of altering various conditions (temperature, pressure, and concentration ratios) on the efficiency of the process. When interacting with the computer, the students enter simple replies to the computer's requests for information. The figure shows a sample print out, with the user's inputs again italicized.

For a more general discussion of the role of simulation exercises in education and training, see Chapter 6.

Use of Computers in an Administrative or Managerial Role

Yet another area in which computers have been used in education is in an administrative or managerial role, helping with, for example, the overall administration of the system, timetable planning, budgetary control and the management of the teaching/learning process.

In this last role, which is known as *computer-managed learning* (CML), the computer does not make a direct contribution to the teaching/learning process, as is the case in CAL. Rather, it acts in a supportive and/or supervisory role, relieving the teacher or trainer of various tedious or time-consuming managerial tasks and thus allowing him to devote more time to teaching and to meeting the specific needs of individual students. Thus, in a smoothly running CML environment, there is a balanced partnership between the teacher, the students and the computer.

In CML, the role of the computer is largely clerical, although it can be argued that it is more efficient and cost-effective than human clerical assistance could ever be. There are four roles normally associated with the computer in a CML system. First, it can generate, mark and analyse tests for diagnostic or assessment purposes. Second, based on what is previously known about each student and about the

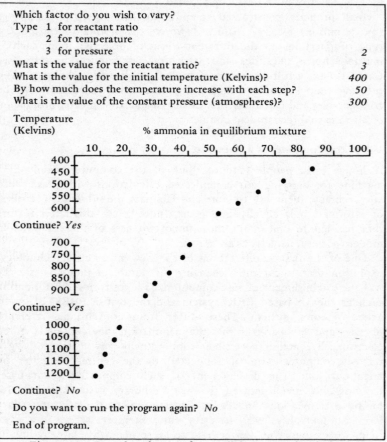

Which factor do you wish to vary?
Type   1   for reactant ratio
       2   for temperature
       3   for pressure   2
What is the value for the reactant ratio?   3
What is the value for the initial temperature (Kelvins)?   400
By how much does the temperature increase with each step?   50
What is the value of the constant pressure (atmospheres)?   300

Temperature
(Kelvins)   % ammonia in equilibrium mixture

Continue? Yes

Continue? Yes

Continue? No

Do you want to run the program again? No

End of program.

Figure 10.3 **Sample print out from a 'laboratory simulation'
mode CAL exercise**

structure of the course, it can provide individual guidance to each
student, directing or advising him on the best choice of route through
a structured set of course materials or modules. This is normally based
on the assumption that the majority of students should follow one of
a limited number of well-defined routes. Third, the computer can be
used to store and update records of test performances and progress
through the course. Finally, from its accumulated records, it can report
on the progress of the student body as a whole, and on the operation
of the course in general, to individual students, the course tutors, and
the course planners. The emphasis on each of these four factors will
obviously vary according to the particular requirements of a given
CML approach, although the administration and operation of assessment

is at the heart of most CML applications.

With properly constructed computer-marked tests, the marking is (by definition) totally reliable. However, this normally restricts the type of questions to the different forms of objective items such as multiple-choice questions and structural communication tests (see Chapter 7 for a full discussion of student assessment techniques). The tutoring time saved by utilizing computer-based assessment can be considerable, and can allow the teacher to allocate a greater proportion of his time to direct student contact.

Use of the Computer as a Data-Base

Although most people tend to think of the computer mainly as a machine for carrying out complicated calculations with great speed and accuracy, its ability to store and facilitate the subsequent retrieval of information is equally important. Indeed, it is this latter feature that has led to one of the most important uses of the computer in modern society, namely, as a *data-base*.

One of the first manifestations of the 'new information technology' explosion that is currently changing the nature of industrial society was the establishment of vast computerized repositories of information such as the US-based ERIC system and the British PRESTEL interactive videotex system. These differ from conventional reference libraries and data-banks in that the information they contain is stored electronically, and is accessible from virtually any distance using a remote computer terminal connected to the central computer by telephone link. The development of such computerized data-bases has not only revolutionized the world's library systems, but is also having a tremendous impact on education — particularly at tertiary level. Students who wish to carry out a literature search in a given field, for example, no longer have to do so manually, but, by linking up with the appropriate bibliographic data-base (which is often located on the other side of the world) can obtain abstracts of virtually every paper, article or book that has ever been written on the subject. Some of the long-term implications of developments of this type will be discussed in greater detail in the next chapter.

It is, of course, also possible to make use of the information-storing capabilities of the computer at a more 'local' level — by, for example, creating custom-built data-bases for specific educational purposes like the two described below.

EXAMPLE 1

Much of the work that is requested of students is often boring and repetitive. If, for example, it is necessary to take 20 readings during the course of a lengthy scientific experiment, it may not be educationally necessary, or desirable, for the students to repeat the actual practical activity more than a couple of times. By feeding a student's first few results into a computer in which a suitable data-base has been established, the computer may then generate the required number of additional readings, which the student can then examine and interpret just as if he had obtained them himself. In a similar way, use of a suitable computer data-base can save students from having to carry out repetitive calculations.

When using the computer in this manner, it is necessary for the teacher to distinguish between appropriate tasks and inappropriate (often time-consuming) tasks associated with the achievement of given goals. Very often, a balance can be struck in which the computer can be used to eliminate the main burden of the latter while still retaining those tasks that are essential to the student's development.

EXAMPLE 2

As we saw in Chapter 7, writing and validating objective test questions is a difficult and time-consuming task. Thus, once a suitable question of this type has been produced, it seems sensible that it should not simply be used on a 'once off' basis, but should be stored for future use. The computer represents an ideal vehicle for this type of storage, and can be used to build up an extensive bank of objective questions over the years. Specific questions can then be culled from such a bank for particular purposes — by, for example, calling up all questions containing certain keywords and then selecting the most suitable by inspection.

Factors Affecting the Educational Use of Computers

There is no doubt that computers and new information technology are potentially capable of causing profound and far-reaching changes in our educational system — changes that are at least comparable to those that were eventually brought about by the mass use of the old information technology of the printing press. We will look at some of these in the final chapter of this book, but first let us discuss some of the factors that are likely to determine to what extent, and at what rate, the computer revolution will be realized.

Technical Factors

Although enormous progress has been made during the last 10 years, there are still a number of technical factors that militate against the use of computers in our schools and colleges becoming even more widespread and far-reaching.

Probably the most important is the fact that it is still generally necessary to learn what are basically new languages (the various program languages) in order to be able to communicate effectively with computers — something that undoubtedly prevents large numbers of people from even trying to use computers in their work or studies. It is true that 'user friendly' software packages, which do not require users to be familiar with the program language in which the program is written, are becoming increasingly available, but there is still a long way to go before the communication barrier is completely broken down. Indeed, some commentators believe that computers will only achieve universal acceptance when users can actually talk to them using ordinary language — as in science fiction situations such as 'Star Trek'. Given the phenomenal rate of progress in computer development, that day may not be all that far off.

Other technical problems relate to the use of the large time-sharing mainframe computers that have now been set up in most of our large colleges and universities. Here, students gain access to the machine via remote terminals, and (unless they are lucky enough to be carrying out their studies in an institution that has enough terminals to meet the peak demand) often experience difficulties in gaining access to a terminal when they want it. Even when they do succeed in gaining such access, they often find that the machine is so overloaded with work from other people that they experience long and frustrating delays in having their own material processed. Over a period of time, an equilibrium is generally established, but not necessarily one that meets the needs of the students, who often have their motivation to use the computer reduced as a result. Nor is the problem necessarily removed by increasing the capacity of the machine, since each successive enhancement merely leads to an increase in usage which very quickly causes the system to become saturated once again. Thus, most central computer service units in colleges and universities find themselves trapped in a perpetual 'Catch 22' situation! No doubt these problems will eventually disappear as time-sharing machines become progressively capable of handling more and more users without undue delays, but, for the foreseeable future at any rate, they will probably remain with us.

Technical problems are not limited to the 'hardware' side of computer operations, since serious difficulties can often arise regarding the compatibility of software, that is, the use of software that has been designed for use with one type of machine on other machines. Such problems even arise with software 'packages' that are designed for use with a variety of machines, since technical standards regarding programs and supportive documentation are seldom rigidly adhered to. Compatibility problems have become even greater in recent years with the proliferation of different types of microcomputers, but, as in the case of the other technical problems that are associated with the educational use of computers, these are probably merely teething troubles that will be overcome in the not-too-distant future, and there appears to be no intrinsic reason why this should not prove to be the case.

Factors Relating to the Availability of Software

With the advent of inexpensive, portable microcomputers, it seems likely that virtually every educational and training establishment in the developed world will soon have access to *some* form of computer hardware. However, while hardware costs are steadily decreasing and computer capacity and sophistication are steadily increasing, appropriate educationally-useful software packages still need to be developed, and this is proving both difficult and time-consuming. Thus, many institutions are finding themselves in a position where they have access to highly-sophisticated computer hardware, but are not in a position to make proper use of it due to lack of suitable software. It was in fact just such a lack of software that prevented teaching machines from making any lasting impact on our educational system.

Given that it can take up to several hundred skilled man-hours to produce, document and validate a single hour of high-quality computer-assisted learning material, it is clearly not realistic to expect the average classroom teacher or college lecturer to produce all his own software. Even if he had all the appropriate skills (a high degree of programming ability, a feel for educational design, ability to write supportive documentation, and so on) the time element would effectively preclude his producing anything more than a tiny fraction of the material he would need to support even a comparatively short course.

Provided that high-quality material was available from other sources, this would cause no real cause for concern (after all, no one expects teachers and lecturers to write their own textbooks). However, with a few honourable exceptions (for example, the packages produced by centres of excellence such as Chelsea College, London and the State University of New York), much of the commercially-available CAL software that has been produced to date is (to quote Megarry (1983)) 'of dismal quality, poorly documented, gimmicky and unimaginative, some of it actually dangerous in the sense that prolonged inexperienced use could lead to the perpetuation of maladaptive strategies and the learning of errors'. No doubt the situation will improve, but, unless there is a really massive commitment to the production of high-quality software that is capable of making a significant contribution to the main-line teaching work of our schools and colleges, it is doubtful whether computer-assisted learning will ever make the impact of which it is potentially capable.

Attitudinal Factors

Another factor that will almost certainly have a considerable influence on the extent to which computers are used in our educational system is the attitude of teachers and lecturers. Here, as in the case of other fields in which an attempt is being made to introduce revolutionary new technology, there is a very real danger that the people who will actually have to use it will see it as a threat to their jobs, authority or traditional role, and, as a result, will fail to provide the co-operation that is necessary for the success of the innovation.

Gray (1983) cites two examples that clearly illustrate these potential problems. The first was an attempt by one of the largest school districts in the American State of Utah to introduce a comprehensive computer-managed learning system covering virtually the entire curriculum. Based on the concepts of skill mastery learning, the system established specified goals, and provided schools with criterion-based pre- and post-tests together with the appropriate learning strategies and resource materials. The entire system was monitored and administered via the district's central computer, which marked the tests, indicated remedial strategies where appropriate and decided when students should progress to new work.

This highly sophisticated and innovative scheme was developed by dedicated teams of teachers and curriculum specialists, all of whom subsequently spoke with considerable enthusiasm about the resulting educational benefits. However, in the case of the great majority of teachers, who had not been directly involved in the development process, the attitude to the scheme was radically different. Many of these felt that their traditional role had been usurped by the computer, and also resented the fact that their efficiency as teachers was effectively being measured by the on-going programme of diagnostic tests. Thus, although there had hitherto been no history of teacher union militancy in Utah, the teachers demanded — and eventually achieved — the partial dismantling of the control mechanisms and the adoption of a more voluntarist strategy on the part of the district administration.

The second example cited by Gray involved an attempt by an (unnamed) English polytechnic to introduce a comprehensive personnel management system, based on the use of a central computer to store detailed information about the expertise, timetables and availability of individual members of staff. It was intended that this information would be used to monitor the accuracy of timetabled information, and to provide more precise data concerning the distribution of teaching activities, student group attendance, teacher's work loads, etc. In the event, requests for the relevant information were simply ignored by the majority of staff involved, thus rendering the system ineffective.

In both these examples, the availability of new computer-based technology encouraged educational administrators to attempt to introduce systems which they confidently expected would improve the efficiency of their organizations. In both cases, however, the innovations met with strong resistance from the teaching staff involved, who felt that their traditional working practices and professional autonomy were under threat. Clearly, any attempts to introduce innovations of this type are foredoomed to failure unless the co-operation of the teachers involved can be obtained, and it is obviously necessary to proceed with great caution.

Other Educational Factors

Other factors that are likely to affect the extent to which computers are eventually used in our educational system are of a philosophical rather than a practical nature. There is, for example, a very real fear among some educationalists that the ever-increasing use of computers and other aspects of new information technology will lead to an over-dependence on *mediated learning*, as opposed to learning through direct experience (what Bruner and his co-workers called *enactive learning*). Such educationalists argue that there is a need to preserve a balance between the two types of learning, since it will never be possible to provide children with a properly-rounded education by mediated learning alone — a view with which we wholeheartedly agree.

Another argument that is sometimes put forward against the increased use of computer-based technology in our schools is that there is a danger that it will lead to a new form of educational elitism. Some children (it is argued), but not the majority, will gain 'computer literacy' and take advantage of whatever becomes available through the technology that this literacy opens up to them. The very real danger of the emergence of such a new elitism is recognized by several commentators, including computer enthusiasts such as Evans (1981) who concedes that some children will take to computers more readily than others, whether or not the same facilities are made available to all children.

Finally, there is concern in some quarters that the increasing reliance on computer-based learning and new information technology will weaken our traditional public educational systems, thus causing lasting and possibly irreparable damage to the fabric of society. Two arguments are put forward in support of this view. The first maintains that new information technology is likely to prove too expensive to be adopted on a really large scale by the State educational sector, and that its undoubted benefits will therefore be limited to the private sector, which will progressively 'cream off' substantial numbers of able students whose parents can afford to pay for their education. This, it is argued, could lead to the eventual demise of the State system as an effective educational force — with all the potential social damage that this would produce. The second argument maintains that new information technology will eventually become so cheap and efficient that existing educational systems will be rendered obsolete, being replaced by individualized learning carried out at home or at work. Thus, face-to-face instruction will become a rarity, with a resulting imbalance between mediated and enactive learning that will be extremely undesirable from an educational point of view.

All the above issues are discussed in detail in a recent book by Hawkridge (1982), and interested readers are referred to this.

Conclusion

If computers are to be used *effectively* in education and training, then they must be used *appropriately*, and their use will certainly not flourish if they are seen merely as an expensive alternative to the classroom teacher. Care must be taken to identify and develop, through the computer, learning opportunities which cannot easily be provided in any other way. In other words, the undoubted strengths of computers must be made the most of; it is in no one's interest simply to use them because of their availability, or to employ them as 'gimmicks', as is all too often the case at the moment. Computers have, in principle, the potential to revolutionize our educational system; let us hope that the opportunity is not lost due to lack of action or mis-use, and that they do not suffer the same fate as the teaching machines which showed such early promise during the 1960s.

CHAPTER 11

A Glimpse into the Future

Introduction

In Chapter 1, we looked at the past history of educational technology, showing how it has developed and (it is to be hoped) matured since the end of the Second World War. In this, the final chapter of our book, we will attempt to look into the future, trying to identify current trends in educational technology and making informed guesses as to how these will affect the educational scene of tomorrow. We hope that this final chapter will help to pull together the various topics that have been examined in earlier chapters, and will thus help readers to put educational technology in its proper perspective.

Current Trends in Educational Technology

We believe that we can identify at least three important underlying trends in current educational technology. The first is a gradual shift towards a more student-centred approach to learning, a shift that is manifesting itself in a steady increase in the use of individualized learning in all its various forms. The second is an ever-widening realization that there is more to education than teaching basic facts and principles, and that a serious attempt should also be made to cultivate the various non-cognitive skills and attitudes that are so important for success in later life; this is leading to a much greater use of group learning methods, which, as we have seen, are ideally suited to this type of role. The third, and probably the most important in the long term, is an almost explosive increase in the use of new information technology in practically all aspects of education and training. Let us now examine these three trends in more detail.

The Shift Towards a More Student-Centred Approach

Traditionally, our educational system has been almost entirely based on the teacher/institution-centred approach described in Chapter 2, a system in which the individual student has little or no say regarding what he learns and how he learns it. Since the end of the Second World

War, however, there has been a gradual but definite shift away from this traditional paradigm towards a more student-centred approach, a shift that has, in our opinion, shown definite signs of accelerating during recent years.

First, let us consider our 'formal' educational system — the network of schools, colleges and universities in which most of our education still takes place. Here, the traditional teacher/institution-centred approach still dominates, and we have no reason to suppose that it will not continue to dominate for many years to come. However, it is probably also fair to claim that there has been a slow but steady increase in the use that is made of student-centred learning *within* the traditional system, as evidenced by the much wider use that is now being made of resources centres and of mediated and individualized learning in all their various forms. Thanks, we believe, to the influence of educational technology, more and more teachers and curriculum developers are beginning to appreciate that such techniques are capable of making a valuable contribution to the educational process, and, as a result, are building them into increasing numbers of courses. We confidently expect this trend to continue at all levels of education — from primary schools right through to polytechnics and universities — and are also fairly certain that it will receive a considerable boost by the current information technology 'explosion', which, as we will see below, is making student-centred learning progressively more practicable by making available new and more effective vehicles for mediated learning.

It is, however, outside the traditional educational system that we see the main developments in student-centred learning taking place. Here, the fundamental (and, we believe) irreversible changes that are currently taking place in the fabric of Western industrial society seem certain to bring about a massive increase in the demand for education, a large proportion of which seems likely to be supplied in student-centred form. More and more people, for example, are finding that they *have* to continue to study after they finish their full-time schooling in order to gain the extra qualifications and expertise that they need to survive in what is becoming an increasingly technical and computer-based society. Since the traditional educational system is not, in its existing form, ideally suited to meet this need, a number of completely new educational and training systems are currently being set up — many, like the British 'Open Tech' system, being largely student-centred in approach. With the increasing need to retrain people for completely new jobs at regular intervals throughout their working lives, the importance of this type of system seems almost certain to increase.

Equally important, more and more people are now continuing to study because they *want* to, and are enrolling in ever-increasing numbers with institutions such as the Open University which provide flexible, student-centred courses of the type that they can fit into their normal lives without undue disruption. As the working week becomes progressively shorter, and more and more people find themselves at a loose end because of long-term unemployment or early retirement, the demand for this type of course seems almost certain to increase, and we expect that the provision of student-centred 'continuing education' courses will become one of the growth industries of the 1980s and 1990s.

The Spread of Group Learning

We saw in Chapter 1 that, according to Professor Lewis Elton, educational technology has gone through three overlapping phases since the end of the Second World War, concentrating on the development first of mass communication, then of individualized learning, and, finally, of group learning (see Figure 1.5). We also saw that the various techniques that are associated with group learning (games and simulations, interactive case studies, structured communication exercises, etc) are now starting to achieve increasingly widespread use in our educational system. We believe that this trend will continue throughout the 1980s, since such techniques are ideally suited for use in teaching towards the various higher-cognitive and non-cognitive skills (for example, decision-making, communication and interpersonal skills) and desirable attitudinal traits that are now regarded as being such an important part of a properly-rounded education.

Since the early 1970s, we ourselves have both been heavily involved in the 'group learning' movement through our work on the development of science- and technology-based games, simulations and case studies. During this time, we have seen such exercises change from being optional extras, employed by a few isolated enthusiasts, to becoming an integral part of an increasing number of courses and curricula, at both local and national level.

In our own colleges, for example, games, simulations and interactive case studies have now been built into the curricula of a large number of science and engineering courses, where they are used in two basic roles. First, they are used as vehicles for teaching towards the various higher-cognitive and non-cognitive skills mentioned above, and, in particular, for the teaching of communication studies; indeed, the staff responsible for this rapidly-expanding area of the curriculum have adopted such exercises as one of their main teaching methods. Second, they are used as vehicles for helping students to appreciate the applications and social relevance of the subjects they are studying. This is another area to which progressively greater emphasis has been given in recent years. Feedback from colleagues in other colleges indicates that similar developments appear to be taking place in many other tertiary education establishments, and we confidently expect this trend to continue.

Similarly, the use of group learning methods appears to be increasing at school level, since such techniques are now starting to be built into a number of national curricula. Two such developments of which we have first-hand knowledge are the use of games and simulations in the AO-level 'Science in Society' course that was recently developed by the (UK) Association for Science Education (ASE) and the proposed use of similar exercises in the Foundation-Level Science course currently being developed for use in Scottish secondary schools. In the case of the ASE course, which is now being taught in secondary schools throughout the United Kingdom, the various games and simulations that were custom-built for use in the course have, in the words of Project Director John Lewis, 'proved a great success with all who have tried them,' and are 'clearly a powerful teaching technique'. Feedback received from teachers who have been involved in testing the exercises being developed for use in the Foundation Science course, which is designed for 13 to 15 year olds in the bottom 20 per cent of the ability range, indicates that group learning techniques seem likely to prove equally successful with lower ability pupils — an extremely encouraging result which supports our view that such techniques are capable of making a valuable contribution to education at all levels, and that their use will continue to spread.

The Increasing Use of New Information Technology

One matter on which virtually all educationalists and educational technologists are in agreement is that new information technology seems certain to play an increasingly important role — many would say a dominant role — in future education. It would therefore probably be helpful to start this section by explaining exactly what we mean by the term.

Like 'educational technology', 'new information technology' is not a particularly easy term to define, largely because it denotes a wide-ranging field of activities rather than a single concept or process. Indeed, Hawkridge, in his book on *New Information Technology in Education* (1982) (to which readers are heartily commended) devotes the whole of the first chapter to attempting to answer the question: 'What is New Information Technology?' In essence, however, new information technology can be thought of as the application of new electronic and other technology (computers, communications satellites, fibre optics, videorecording, etc) to the creation, storage, selection, transformation and distribution of information of all kinds. This may not be a completely satisfactory definition, but we hope that it is slightly more helpful to readers than the 'official' definition of new information technology that was recently adopted by UNESCO, namely: 'the scientific, technological and engineering disciplines and the management techniques used in information handling and processing;

their applications; computers and their interaction with men and machines; and associated social, economical and cultural matters'. (The camel has been described as 'a horse designed by a committee' and the above definition could well be described in similar fashion!)

It is self-evident that new information technology in all its various forms and manifestations is making an increasing impact on education as the years go by, and that this trend currently gives every appearance of accelerating rapidly. In formal education, for example, computers and the various mediated learning systems that make use of them are becoming increasingly widely used at all levels. Initially, these were largely confined to the tertiary sector, but, with the recent appearance of the cheap desk-top microcomputer, the use of computers has now spread throughout our secondary schools and is even starting to make an impact at primary level. If microcomputers continue to become progressively cheaper in real terms, and the various technical and other problems that were outlined in the last chapter can be satis-factorily overcome, their use may indeed eventually become universal, as many commentators currently predict. This would clearly have consequences of the most far-reaching nature, consequences that can indeed probably be compared with those that have resulted from the universal use of the old information technology of the printing press.

New information technology also seems likely to have a comparable impact on informal education — the education that both we and our children constantly receive from the activities of everyday life (watching television, reading books and newspapers, etc) rather than in the context of formal school or college courses. Whatever the criticisms that are levelled at the modern child in respect of traditional academic standards, surely no one would seriously deny that he is considerably better informed than the generations that preceded him, largely as a direct consequence of exposure to television from an early age. With the increasing availability in the average home of products of new information technology such as videorecorders, computer-based data retrieval systems, electronic games, mediated instruction systems, etc, an increasingly large proportion of the edu-cation of the child of the future seems likely to take place *outside* school, a development that is again likely to have far-reaching impli-cations both for society and for our educational system.

Education in the Year 2000

Let us now conclude this look at the future by extrapolating the above trends to the end of the century, and trying to predict what changes they are likely to bring to education by then. We appreciate that new technological developments, political and social changes, and other events that are impossible to anticipate at the time of writing, will almost certainly invalidate these predictions in a number of important respects, but we hope that they will prove of interest to readers who would like to know what the future may hold. Readers who regard such speculations as pointless can always close the book now!

Pre-School Education

There seems little doubt that, by the end of the century, most children will have received a significant part of their education before they ever start formal schooling at the age of five or six. Some progress has already been made in this direction, largely due to the presence of a television set in virtually every home, but the possibilities that will be opened up through the mediated learning resources that new information technology seems likely to make available are almost limitless.

By the year 2000, we expect that most homes will contain a basic information/entertainment system, comprising integrated television, sound reproduction, communication, information retrieval and computing facilities. Using this system, members of the household will be able to gain access to multi-channel television networks, probably via optical cable links and/or direct broadcast communications satellites, which will provide programmes of every possible type — including basic educational programmes for pre-school children. These will almost certainly be so interesting, and so attractively presented, that the great majority of children will need no persuasion to make extensive use of them. Similarly, children will very quickly learn to make use of the wide range of packaged material that will be available on videodisc, videocassette and similar media, including electronic games (many of which will have a built-in educational content) and interactive video presentations. Using these mediated resources, many children will probably learn the basics of the 'three Rs' long before they start school, and, once they do, they will be able to make use of an even wider range of computer-mediated resources, including interactive videotex systems and data-bases, which will both no doubt contain large amounts of material specially designed for the entertainment and education of the pre-school child.

Thus, by the time they start school, children will not only be thoroughly familiar with new information technology, but will, through the medium of such technology, have already mastered a significant proportion of the material that they would previously have learned during the first few years of formal schooling.

Primary Education

Despite some dire predictions of the virtual total disappearance of schools, we do not expect the educational system to have changed greatly in terms of its overall structure by the year 2000. Children will still, for example, start full-time schooling at the age of roughly five or six, and will then spend six or seven years in a primary school that is similar in many ways to those we have today. Indeed, most of them will probably still occupy the same buildings, because of the ever-increasing cost (in real terms) of constructing new ones.

We also expect that primary schools will continue to be organized along much the same lines as today, with most children being taught in single-age groups of between 20 and 30 and being under the direction of a single teacher for most of the time. (This is a system that has proved extremely flexible in incorporating all the various educational innovations that have appeared during the last 30 years, so we see no reason why it should not prove to be equally flexible in respect of the challenges posed by the advent of new information technology).

With regard to the activities that will take place in the average primary school, we again expect that these will be similar in many ways to those that take place in the more progressive primary schools of the present day. Already, most of the work in these schools is organized on pupil-centred lines, with the teacher acting as a manager and supervisor of learning activities rather than a 'fount of knowledge' of the traditional type. The main changes will be in respect of the range of resource materials to which pupils will have access, which will, in addition to the textbooks, work cards and resource sheets of the present classroom, include interactive video and multi-channel cable and satellite television systems, computer-mediated systems such as interactive videotex, word processors and data-bases, and a wide range of mediated learning packages. Mediated individualized learning, based on the use of these systems, will be complemented by a variety of group activities designed to cultivate social, interpersonal, communication and other skills, and also by a certain amount of 'plenary' face-to-face teaching, which will still have an important part to play in primary education.

By the time they reach the end of their primary schooling, children will probably vary greatly in the academic level that they have reached — almost certainly much more so than today because of the greatly increased learning opportunities that new information technology will make available to the 'high fliers'. Nevertheless, we expect the overall standard to be significantly higher than today, with virtually all children being brought to a level where they can benefit from the more advanced education that they will receive in secondary schools.

Secondary Education

As in the case of primary education, we do not expect that secondary education will be all that different in terms of its overall organization from that which we see today. Children will still start their secondary education at the age of about 12, and will still spend a minimum of four or five years in the system, with most of them probably spending even longer at school because of the poor job prospects for unqualified school leavers (which will almost certainly be even worse than they are today). Similarly, most secondary schools will probably occupy the same buildings that they do today.

With regard to their internal organization, we again do not expect any major changes to take place between now and the end of the century. The specialized nature of secondary teaching will still make it necessary for most of the work to be carried out on a single-subject or related-subject basis, although we expect that there will be a significantly greater emphasis on cross-disciplinary studies than is the case at the moment, probably under the direction of teams of teachers with different subject backgrounds. Such studies will probably make extensive use of group learning techniques, such as games and simulations, which, as we have seen, are ideally suited for use as vehicles for cross-disciplinary work.

Although the activities that take place in the actual classroom will obviously vary considerably from subject to subject, there will probably be much less emphasis on conventional face-to-face teaching than is the case at the moment. Pupils will spend a large proportion of their time carrying out individualized study of one form or another, much of it based on mediated resource material (although we expect that textbooks and other printed materials will still have an important role to play). This will be complemented by other, more traditional activities such as practical work, as well as by a wide variety of group learning techniques, with the curriculum in each subject, and the overall curriculum, being designed in such a way as to provide each child with a balanced, rounded education tailored to his particular needs.

Needless to say, tomorrow's secondary schools will make extensive use of the products and techniques of new information technology. In many schools, for example, practically all mathematics and computer studies teaching will actually be carried out via computers, probably using rows of microcomputers or time-sharing terminals laid out in a similar fashion to a present-day language laboratory. Science classrooms will also make heavy use of computers, both for basic teaching and calculation purposes and also to provide computer simulations of laboratory situations. Even non-mathematical subjects such as English and history will almost certainly make considerable use of the new technology. Most English classrooms, for example, will probably contain banks of word-processors (for creative writing) and video terminals (for studying literature contained in data-banks, consulting computerized dictionaries, etc), while history classrooms will probably contain libraries of audio- and videorecordings of archive material, together with the hardware needed to study them on an individual or group basis.

Tertiary and Continuing Education

The area of education that will probably have undergone the greatest change by the end of the century is the tertiary sector — the sector that includes all today's further and higher education colleges, universities, polytechnics, teacher training colleges, and so on. Such establishments will no doubt still exist in the year 2000, but we expect that their function will have undergone a significant change. At the moment, the primary role of most tertiary education establishments is to provide long 'one-off' courses that are designed to equip students to hold down a job for the rest of their working lives. No doubt this will continue to be an extremely important part of the work of such establishments, but we expect that they will also become much more heavily involved in providing other types of courses — short updating, extension and re-training courses that people will undertake at regular intervals throughout their working lives, for example, and also courses designed specifically for the unemployed, the retired, non-working mothers, and so on. Indeed, by the year 2000, we feel that continuing education of this type — backed up with almost unlimited opportunities for informal education via the various mediated techniques that information technology will make available — could well have become one of the mainstays of post-industrial society.

The organization of most tertiary-level courses will probably also have undergone a number of significant changes by the year 2000. We expect that they will be much more strongly student-centred than is the case today, with much less emphasis on formal 'face-to-face' teaching and more emphasis on individualized and resource-based learning and on group learning. As in the case of primary and secondary education, much of the former will be based on new information technology, with which the students of the year 2000 will be just as familiar as they are with textbooks today. They will, for example, make extensive use of computer terminals, both to gain access to mediated learning programmes and data-banks and to carry out calculations, simulated laboratory work, exercises and creative work. Essays and assignments, for example, will probably be carried out using word-processors, which teaching staff will probably also use to scrutinize, mark and annotate students' work.

As a result of the above changes, teaching staff will spend much less of their time in timetabled contact with their students and much more creating, modifying and updating teaching packages and resource materials of one form or another. Much of their work will probably be done via computers, with each member of staff having his own personal terminal via which he can gain access to data-banks, create new material, carry out research, and so on.

Final Word

Needless to say, one extremely important aspect of tomorrow's educational system will be the training of teaching staff, something that will probably take place on a regular on-going basis rather than on a once-off pre-service basis as is usually the case at the moment. Such training will be designed to ensure that teachers and lecturers are not only thoroughly familiar with and proficient in the use of the new techniques that information technology has made available, but are also able to organize the learning activities of their pupils or students in a systematic and effective way, making appropriate use of group learning and individualized learning as well as conventional expository teaching. They will, in other words, be expected to have a thorough understanding of the principles and practice of educational technology. We hope that this book will go some little way towards helping the teachers and lecturers of today to gain such an understanding, and realize that educational technology is a discipline that can be of considerable assistance and benefit to them in their everyday work.

Glossary of Terms used in Educational Technology

A

Ability profile a chart or diagram which provides a graphical representation of an individual's scores in respect of a number of separately-
assessed aptitudes and abilities, and which thus gives a balanced picture
of his overall ability.

Achievement test a test designed to measure a person's knowledge,
skills, understanding, etc, in a given area at a particular time; as opposed
to his potential for learning.

Acoustic coupler a device that enables a remote terminal to be
connected to a computer via an ordinary telephone link by using a
modem to convert the digital signal into an analogue signal and then
converting it back into digital form after transmission.

Active, activity learning learning which involves active participation on
the part of the learner.

Adjunctive programme a type of instructional programme which
incorporates a set of questions which are presented to the learner at
the end of a text (or section of a text) in order to determine what has
been learned.

Advance cue, signal synonyms for *synchronizing signal.*

Affective (adjective) relating to attitudes, feelings or values; see also
affective domain.

Affective domain one of the three broad sets into which Bloom and his
colleagues classify learning objectives, containing all those connected
with attitudes, feelings and values (see Chapter 3).

Agricultural/botanical approach (to evaluation) a scientific approach
to evaluation that involves measuring the extent to which specific
objectives are achieved by an instructional system under controlled
conditions; contrast with *social/anthropological approach* (see Chapter
8).

Aims the desired outcomes of an exercise, programme etc expressed in fairly general terms.

Algorithm a series of instructions or procedural steps in the solution of a specific problem.

Analog(ue) a term applied to an information processing, storage or transfer system in which the signal is *not* translated into binary code before processing, storage or transmission.

Analysis a *cognitive* process which involves breaking down an idea, system, process, etc into its constituent parts and examining the relationships between those parts; level 4 of Bloom's *cognitive domain* (see Chapter 3).

Analytic(al) method of marking a method of marking essays, projects, etc based on a separate assessment of specific aspects or features.

Application a *cognitive* process in which a learner, given a new problem, will be able to make use of the appropriate theories, principles, facts, etc needed to tackle it; level 3 of Bloom's *cognitive domain* (see Chapter 3).

Assessment grid a table or grid used in the *analytical method of marking* in order to help the marker assess specific aspects of an essay, project, etc independently.

Attention span the time during which a learner can give his full attention to a topic, programme, etc (see Chapter 4).

Attitude scale a linear instrument designed to assess a person's attitude to a specific issue, phenomenon, etc by determining his position on some form of *rating scale.*

Audible advance a term applied to a synchronized sound/vision presentation with an audible *synchronizing signal* which indicates when the next frame should be shown.

Audio aids instructional aids such as sound discs and audiotapes which rely solely on sound for their effect.

Audio recording any recording of sound on disc, tape, etc.

Audio signal an electronic signal, either in *analogue* or *digital* form, representing a specific sound and capable of being used to reproduce that sound.

Audiovisual specifically, a term used to describe instructional materials or systems which use both sound and vision; more generally, a term used to describe all educational communications media.

Autoinstructional aid, device a general term for an audiovisual aid used for individualized instruction.

Autonomous learner, student a learner or student who controls the selection and content of his learning material and who also has control over his pace of learning.

B

Backing store an extension to the *main store* of a computer, generally physically distinct from it.

Back projector projection of an image on to the back of a translucent screen for viewing from the opposite side.

Backward branching a type of *branching* in programmed instruction in which the learner is sent back to repeat items which he has not yet mastered; also known as *washback*.

Bandwidth the range of frequencies over which a communications channel or piece of equipment is capable of operating or is capable of carrying.

Barrel distortion distortion of a projected image whereby straight lines parallel to the edges of the field curve inwards at their ends.

Batch mode, processing, system a method of using a computer in which all the data relating to a given task (or set of tasks) are fed into the computer at one time and processed to give a specific output (or set of outputs) based on this.

Battery any group of tests, scales, etc that are normally administered consecutively over a short period, the results being used to give an overall picture of performance, ability, attitude, etc in the area of interest.

Beaded screen a projection screen with a surface which consists of a very large number of tiny glass beads, thus giving high forward reflection.

Beginning spurt a (generally short) period of abnormally fast work or high concentration at the start of a lesson, activity, etc; see also *end spurt*.

Behaviour the observable activity of an individual or group; the response or responses of an individual or group to stimuli.

Behavioural instruction a term that is sometimes applied to instructional systems such as the *Keller Plan* (see Chapter 2) where the learning process is based on mastery of successive units, with testing and tutoring carried out largely by the learners themselves, or by monitors.

Behavioural objective a precise statement indicating the performance expected of a learner (in terms of specific skills) as a result of exposure to given instructional material; see also *Magerian objective*.

Behavioural(-ist) psychology the school of psychology which holds that all behaviour of an organism can be explained in terms of the *stimulus-response mechanism.*

Behaviourism a name sometimes given to *behavioural psychology.*

Binaural recording (reproduction) audio recording (reproduction) that employs separate sound channels for the signals heard by the left and right ears; often used synonymously for *stereophonic recording* (reproduction).

Black box a term (originating from the name of Professor Black, an early worker in the field of systems theory) for an electronic device whose internal mechanism is hidden from (or is irrelevant to) the user, or, more generally, any system whose input and output are much more important than its internal mode of operation.

Bloom's taxonomies a set of taxonomies of learning objectives, compiled by the American psychologist B S Bloom and his co-workers, in which all such objectives are classified into three broad groups, or domains — the *cognitive, affective* and *psychomotor domains* (see Chapter 3).

Branstorming a technique for generating ideas, solving problems, etc whereby members of a group are encouraged to originate ideas, no matter how wild or apparently unrelated to the topic under discussion, and then to consider their potential.

Branch a point of choice in a *programmed learning* sequence at which the learner is directed to alternative items depending on his response to the previous item tackled (see Chapter 1).

Branching programme a *programmed learning* sequence that makes use of branches.

Briefing an introductory session for the participants in a game, simulation or other exercise that is used to describe the background to the exercise, assign roles, etc.

Broadcasting simultaneous dissemination of information to a large number of receivers, usually via electromagnetic carrier waves as in radio and television broadcasting.

Broadcasting videotex(t) *videotex(t)* in which a limited number of pages of information are incorporated into ordinary television transmissions and can be 'called up' by owners of receivers that incorporate the necessary decoding facilities; the British CEEFAX and ORACLE systems are typical examples.

Bulletin board a panel of cork, wood or other soft material to which pictures, notices and other display materials may be pinned.

Bulletin typewriter a manual or electric typewriter which produces very large print, suitable for use on *OHP transparencies*.

Buzz session a short period in a lesson or exercise in which small groups of people (buzz groups) intensively discuss a given topic.

C

Cablecasting dissemination of information via cables, as in *cable television*.

Cable television a television system in which the signal is distributed to subscribers via cable rather than by broadcasting; cable systems can carry a much larger number of channels than broadcast systems, and (in some cases) also enable users to communicate with the distribution centre; see also *switched-star system, tree-and-branch system*.

Carrel a small enclosed space in a library, resources centre, language laboratory, etc designed for individual or private study.

Carrier wave, signal a high-frequency electromagnetic wave or signal used to carry a signal of lower frequency, as in radio and television broadcasting.

Cartridge a type of cassette carrying a closed loop of audiotape, videotape or film that does not require re-winding.

Case study an in-depth examination of a real-life or simulated situation carried out in order to illustrate special and/or general characteristics.

Cassette a closed container of film or magnetic tape designed for loading and unloading into a suitable projector, reader or recorder without prior threading.

Central processor, processing unit (CPU) the main part of a computer system, comprising the main store, arithmetic unit and control unit, or (in the case of some modern computers) simply the arithmetic and control units, see Chapter 10.

Central service unit a name given to an organizational unit (such as a library, educational technology unit or computer services unit) which houses, under one structure, a service available to all departments of an educational institution.

Chalk-and-talk a traditional expository method of teaching that involves talking to a class and illustrating what is said by writing and/or drawing on a chalkboard or similar aid.

Changeover cue another name for a *synchronizing signal*.

Characterization an *affective* process that involves the organization of values into a total and consistent philosophy; the highest level (level 5) of Bloom's *affective domain* (see Chapter 3).

Chronological age an individual's physical age expressed in years and months as opposed to his *mental age.*

Circuit time a term used in *distance learning* to denote the 'turn around' time needed to process student assignments, queries etc.

Class analysis chart a chart on which the relative performances of the members of a class of pupils or students are displayed in graphical form.

Class interval the range of scores between the upper and lower boundaries of a class of score in a test or other assessment.

Clip a term used to describe a short excerpt from a motion picture film or videotape, especially when it is used in a different context (eg in a lesson, or as part of a larger presentation).

Clip art ready-to-use illustrations that can be transferred on to artwork, overhead transparencies, etc from plastic sheets.

Closed access a practice whereby users are not normally given direct access to the stock of a library or resources centre or to parts thereof, such access being restricted to the staff of the library or centre (see Chapter 9).

Closed-circuit television (CCTV) a television system which limits distribution of the signal to those receivers or monitors which are directly connected to the origination point by coaxial cable, optical fibre or microwave link; see also *cable television.*

Closed question an examination or test question in which a unique answer is required and where there is no scope for divergent thinking, evaluation, explanation, etc.

Cognition a generic term for the rational processes of perception, discovery, recognition, imagining, judging, memorizing, learning and thinking through which an individual obtains knowledge and conceptual understanding.

Cognitive domain one of the three broad sets into which Bloom and his co-workers classify learning objectives, containing all those associated with the acquisition of knowledge or knowledge-related skills (see Chapter 3).

Cognitive skill a skill associated with the acquisition, application or manipulation of knowledge, relating to *cognition* or the *cognitive domain.*

Cognitive style an alternative name for *learning style.*

Commercial materials instructional materials produced and/or distributed by a commercial firm.

Compact cassette the most commonly used type of audiotape cassette, containing tape 4mm wide and having separate supply and take-up spools.

Compact disc a recently-developed ultra-high-fidelity *sound disc* on which the signal is recorded in *digital* form; such discs are only 5″ in diameter (hence the name) and are played in a similar way to an *optical videodisc*, using a laser to read the signal.

Compact slide a 2″ x 2″ (35mm) slide, as opposed to a *lantern slide.*

Compatibility (of learning resources) the suitability of one learning resource as it relates to other learning resources in terms of content, format, target, population, etc.

Competency-based learning a form of individualized, self-instructional learning in which the learner is not allowed to progress to the next stage of the learning programme until he has demonstrated complete mastery of the present stage.

Completion item a test *item* in which an incomplete statement, calculation, figure, etc has to be finished by the person taking the test, usually by supplying a missing word, symbol, number, section, etc.

Component behaviour a specific component of the *criterion behaviour* which a learner is expected to master in a course of instruction or learning situation.

Component resources learning resources that are relatively unstructured, user-acceptable and generally available, so that they can be used as components of a wide range of instructional programmes.

Comprehension a *cognitive* process whereby an individual understands a particular idea, set of knowledge, etc without necessarily being able to relate it to other material or appreciate its wider implications; level 2 of Bloom's *cognitive domain* (see Chapter 3).

Computer any device, usually electronic, which is able to accept information, apply some processing procedure to it, and supply the resulting information in a form suitable to the user; see also *mainframe computer, minicomputer, microcomputer.*

Computer-aided (assisted) assessment, examination, test an assessment, examination or test that is constructed and/or administered and/or marked with the aid of a computer.

Computer-aided (assisted) instruction (CAI) use of a computer as an integral part of an instructional system, the learner generally engaging in two-way interaction with the computer via a terminal (see Chapter 10).

Computer-aided (assisted) learning (CAL) learning with the aid of a computer through *computer-aided instruction, computer simulations,* etc.

Computer game a *game* that involves the use of an external *mainframe computer* or *microcomputer*.

Computer graphics the generation and/or display of graphic materials by computers, either on a *video display unit* or as *hard copy* produced by an electronic or mechanical plotter.

Computer-managed instruction (CMI) the use of a computer in a managerial or supervisory role, the computer prescribing work schedules, carrying out assessment, etc (see Chapter 10).

Computer-managed learning (CML) a term used virtually synonymously with *computer-managed instruction*.

Computer-marked assignment a technique (pioneered by the UK Open University) whereby a computer is used to mark assignments completed by students at home; the student fills in his responses on special sheets which can be read by the computer.

Computer program the coded instructions that are given to a computer in order to enable it to carry out a specific set of actions.

Computer simulation a *simulation* that involves the use of an external *mainframe computer* or *microcomputer*.

Computer terminal an electronic device which permits communication between a user/learner and a computer; see also *data tablet, graphics terminal, intelligent terminal, keyboard terminal, remote terminal, smart terminal*.

Computerized item bank an *item bank* which is held in a computer store and can be accessed via a computer terminal.

Concept cards information-carrying cards included in *resource materials* to stimulate awareness of key concepts in a particular topic or subject.

Concept film, tape a short sequence, recorded on film or tape, which gives an illustration or demonstration of a single concept or idea.

Concrete materials physical objects (eg models) used in teaching.

Conditioning manipulation or *reinforcement* of *behaviour* in an individual.

Confidence testing a method for discriminating between levels of partial knowledge relating to the content of a test item in which the testee indicates his degree of confidence in the answer chosen.

Conflation the fusing together of two sets of scores to give a single overall mark, eg combining a *continuous assessment* score with a *terminal assessment* score.

Contact videodisc a type of *videodisc* on which the signal is read by electrical means using a stylus that is in actual contact with the surface of the disc.

Content-centred exercise an exercise in which the subject matter plays an important role.

Continuous assessment on-going assessment of a learner throughout a course of instruction.

Controlled discussion a discussion in which learners may raise questions or make relevant comments, but whose general direction is under the strict control of the teacher, tutor or instructor (see Chapter 6).

Convergent thinking a rational, systematic approach to problem-solving, normally leading to the single correct, best, most conventional, or most logical solution.

Conversational language natural language used to communicate with an on-line computer; see also *conversational mode*.

Conversational mode on-line dialogue between a computer and a user.

Cookbook laboratory experiment a laboratory exercise which consists of following detailed instructions, without any element of discovery or problem-solving.

Core course (a) a teaching course in which a skeleton framework of ideas and teaching activities is provided and in which the individual teacher is able to add his own methods, ideas, etc; (b) a course that has to be taken as part of the *core curriculum* of a school, college, etc.

Core curriculum (a) key elements or subjects in the curriculum operated by a school, college, etc that are taken by all pupils or students; (b) basic elements in a course that have to be taken by all students, regardless of their selection of optional modules, materials, etc.

Core module, subject a *module* or subject that forms part of the *core curriculum* of a course.

Correspondence course a form of *distance learning* course that relies mainly on the postal service to provide a link between the individual learner and the person or organization running the course.

Counselling (a) advice and support given to participants during a *game, simulation* or similar exercise; (b) guidance given to pupils or students regarding their courses, future careers, etc.

Courseware a general term applied to teaching materials that store information in forms that are compatible with *new information technology* (videotapes, videodiscs, films, multi-media packages, etc); often used as a synonym for *software* (in its broadest sense).

Criterion a characteristic or measurement with which other characteristics or measurements are compared.

Criterion behaviour in *programmed learning*, the detailed *behaviour* that is expected of an individual at the end of the programme or after a specific part thereof.

Criterion-referenced assessment assessment designed to determine an individual's achievement with reference to predetermined, clearly-defined performance standards (see Chapter 7).

Cross-fade to fade out the image from one slide projector at the same time as the image from a second projector (focused on the same screen) is faded in; a technique used to present slide or tape-slide programmes without any 'gaps' between successive slides.

Cross-media approach a methodology based on the principle that a variety of audiovisual media and experiences, correlated with other instructional materials, overlap and reinforce the value of one another.

Curriculum the subject areas or sections covered within a specified course of study.

Curriculum design, development the process of planning, validating, implementing and evaluating new curricula, etc.

D

Data-base a collection of data, bibliographic information, etc held on file and available for extraction or reference, usually via a computer terminal.

Data tablet a device whereby graphic material can be inputed into a computer by 'writing' on its (electromagnetically-sensitive) surface using a *light pen* or other forms of electronic stylus.

Daylight projection a projection system that produces an image bright enough to be seen without darkening the room.

Daylight screen a projection screen so constructed that clear images from a projector are visible in an undarkened room.

Debriefing review and discussion of the processes and outcome of a *game, simulation* or similar exercise.

Decoy another term for a *distractor* in multiple-choice testing.

Dedicated a term applied to a computer, machine, system, etc that is set apart for special use.

Deductive method a method of teaching, study or argument which proceeds from general or universally-applicable principles to particular applications of these principles and shows the validity of the conclusions.

Design criteria, specifications a set of detailed written instructions and descriptions for developing specific *instructional system components* (ISCs), including how each instructional event, and the overall instructional strategy and sequence, will be presented through each ISC in the overall instructional system or product.

Diagnosis the process of determining the existing capabilities of a learner by analysing his performance of a hierarchy of essential tasks in a specific subject, with the object of facilitating his learning by assigning appropriate remedial or advanced learning tasks.

Diascope a (seldom used) name for a device used to project still images held on transparent materials on to an external screen.

Didactic method a method of instruction that emphasizes rules, principles, standards of conduct and authoritarian guidelines, usually told directly to the learner by someone else.

Didactogram a diagram that shows how students perform in *programmed learning*; such diagrams are used in programme analysis, eg during programme development.

Didule the fundamental instructional unit in programmed learning; it constitutes one part of a *frame*, which comprises both instructional and presentational elements.

Differential weighting assigning different weights (marks) to different options in a multiple-choice question in order to give some reward for partly correct answers.

Difficulty index another name for *facility value*.

Digital a term applied to an information processing, storage or transfer system in which the signal is translated into binary code before processing, storage or transmission.

Diorama a three-dimensional representation of a scene, usually created by placing objects, figures, etc in front of a two-dimensional painted background.

Directed observation guided observation provided for the purpose of improving the study, understanding and evaluation of that which is observed.

Directed private study individualized instruction, normally carried out at home, that is built into a course which also uses other methods such as face-to-face instruction.

Directed reading a type of *directed private study* that involves reading specific books or sections thereof.

Directed (direct) teaching a type of teaching in which there is a strong element of teacher direction and guidance.

Discovery area a portion of an *open classroom* which is provided with reading, audiovisual and manipulative materials relating to one particular interest, activity or subject.

Discovery learning a method of instruction that attempts to teach principles or general concepts by providing the learner with a set of relevant experiences from which it is hoped he will arrive at the principles or concepts by the process of induction; see also *inductive method.*

Discrimination index a measure of the ability of an *item* in a *multiple-choice test* to discriminate between students of high and low ability; it is equal to the difference between the *facility values* for the top and bottom thirds of the candidates (see Chapter 7).

Display (a) (noun) in instructional design, that material constituting a single presentation; (b) (verb) to present an organized pattern of sensory data to a learner.

Dissolve control a device which controls the illumination or signal strength from two or more projectors or sources so that images on a projection or television screen seem to dissolve from one into another.

Distance learning learning carried out by a student who is geographically remote from the body or person organizing the instruction (see Chapter 5).

Distractor a wrong answer in a *multiple-choice item* (see Chapter 7).

Divergent thinking a creative approach to solving problems and tackling tasks which produces a range of original solutions, procedures, etc.

Double-band projector a motion film projector (usually 16mm) that has, in addition to the normal film channel, a sound recording channel that uses sprocketted tape; the two channels are mechanically coupled to ensure synchronization.

Double-frame a term used to describe a *filmstrip* where the horizontal axis of the pictures is parallel to the length of the film; also known as *full frame.*

Down-time the period (absolute or fractional) for which a learning resource (usually a device or system) is out of action due to breakdown, routine servicing, etc cf *up-time.*

Drill an ordered, repetitive learning activity intended to help develop or fix a specific skill or aspect of knowledge.

Dual 8mm film projector a film projector designed to project both *standard 8* and *super 8* motion picture films.

E

Easement a legal process whereby a copyright holder grants limited performance, reproduction, publication or other rights to another person, body, etc while retaining ownership of the actual copyright.

Eclectic programme an instructional programme that uses more than one type of programming technique.

Editing (a) selecting and re-arranging recorded audio and/or video signals or film into a new continuity by manual or electronic means; (b) removing unwanted material from and/or inserting new material into a document, file, computer file, etc prior to storage, publication or use.

Educational broadcasting television or radio broadcasting whose primary aim is to educate, or assist in the education of, its viewers or listeners.

Educational technology (a) the development, application and evaluation of systems, techniques and aids to improve the process of human learning; (b) the application of scientific knowledge about learning, and the conditions of learning, to improve the effectiveness and efficiency of teaching and training. In the absence of scientifically established principles, educational technology implements techniques of empirical testing to improve learning situations; (c) a systematic way of designing, implementing and evaluating the total process of learning and teaching in terms of specific objectives, based on research in human learning and communication and employing a combination of human and non-human resources to bring about more effective instruction (see Chapter 1).

Educational television a broadcast or closed-circuit television programme or system whose main purpose is education or cultural development rather than pure entertainment.

Eidophor a type of television projector which first produces an intense primary image by electronic means and then projects this by means of a system of lenses similar to those in a film projector.

Eight millimetre (8mm) film a standard size of motion picture film 8mm wide and with sprocket holes along only one edge; see also *standard 8, super 8.*

Eight-track a term applied to an audiotape (usually in a cartridge) with eight separate tracks of sound recorded on it; the term may also apply to the players and recorders used with such audiotapes.

Electronic editing a form of videotape editing in which the signal from one videotape recorder is re-recorded on another machine using special electronic circuitry to ensure synchronization and compatibility.

Electronic game a *game* that makes use of an internal electronic data-processing device or an external computer; see also *computer game*.

Electronic reproduction materials audiovisual materials which rely on electronic means of reproduction for their use.

Electrostatic copying a reprographic process that first produces an electrostatically-charged image of the original material on a plate or drum and then uses this to transfer pigment particles to the copy paper; also known as *xerography*.

Elliptic questioning a method of question writing (widely used in *programmed learning*) whereby a learner is not asked questions directly but is left to complete statements by adding missing words.

Enactive learning a term (first used by Olson and Bruner) to denote learning through direct experience as opposed to learning via *media* of some sort *(mediated learning)*.

End spurt in learning, a final increase in effort made at the end of a period or sequence of work; see also *beginning spurt*.

Enhancement materials instructional materials which are used to extend understanding of basic course material in specific areas.

Entry behaviour the set of skills which a learner possesses at the time he enters or begins a sequence of instruction.

Entry level performance a set of statements specifying the prior skills and concepts necessary for undertaking a particular learning task.

Entry skills another term for *entry behaviour*.

Epidiascope a device that can project images held on both opaque and transparent materials on to a screen, ie a combined *episcope* and *diascope*.

Episcope another name for *opaque projector*.

Essay test, examination a test or examination that involves writing essays of a given length on one or more topics (see Chapter 7).

Evaluation (a) a *cognitive* process which involves making judgements about the value of ideas, works, solutions, methods, materials, etc for some specific purpose; the highest level (level 6) of Bloom's *cognitive domain* (see Chapter 3); (b) a series of activities designed to measure the effectiveness of a teaching/learning system as a whole (see Chapter 8).

Evaluation instrument any of the means by which one obtains information for the purpose of *evaluation*, eg questionnaires, rating scales.

Examples class a science teaching technique used in colleges, universities, etc in which demonstrators, junior members of staff, or postgraduate students work through problems with small tutorial groups.

Experiential laboratory a *simulation* of a situation outside a school, college, etc used for teaching purposes.

Experiential learning learning which is based on participants' reactions to the activities experienced during an exercise.

Expert witness method a group instruction technique in which students question or cross-examine one or more experts in a particular field.

Expository display a display which presents information only.

Expository teaching methods teaching methods that are based on exposition, ie presentation of material to a class in a lesson, lecture, etc.

F

Facilitator a group discussion leader whose primary function is to act as a catalyst in stimulating discussion rather than providing information.

Facility value the fraction (expressed as a decimal) of candidates choosing the correct answer or *key* in a multiple-choice question (see Chapter 7).

Feedback (a) the information recieved by a learner immediately after each of his responses during a sequence of programmed instruction which indicates the correctness (or otherwise) of the response; (b) communication of responses to a teacher by learners, as in a *feedback classroom*.

Feedback classroom a special classroom where student positions are electronically or electrically connected to the teacher's desk so that responses to multiple-choice questions can be monitored by the teacher.

Feltboard a flat display surface covered with felt, flannel or similar material on to which pictures, symbols or shapes backed with the same or similar material will adhere; also called a *flannel board* or *flannelgraph*.

Fibrevision a cable television distribution system that employs optical fibres to carry the signals; such systems can carry many more channels than conventional systems; see also *switched-star system*.

Field test, trial the assessment of a near-final system (eg an instructional exercise or programme) in an appropriate realistic setting prior to full-scale production and/or use.

Film clip a short sequence of motion picture film used as an insert in a presentation to illustrate a specific point.

Film gauge the width of a motion picture or photographic film; the most commonly used gauges are 8mm, 16mm, 35mm and 70mm.

Film loop another name for a *loop film.*

Filmstrip a strip of 35mm film carrying a sequence of positive photographic images intended for projection (or viewing) as still pictures (see Chapter 4).

Fishbowl session a group discussion technique whereby a number of the class sit in an inner circle and hold a discussion while the remaining members sit around the outside and observe the interaction.

Fixed-response item a type of objective test item which provides all the options from which a testee must select correct responses.

Fixed tracking use of tightly-structured, inflexible programmes of study in a course, so that students have little or no scope for individual curriculum selection.

Flannelboard, flannelgraph alternative names for a *feltboard.*

Flashcard a card or other opaque material carrying words, pictures or other information designed to be displayed briefly, usually by hand, during a programme of instruction.

Flexible schedule a technique for organizing time more effectively to meet the needs of instruction by dividing the working day into uniform time modules which can be combined on an *ad hoc* basis as required.

Flexistudy an individualized learning system in which students are provided with learning materials for home-based study, counselling, tutorial support and access to college facilities (see Chapter 5).

Flip chart a set of large sheets of paper attached to an easel unit so that they can be flipped over the top of the unit into or out of view as a presentation progresses (see Chapter 4).

Flurorescent chalk special chalk that becomes luminescent in a darkened room under ultraviolet lighting.

Fog index a numerical indicator of the readability of a text.

Forced-choice item another term for a *fixed-response item.*

Formative evaluation evaluation of instructional programmes or materials while they are still in some stage of development (see Chapter 8).

Forward branching in programmed learning, *branching* in which the learner is sent forward by several frames if he makes a correct response; also known as *washahead.*

Foundation course (studies) a course designed to provide a basis for more advanced or more extended studies.

Four-track a term applied to an audiotape with four separate sound recording tracks.

Frame (a) each separate presentation of a small basic unit of material, eg an individual picture in a series of pictures such as a motion picture film or filmstrip; (b) one of the discrete stages into which a programmed learning sequence is broken down, ie a *step*.

Frame game a type of *game* or *simulation* which is structured in such a way that a variety of roles, ideas and relationships may be inserted as and when required or appropriate.

Free-group discussion a group discussion in which the specific topics covered and the direction that the discussion takes are largely controlled by the learners (see Chapter 6).

Free-response item a test *item* in which responses can be made freely, provided that they satisfy set criteria, eg as in a *completion item*.

Frieze a long wallchart on which scenes are built up by pupils.

Front projection projection of an image on to the front of an opaque screen, for viewing from the same side as the projector.

Full-frame another term for *double-frame*, as applied to a filmstrip.

Full-track a term applied to an audiotape with a single recording track covering almost the whole width of the tape.

Function in instructional design, a cluster of tasks which have a common or unique set of activities, outcomes or purposes.

Functional reading reading activities that are a purposeful extension of classroom work.

Fused curriculum a curriculum which combines two or more subjects and studies their inter-relationship.

G

Gain score the measured amount of favourable change in an individual of some trait or variable due to treatment or instruction.

Game any contest or exercise in which adversaries (players) operate under constraints (rules) for an objective (winning, victory or pay-off).

Gate-keeper function the 'qualifying' function of an examination or assessment that has to be passed in order to progress to further instruction.

Gateway course a course that is taken with the specific object of attaining the qualifying standard for another course such as a first or higher degree.

Generative CAI (CAL) a type of CAI or CAL system in which all possible lessons are *not* stored in the form of a single vast *branching programme*; instead, a few basic *algorithms* are used to generate a wide range of presentations and problems suited to meet the needs of individual students.

Ghost (a) an 'after image' that remains on a chalkboard, whiteboard, etc after material has been rubbed or wiped off; (b) a secondary image on a television screen, due to faulty transmission or reception.

Global learning remembering material as a whole unit rather than by splitting it up into manageable sections.

Goal (a) a general statement of intent or aspiration; (b) an expression (in broad terms) of the desires and expectations of the designers or planners of an instructional exercise or programme; see also *aims*.

Goal-free evaluation *evaluation* in which the evaluator examines the actual effects of a programme without prior consideration of the programme goals.

Goal specification the detailed description of the desired results of an action or programme prior to the action or programme.

Graded difficulty a term applied to a series of tasks that are made progressively more difficult in order to extend a learner's capabilities gradually; a technique commonly used in *programmed learning*.

Grading on the curve a grading system in which grades or marks are allocated to the students in a class or large group so that they conform to the *normal distribution*; a form of *norm-referenced assessment* (see Chapter 7).

Graphic(al) materials, graphics a general term for two-dimensional illustrative representational materials (often incorporating words and/or symbols) designed to communicate a brief message.

Graphical plotter an electro-mechanical device that can draw graphs, diagrams, etc on the basis of signals supplied by a computer.

Graphics terminal a *computer terminal* on which graphical materials may be created, altered, displayed, etc.

Grey scale the variation in tonal value from white, through different shades of grey, to black on the screen of a monochrome television set.

Group dynamics the methods by which a group of people function as a collective whole.

Group instruction the act of attempting to teach a number of learners the same lesson at the same time; not to be confused with *group learning* or *group teaching*.

Group learning *learning* that takes place through some form of interactive small-group activity, eg in a game or simulation; not to be confused with *group instruction* or *group teaching* (see Chapter 6).

Group pacing a type of programmed group instruction in which all the members of the group progress in lockstep (that is, all doing the same tasks at the same time).

Groupogram a *group learning* technique that uses an audiotape cassette to provide a structure and input to, and also to regulate the timing of, a group activity.

Group teaching dividing a class of pupils into groups according to some aspect(s) of ability, and then teaching them in these groups; not to be confused with *group instruction* or *group learning*.

Group work a process in which members of a group, working co-operatively rather than individually, formulate and work towards common objectives under the guidance of one or more leaders (see Chapter 6).

Guided discovery learning a form of *discovery learning* in which the activities of the learner are partly structured or pre-determined by the teacher.

Guided reading another name for *directed reading*.

H

Half-frame another term for *single-frame*, as applied to a filmstrip.

Half-track a term applied to an audiotape with two separate recording tracks on it, each approximately half the width of the tape.

Hard copy information printed, typed or otherwise reproduced on paper, as opposed to information temporarily displayed on a screen, held in a store, coded on tape, etc (known as *soft copy*).

Hardware a generic term for a piece of equipment used to handle or transmit information stored on materials of some sort.

Hawthorne effect in learning, where improvement apparently brought about by the use of a new technique is wholly or partly due to the increased interest and motivation produced by the use of the technique rather than to the intrinsic properties of the technique itself.

Head a component of an audiotape or videotape recorder or player used to transfer a signal to or from the tape or to erase an existing signal.

Headset a device consisting of one or (usually) two small audio transducers connected to a headband for individual listening to audio sources; also known as headphones or earphones.

Hectograph (gelatin) duplication a type of *spirit duplicating* process in which copies of writing, drawing, etc are made from a pre-prepared gelatin surface to which the original image has been transferred.

Helical scanning a video recording technique in which the tape is wrapped helically round a fixed drum while the recording head rotates within a slot in the side of the tube, thus producing a diagonal scan across the tape as it moves through the machine.

Heuristic a term used to describe a method of instruction or problem-solving that involves using successive evaluations of trial and error in an attempt to arrive at a final result; see also *discovery learning*.

Hierarchy an arrangement of elements to show subordinate and super-ordinate relationships, for example Bloom's taxonomies of educational objectives, as discussed in Chapter 3.

High fidelity a qualitative term used to describe a sound recording or reproducing system capable of handling the full audible range of frequencies (roughly 20 - 20,000 Hz) at low distortion.

High-level (programming) language a computer programming language (such as ALGOL, BASIC or FORTRAN) which provides a range of facilities and standard constructions designed to simplify the writing of computer programs.

Hitch-hiking in education, using existing ideas as a basis for stimulating new ideas.

Hologram a visual recording, produced using a laser, which presents the illusion of three dimensions, including parallax.

Home experiment kit a package supplied or sold to students so that they can perform practical experiments at home, eg as part of a *distance learning* course.

Home study (a) course-related work carried out by pupils or students at home in their own time; (b) study carried out at home for a distance learning course, correspondence course, etc.

Hook-and-loop board a display board covered with a nylon (or nylon-type) surface containing a large number of tiny loops on to which materials backed with tape strips carrying tiny hooks will adhere firmly.

Horizontal panel book a programmed text in which pages are divided into panels which are not read in any logical sequence but on the basis of test item performance.

Horizontal transfer (of learning) a form of *transfer of learning* in which no new higher-order skills are learned, but in which existing skills are applied to a new task (or set of tasks) of similar level of difficulty; also known as *lateral transfer*.

Humanist psychology a school of psychology that emphasizes the concepts of 'self' and 'person' and the study of man's 'humanness' in an integrated or holistic manner as opposed to an analytical or psychometric style (see Chapter 1).

I

Ice breaker (a) an activity designed to establish rapport and generate a receptive atmosphere in a group of people who are about to take part in an exercise, course, etc; (b) a preliminary question or short paper taken by students before starting an examination in order to accustom them to the examination room environment and help overcome nervousness; it is not usually marked as part of the examination proper.

Illuminative evaluation another name for the *social/anthropological approach (to evaluation)*.

Impression method of marking a technique of marking a composition, essay, etc purely on the basis of the overall impression it creates.

Inaudible advance a term applied to a synchronized sound/vision presentation with an inaudible synchronizing signal.

In-basket (in-tray) technique a method of training or instruction in which an individual is called upon to play a specific role and must, in isolation, respond to a number of hypothetical situations as they arise.

Independent learning, study an instructional system in which learners, carrying on their studies without attending formal classes, consult periodically with instructors or tutors for direction and assistance (see Chapter 5).

Individualized instruction, teaching, learning the tailoring of instruction, teaching or learning to meet the needs of the individual learner rather than the learning group as a whole (see Chapter 5).

Inductive method a method of instruction that involves presenting the learner with a sufficient number of specific examples to enable him to arrive at a definite rule, principle or fact embracing the examples; contrast with *didactic method, deductive method.*

Information technology the technology associated with the creation, storage, selection, transformation and distribution of information of all kinds; see also *new information technology.*

Initial ability, behaviour the ability or behaviour of a learner at the start of a programme of instruction, before he takes part in an exercise, etc.

Inlay an image inserted or incorporated in another image, as, for example, in television production.

Inquisitory display a display which asks a question; contrast with *expository display.*

Instant lettering rub-down adhesive letters which can be transferred from plastic or paper carrier sheets on to artwork.

Instructional media the physical tools of educational technology, including printed words, film, tape, records, slides and the various combinations thereof.

Instructional sequence the sequence in which instructional objectives are to be overtaken and in which the instructional events associated with each objective are to be presented.

Instructional system a combination of *instructional system components* and an overall management pattern for their use to bring about directed and controlled learning.

Instructional system component (ISC) a collection of learning resource materials, together with the method in which they are used, which forms an identifiable part of an instructional system.

Integrated experience approach a 'gestalt' approach to instruction that involves using a whole range of experiences to achieve an integrated, comprehensive set of objectives.

Integrated learning system an instructional system that makes combined and planned use of a variety of methods of instruction and teaching aids in order to achieve specific goals.

Intelligent terminal a computer terminal which can be used to perform some local data processing without the assistance of a central processor.

Interactive a term used to describe an exercise which involves participants in communicating with one another in some way; see also *interactive mode.*

Interactive courseware development a technique whereby a teacher plans, writes and evaluates a computer-based course or instructional programme using a computer terminal.

Interactive mode a method of using a *computer* whereby the user carries out an *on-line* dialogue with the computer via a suitable terminal.

Interactive video a hybrid individualized learning system in which a *videocassette* or *videodisc* recorder is linked to a computer.

Interactive videotex(t) *videotex(t)* in which the user is connected to a computer *data-base* by cable (usually a telephone line) and can therefore interact directly with the data-base; the British PRESTEL system is a typical example.

Interdisciplinary a term used to describe an exercise, programme, course, etc that draws its material from a number of different subject areas and illustrates the links and relationships that exist between them.

Intrinsic programme another term for a *branching programme.*

Inventory test (a) a general term for personality tests and question-naires designed to assess or identify attitudes, traits or personality characteristics; (b) a stock-taking test used to determine the level of prior knowledge or later achievement in short components of a course of instruction; see also *pre-test* and *post-test.*

Item (a) in assessment, a single component in a test; (b) in programmed learning, another name for a *frame* or *step.*

Item bank a bank of multiple-choice *items* from which multiple-choice tests can be made up by selecting suitable items.

Item difficulty gradient the extent to which items in a test or examin-ation are arranged in order of increasing difficulty (a common practice in objective tests).

Item editing, trial testing, validation see *shredding.*

J

Job aid any form of 'aide memoire' designed to facilitate either the learning or the performance of a task.

Joystick a lever used to control a cursor, 'write' on a *video display unit*, etc.

K

Keller Plan a type of individualized learning strategy based on the self-paced study of (mainly) written material backed up by tutoring and monitored by means of mastery tests at the end of each unit (see Chapter 5).

Key the correct answer to a *multiple-choice item* (see Chapter 7).

Keyboard terminal a computer terminal that incorporates a keyboard similar to that on a typewriter.

Keypad a small hand-held keyboard of the type used to call up pages of a videotex(t) system.

Keystoning the production of a trapezoid (out-of-square) image on a projection screen due to the fact that the screen is not perpendicular to the projection direction.

Kit a collection of resources, involving more than one type of *instruc-tional system component*, that are subject-related and intended for use as an instructional unit.

Knowledge a cognitive process which involves the remembering of facts, ideas, etc without necessarily understanding them or being able to make use of or manipulate them; the lowest level (level 1) of Bloom's *cognitive domain* (see Chapter 3).

L

Language laboratory a room equipped for language instruction in which taperecorders, projectors, record players and other devices are used singly or in combination in order to present material, provide feedback, etc.

Lantern slide a slide with an image area 3¼" x 4" or 3¼" x 3¼".

Lateral thinking a term (first used by de Bono) that describes the process of solving a problem by indirect or interactive methods rather than by adopting a logical, direct approach.

Lateral transfer another name for *horizontal transfer*.

Lead-lecture a lecture designed to present material and information for later discussion or given in preparation for participative work.

Learning (a) in behavioural psychology, a change in the stable relationship between (i) a *stimulus* that an individual organism perceives and (ii) a *response* that the organism makes, either covertly or overtly; (b) a relatively permanent change in *behaviour* that results from past experience, produced either inadvertently or deliberately.

Learning (aids) laboratory an alternative name for a *resources centre*.

Learning-by-appointment system a system in which learners can obtain access to teachers, instructors, self-instructional materials, hardware, etc as and when they need them by making appropriate appointments or booking arrangements.

Learning curve a graphic representation of the rate of progress of a learner (or group of learners) produced by plotting some appropriate measurable variable against time.

Learning package a self-contained collection of subject-related materials accompanied by specific instructions for learner use.

Learning resources all the *resources* which may be used by a learner (in isolation or in combination with other learners) to facilitate learning.

Learning resources centre an alternative name for a *resources centre*.
learning that is employed by an individual; sometimes called cognitive style.

Learning style the preferred mode of problem-solving, thinking or learning that is employed by an individual; sometimes called *cognitive style*.

Lecture method an approach to instruction which relies solely or heavily on lectures to impart information to learners.

Lenticular screen a silver projection screen with tiny corrugations on its surface in order to increase the brilliance of the image when viewed from a direction close to the line of projection.

Lesson plan an outline of the important points of a lesson arranged in the order in which they are to be presented to the learners by the teacher.

Lesson unit a discrete individual lesson designed to form part of a larger course or sequence of lessons.

Light box a back-illuminated translucent surface used for viewing and working with transparent graphic and photographic materials.

Light pen a pen-like implement that may be moved across the face of a computer *data tablet* in order to enter new data or alter existing data.

Likert scale an *attitude scale* involving the use of a list of statements to which an individual has to respond, normally from a range of degrees of agreement/disagreement (see Chapter 8).

Linear programme a type of instructional programme in which no *branching* occurs (see Chapter 1).

Line printer a printer mechanism that produces a *hard copy* readout from a computer, word processor, etc one line at a time.

Liquid crystal display a data display technique that produces visible characters as opaque liquid crystals by application of suitable electric fields.

Listening centre an audio distribution device to which several headsets can be connected in order to enable more than one learner to hear an audio programme at the same time.

Listening group an organized group that meets to hear an audio presentation of some sort (eg a radio broadcast or audiotape) as part of an instructional programme.

Loop film a length of motion picture film joined as an endless band to facilitate continuously-repeated projection; usually contained in a cartridge.

Low-level (programming) language a computer *programming language* (such as *machine code*) which requires the programmer to specify his program in minute detail, but also gives access to the more intimate facilities of the hardware.

M

Machine code a *low-level (programming) language* in which the instructions that cause a particular computer to operate are written.

Machine-dependent instruction a type of instructional system in which a machine (or set of machines) is so integral to the system that its removal would cause the system to fail.

Machine-independent instruction a type of instructional system in which the removal of machines may cause inconvenience, or reduction of efficiency or quality, but not complete failure of the system.

Machine-paced instruction a type of *programmed instruction* in which a *teaching machine* controls the rate of a learner's work by controlling the amount of time for which each stimulus is visible, the time the learner has to respond, the time for which the feedback is visible, and the time before the appearance of the next frame.

Magazine a container for slides, a filmstrip, a film, etc for use in conjunction with a projector.

Magerian objective a *behavioural objective* which indicates what the learner should be able to do, under what conditions, and at what level of competence (see Chapter 3).

Magnetic board a flat sheet of ferromagnetic material (or steel) to which objects may be stuck with magnets for display purposes (see Chapter 4).

Magnetic film a type of motion picture that uses a *magnetic soundtrack*.

Magnetic letters pre-cut letters with magnetized backs that can be used to make up words for display on a magnetic board or other ferromagnetic surfaces.

Magnetic recording film sprocketted 35mm or 16mm recording tape on which the soundtrack of a motion picture is recorded independently of the picture film.

Magnetic soundtrack a strip of magnetic oxide along one edge of a motion picture film used to carry the sound signal.

Magnetic tape (a) magnetic oxide-coated tape on which audio or video signals or data can be recorded; (b) heavy magnetized tape used for attaching light materials to a magnetic board or preparing displays for use on such boards.

Mainframe computer a large, 'fixed' computer facility (see Chapter 10); see also *mini-computer* and *microcomputer*.

Main store the rapid-access memory system incorporated in the central processing unit of a computer.

Maintenance costs the total expenditure of funds involved in keeping a learning resource (usually a device or system) in an operational state.

Manual (a) (noun) a detailed and comprehensive guide to practice, use. manufacture or service, usually in book or booklet form; (b) (adjective) a term applied to an exercise such as an educational game that does not involve the use of an internal or external computer or data processor.

Marker board a smooth surface on which display material may be written or drawn using crayons, felt pens or other easily erased materials (see Chapter 4).

Marking scales scales that are established by examining bodies, schools, etc in order to guide examiners in marking examination papers (see Chapter 7).

Marking scheme any system that is used for evaluating and reporting achievement in a learner's work.

Master a copy or, in some cases, the original of a document, tape, film, etc from which further copies (or extracts) can be made.

Mastery learning the theory that mastery of a topic, subject, field, etc is (in principle) possible for *all* individuals provided that the appropriate amount of teaching time and the optimum quality of instruction are given to each student.

Mastery model the model for correct, error-free or minimally-acceptable performance of a task or set of tasks.

Mastery requirements another name for *unit-perfection requirement.*

Matching item a type of objective test item which requires the testee to pair one word, object, symbol, etc with an associated response.

Matt(e) screen a projection screen with a flat, even surface and dull finish which provides an even brilliance at all viewing angles.

Media (a) the physical tools of educational technology, including printed words, film, tape, records, slides and the various combinations thereof; (b) the various channels of mass communication, including the press, radio and television.

Mediated learning a term (first used by Olson and Bruner) to denote learning via media of some sort as opposed to learning through direct experience (*enactive learning*).

Mediated observation observation of a situation carried out using some type of audiovisual medium (eg film or television) rather than direct observation.

Mediated self-confrontation use of *media* (audio recording, video-recording, film, etc) to show a learner how he is coping with a specific task or situation; see also *microteaching.*

Mediated self-instruction a combination of learning resource materials (often audiovisual) and a system for their use designed to enable a learner to achieve a specified set of instructional objectives without additional input from other sources (eg people).

Medium (a) the material in or on which a physical variable (such as an electrical signal or magnetic field) may represent data or information;

also, the physical variable itself; (b) in a wider sense, the means (eg audible signals, visual images) and/or the process (eg television transmission) by which information is conveyed to the senses. See also *media*.

Memory span in learning, the number of related or unrelated items that can be recalled after one presentation.

Mental age an estimate of the intellectual development of an individual given in terms of the *chronological age* of the average population to which he is equivalent in intellectual terms.

Microcard a card on which a matrix of *micro-images* are recorded; a type of *micro-opaque*.

Microcomputer a small, portable computer based on microcircuit technology; see also *mainframe computer* and *minicomputer*.

Microcopy a copy of printed or other material so reduced in size in comparison with the original that it cannot be read without the aid of a suitable magnifying device.

Microfiche a transparent sheet of photographic film bearing a matrix of *micro-images* (usually pages of text) together with an eye-legible title strip.

Microfiche reader a projector by means of which an eye-readable image of one or more pages of a microfiche can be produced for individual or group study.

Microfilm a roll or strip of photographic film carrying a series of *micro-images*.

Microfilm reader a projector by means of which an eye-readable image of one or more frames of a *microfilm* can be produced for individual or group study.

Microform a general term for any medium used to record *micro-images*.

Microgroove a term used to describe a conventional *sound disc* with more than 350 lines to the inch.

Micro-image an image, obtained by means of an optical device, so reduced in size in comparison with the original that it cannot be read or studied with the naked eye.

Micro-opaque a matrix of *micro-images* recorded on an opaque medium such as a card or sheet of photographic paper.

Microphone a device which converts sounds into electrical signals, usually for feeding into an amplifying, mixing or sound recording system of some sort.

Microphone characteristic the directional properties of a microphone, usually given in terms of a polar response diagram that indicates its relative sensitivities in different directions.

Microprint a matrix of *micro-images* recorded on a sheet of photographic paper; a type of *micro-opaque*.

Microprocessor a self-contained solid-state microcircuit unit that can be used to build more complicated devices such as computers and control systems.

Microprojector a device designed to enlarge and project microscopic transparencies such as microscope slides for viewing by large groups.

Microsleep a term for the type of attention break that a learner undergoes periodically during a lecture, talk, etc that lasts longer than his *attention span* (see Chapter 4).

Microteaching training of teachers, lecturers, etc in specific skills or sets of skills in a scaled-down teaching situation, often using techniques such as *mediated self-confrontation*.

Mimeograph, mimeographing see *rotary stencil duplication*.

Mimeoscope another name for a *light box*.

Minicomputer a term that is used to denote a computer intermediate in size between a *mainframe computer* and a *microcomputer*.

Model a physical or conceptual representation of an object or system, incorporating certain specific features of the original.

Modem in computing, a contraction of *modulator-demodulator* — a device that can be used to convert a *digital* signal into an *analogue* signal capable of being transmitted along an ordinary telephone line or to re-convert such an analogue signal back into digital form after transmission.

Moderator an internal or external examiner who checks the standard of marking and/or examining in a course or section thereof.

Modulation the addition of information to an electromagnetic wave or electrical signal by adjusting its amplitude (amplitude modulation), frequency (frequency modulation) or phase (phase modulation).

Module (a) an organized collection of learning experiences assembled in order to achieve a specified group of related objectives; (b) a self-contained section of a course or programme of instruction.

Modular course a flexible course that allows individual learners to select the course programme that best suits them from a structural hierarchy of *modules*, some of which are compulsory and some optional.

Modulator-demodulator see *modem*.

Modular examination an examination in which candidates can elect to take a number of optional elements of equal difficulty in related subjects, topics or areas.

Moirée pattern, fringes patterns produced when two separate sets of parallel lines are superimposed at a small angle to one another.

Monaural a term used to describe a sound recording or sound reproduction system with only a single sound channel.

Monitor (noun) (a) see *television monitor*; (b) a person who acts as a tutor supervisor, or assessor in a *behavioural instruction* system; (c) (verb) to listen to a sound signal as it is being recorded or played back or check a system for correct operation.

Monitoring carrying out an on-going assessment or appraisal of a system while it is in operation.

Monophonic a term used synonymously with *monaural*.

Motion picture a length of photographic film, with or without a magnetic or optical soundtrack, bearing a sequence of images which create an illusion of movement when projected in rapid succession (usually at 18 or 24 frames per second); commonly referred to as a film.

Multi-access a term used to describe a computer system whereby several users or operators may, through multiple or remote terminals, each use the same computer facilities at the same time; see also *time-sharing*.

Multi-choice item, question see *multiple-choice item, question*.

Multi-image of a presentation, the simultaneous use of two or more separate images, usually projected.

Multi-media a term used to describe (a) collections or groups of documents in several media, (b) a work designed to be presented through the integrated use of more than one medium (eg a tape-slide programme).

Multi-media kit, package a package of materials in several media dealing with a specific topic or subject area and forming an integrated whole.

Multiple-choice item, question a type of objective test or questionnaire question in which the testee has to choose the correct answer from a number of alternatives supplied (see Chapter 7).

Multiple-choice questionnaire a questionnaire in which the person being assessed or questioned has to choose his answer to each question from a number of alternatives supplied.

Multiple-choice test a form of *objective test* composed of several multiple-choice items (see Chapter 7).

Multiple-completion item another name for a *multiple-response item.*

Multiple-cut-off approach a technique used in multiple-test assessment to ensure that weakness in one test or paper is not compensated for and/or obscured by high scores in other tests or papers; it involves establishing a minimum cut-off score in each test or paper.

Multiple marking examination, essay, project or other marking carried out independently by more than one person in order to arrive at a collective mark that is (it is to be hoped) free from subjective influence and thus has a greater *reliability* (see Chapter 7).

Multiple-response item an *item* in an objective test of the multiple-choice type in which two or more responses are correct.

Multiple-track a term used to describe (a) a recording tape that carries more than one recording track; (b) a set of programmed materials with more than one track through them, ie a *branching programme.*

Multi-screen a term used to describe a presentation that employs two or more screens for showing projected images simultaneously.

Multi-sensory learning (teaching) aids learning or teaching aids which utilize or bring into play more than one of the physical senses (eg sound film or tape-slide programmes).

N

Narration the verbal comments that are written to accompany a visual presentation.

Narrowcasting a term sometimes applied to cable television and similar systems where distribution of the signal is restricted to those connected to the network; contrast with *broadcasting.*

Natural language ordinary spoken or written language as opposed to an artificial or computer language.

Negative transfer (of learning) a reduction in the efficiency of learning because of earlier learning carried out in a different situation.

New information technology the application of new electronic and other technology (computers, communication satellites, fibre optics, videorecording, etc) to the creation, storage, selection, transformation and distribution of information of all kinds.

No-failure programme a course or programme designed to avoid outright failure by a system of adjustment of tuition and learning materials and/or transfer to other courses.

Non-book (non-print) media *media* that carry or transmit information or instructions by non-typographic means, eg by sound, pictorial representations, projected images, etc.

Non-directive tutorial (group) a tutorial (group) in which students are encouraged to contribute views and questions spontaneously, with the tutor acting as a leader and guide, but not to the extent of dominating the group or firmly structuring the course of the discussion (see Chapter 6).

Non-functioning distractor a *distractor* which attracts less than 5 per cent of the responses to a *multiple-choice item.*

Non-projected visual aids, materials visual materials which do not require the use of a projector for their display; also called *self-display* materials (see Chapter 4).

Non-verbal communication the meaningful transfer of thought or emotion through methods other than words or speaking, eg using body language.

Norm the average performance or measure in a specified function of a specified homogeneous population.

Normal distribution (curve) a symmetrical bell-shaped distribution that has, or approximates to, the shape of a Gaussian distribution; many statistical measures (eg intelligence) are found to follow such a distribution.

Norm-referenced assessment assessment designed to determine an individual's achievement in comparison with the group or population to which he belongs.

O

Objective a desired outcome of an instructional process or programme expressed in highly-specific (generally behavioural) terms; cf *aims* (see Chapter 3).

Objective assessment, examination, test an assessment, examination or test that can be marked with total reliability by anyone, including non-subject specialists, or (in some cases) by computer (see Chapter 7).

Objective item (question) an *item* (question) in an objective assessment, examination or test.

Observational learning learning that takes place through the observation of a model system; see also *discovery learning.*

Obsolescence time the length of time before a learning resource becomes so outdated that it is no longer of any use.

Off-line a computing term applied to a terminal or peripheral that is not at the time in question under the control of the central processing unit, ie is switched off or operating quite separately from the main computer.

OHP transparency see overhead transparency.

One-zero mark scheme a test marking scheme in which one mark is given for a correct answer and zero marks for an incorrect answer or no answer.

On-line a computing term applied to a terminal or peripheral that is under the control of the central processing unit at the time in question; cf off-line.

Opaque projector a device designed to project images of opaque, flat objects on to a screen by using light scattered from the object.

Open access (a) a practice whereby users are given direct access to all or part of the stock of a library or resources centre (see Chapter 9); (b) a system whereby admission to a course is open to anyone who wishes to participate, regardless of his qualifications or experience; (c) an informal *individualized learning* system in which a student can have access to the facilities of the host institution more or less at any time (see Chapter 5).

Open-book examination, test an examination or test in which students are allowed to bring into the examination room, or consult any reference material they wish.

Open classroom a classroom environment based on the concepts of *open education*, generally incorporating a system of *discovery areas*.

Open education an approach to education that includes an emphasis on learning (rather than teaching), personal and affective growth, exploring and questioning, decision-making, and the role of the teacher as a partner and guide rather than as an authoritarian figure (see chapter 2).

Open-ended a term applied to a question, test, examination, exercise, project, etc in which many acceptable answers or outcomes are possible rather than one single correct solution or result.

Open learning an instructional system in which many aspects of the learning process are under the control of the individual learner, who decides what and how to study, usually under some form of guidance (see Chapter 5).

Open plan a learning environment that is designed in an open, flexible manner rather than divided into traditional 'closed-door' classrooms, thus allowing a wide range of teaching and learning methods to be employed (traditional expository teaching, team teaching, group learning, individualized learning, etc).

Open reel a term applied to an unenclosed audiotape, videotape or film reel (as opposed to the enclosed reels contained in cassettes or cartridges) and to audio or video systems which employ such reels.

Operating, operation(al) costs the total recurring expenditure of funds associated with operating a learning resource after any initial purchase and installation costs have been met.

Operational objective another term for a *behavioural objective.*

Opportunistic teaching an unstructured, *ad hoc* style of teaching which is characterized by acting on inspiration, seizing opportunities as they occur and working towards general goals as opposed to pre-planned objectives.

Optical character recognition (OCR) a technique (device) whereby characters that are legible to the (unaided) human eye may be read by optico-electronic means.

Optical pointer an electrically-operated torch which projects a small arrow or spot of light; used in place of a conventional pointer during projection, especially in darkened rooms.

Optical soundtrack a soundtrack which has been recorded and/or printed on a motion picture film in the form of an optical band of varying density or width along one edge of the film.

Optical videodisc a type of *videodisc* in which the signal is read optically, usually using a laser.

Oral examination examination by spoken word and answer, as opposed to a written examination; also known as a *viva voce* examination, or *viva.*

Organization an *affective* process that involves the conceptualization of values and ordered relationships between values; level 4 of Bloom's *affective domain* (see Chapter 3).

Orientation course a short course designed to introduce pupils or students to a subject, course, institution, etc.

Outcome specification in instructional design, a statement of desired terminal learner performance in terms that can be measured or assessed by teachers.

Overhead projector (OHP) a device designed to project easily visible images from transparent materials (usually roughly 10" x 10" in size) on to an external screen in a completely lighted room (see Chapter 4).

Overhead transparency a transparent sheet of material (usually roughly 10" x 10" in size) intended for use with an *overhead projector* or *light box* as a means of showing graphic, textual or other information.

Overhead transparency mount a cardboard or plastic mount designed to hold a standard 10" x 10" overhead transparency.

Overlay a transparent sheet which registers over another sheet or transparency, giving additional or alternative information.

P

Pacing the act of indicating the speed to be achieved by an individual learner, group or class in carrying out a given programme of works; see also *self-pacing*.

Package (a) a collection of all the materials needed to organize, run or participate in an exercise, course or programme of some sort; (b) a computing term for a generalized *program* or set of programs designed to meet the needs of several users.

Page a *viewdata* term for a collection of information that can be called up by means of its page number.

Panel a collection of resource materials made available to a learner while he is working through a particular instructional programme; it may include written texts, audiovisual material, laboratory equipment, computer facilities, etc.

Paper-and-pencil test, examination any test or examination which involves only question papers, answer papers and writing instruments.

Paper tape tape or ribbon that is capable of storing information by means of a pattern of holes punched across its width; also known as punched tape.

Paradigm a unique example; now widely used as a term for an operational model that can serve as an example or guide.

Parent page a term used in *viewdata (interactive videotex)* for the *routing page* immediately prior to the page containing the information that the user requires.

Participative simulation a *simulation* whose main purpose is to enable people to participate in some activity (or group of activities).

Passive learning learning in which the learner has a purely passive role, receiving information from the instructor or from the materials being studied without taking any active part in the proceedings.

Pathway scheme a method of modular course organization in which a student can choose a number of different routes through the course units.

Pedagogy a word re-emerging in educational circles as a term for educational science, that is, the study of classroom methodology and educational techniques.

Peer group a group of individuals sharing similar age, background, qualifications, etc.

Peer teaching, tutoring a technique in which the teaching (tutoring) of learners is not done by a teacher but by other learners, usually either older or the same age, who have already met the learning objectives involved.

Performance-based instruction a (loose) term for instruction that is based on mastery criteria, ie in which the learner has to demonstrate mastery of one unit before being allowed to move on to the next.

Peripheral (equipment, unit) in computer parlance, a terminal or backing store device that is (or can be) connected to the central processing unit of a computer system.

Personal observation an evaluation technique that involves direct observation of the item, system or subject under study.

Photocopy a copy of a document or part thereof produced on or via sensitized material by the action of light, heat, etc.

Pictogram a diagram in which items or objects are drawn in different sizes or quantities in order to represent actual sizes or quantities more forcefully.

Pilot testing carrying out early trials of an exercise, programme, etc during its development; a type of *formative evaluation.*

Pincushion distortion distortion of a projected image whereby straight lines parallel to the edges of the field move outwards at their ends.

Pixel the smallest picture element on a television or video display unit screen.

Platen the flat surface or platform in an *opaque projector* on which the material to be projected is placed.

Plenary session a session involving all the participants in an exercise, programme, course, etc.

Polarized animation simulation of movement in overhead transparencies, slides and other display materials by the use of variably-oriented polarized light transmitted through special materials.

Polarizing spinner a hand-operated or motor-driven spinner carrying a polarizing filter of the type used in *polarized animation.*

Portability a term used to give an indication of the ease with which an educational or other device can be moved and its resistance to damage when being transported.

Positive transfer (of learning) facilitation of learning brought about as a result of learning a previous task which contained similar elements.

Post-test a test carried out after the completion of a course or programme of instruction in order to determine the extent to which the learner has achieved the specified objectives; cf *pre-test.*

Pounce paper transfer a system of transferring an outline of an illustration from one surface to another (eg from paper to a chalkboard) by making small holes along the lines of the original; the pattern can then be transferred to another surface by dusting alone the lines with chalk dust, powder, etc.

Power test a test in which the score or level of performance attained is more important than the time taken to achieve the score or level.

Practice items trial items that are included in a test, examination or questionnaire in order to familiarize the subject with its form.

Precision teaching (PT) a method of teaching or individualized instruction in which the response rates of students are checked by using standard behaviour charts to record each student's improvement relative to prior performances rather than to a fixed standard.

Predictive simulation a *simulation* whose main purpose is to predict future behaviour, performance, trends, etc, as opposed to a *participative simulation*.

Predictive validity the degree to which predictions made by a test (or inferred from test results) are confirmed by the later behaviour of the subject(s) tested.

Pre-knowledge relevant knowledge which a learner or participant should have before embarking on a programme, course, etc or taking part in an exercise.

Pre-recorded materials recorded materials (such as audiotapes or video-tapes) where the recorded signal was present at the time of purchase or acquisition.

Pre-release testing a term for the determination of the effectiveness of an educational package during and after development and before the final edited version is prepared; a type of *formative evaluation*.

Presentation programmer an electronic system which controls the synchronization of sound reproduction and/or projection devices in multi-media or multi-device presentations (eg cross-fade tape-slide programmes).

Presentation session a teaching period (such as a lecture) which is intended primarily for the presentation or imparting of information by the teacher, with little or no student participation and discussion.

Pre-test a test carried out prior to a course or programme of instruction in order to determine the *entry behaviour* of the learner(s); cf *post-test*.

Printout the hard copy output that a computer or word processor provides via a line printer or similar device.

Problem method a method of instruction in which learning is simulated by the creation of challenging situations that demand solution.

Process-centred exercise an *exercise* in which the subject matter is far less important than the activities that the exercise involves; contrast with *content-centred exercise.*

Product testing the empirical testing of instructional materials in order to determine their effectiveness; normally carried out in three phases: developmental testing, validation testing and field testing.

Prognostic test a type of *diagnostic test* that is used to predict the future performance of an individual in a specific task, course of study, etc; see also *predictive validity.*

Program a coded sequence of instructions whereby a programmer communicates with a computer.

Programmable calculator an electronic calculator that possesses a limited amount of memory and logic capability, and can thus carry out some of the functions of a small computer.

Programme an ordered sequence of learning or other activities.

Programmed individual presentation (PIP) an audiovisual system that uses a super 8 film cassette in combination with a tape cassette, both cassettes being played back using a special individual viewing unit known as a cassettescope; the system allows both still and moving sequences to be incorporated in the visual element of programmes.

Programmed instruction, learning a general term for instruction or learning that takes place in a systematic, highly-structured manner, generally in a step-by-step fashion with feedback taking place between steps (see Chapter 1).

Programmed text a set of programmed learning materials produced in the form of a printed text.

Programming language the code that a computer programmer uses to communicate with a computer; see also *high-level programming language, low-level programming language.*

Progressive teaching a general term for teaching methods that are pupil-centred and stress discovery learning, as opposed to the traditional authoritarian teacher-centred approach (see Chapter 2).

Projected television a television display system that produces a large projected picture on an external screen by optical or electronic means; see also *eidophor.*

Projected visual aids visual materials that require the use of a *projector* for their display.

Project method a method of instruction in which learners (individually or in groups) carry out projects, working largely free of supervision or control.

Projector a generic term for devices used to form images on external screens by optical means.

Psychological inventory a type of psychological assessment instrument that differs from a *psychological test* in that it reflects what the person being tested says he feels; a psychological test, on the other hand, measures what he knows or can do.

Psychological test a test devised by psychologists to measure some aspect of ability, knowledge or performance for educational assessment, research or other purposes.

Psychomotor associated with the co-ordination of mind and body in carrying out physical (motor) actions; see also *psychomotor domain*.

Psychomotor domain one of the three broad sets into which Bloom and his co-workers classify learning objectives, containing all those associated with the co-ordination of mind and body in carrying out physical (motor) actions.

Pygmalion effect the theory that a teacher's expectations of a pupil's achievement can sometimes become a self-fulfilling prophecy in that the pupil will perform to meet the teacher's preconceptions of him.

Q

Quadraphonic a term applied to a sound recording or sound reproduction system that makes use of four discrete but related sound tracks, channels or sources.

Quality (rating) scale a type of standard scale used for marking compositions, essays, etc; such a scale consists of a number of standard samples, graded and arranged in order of merit, against which comparisons can be made (see Chapter 7).

Quarter-track a synonym for *four-track*.

Query language a *high-level programming language* that is designed to resemble a *natural language* as closely as possible in order to help inexperienced users carry out information searches in *data-bases*.

Questionnaire a diagnostic instrument in which members of the population being studied are asked to answer a series of questions (usually on a form).

Quiz mode a programmed learning technique that involves providing the learner with the correct response immediately after he has made his response to each item.

R

Radio listening group a group of people who meet in order to listen to and discuss educational radio broadcasts, usually with the help of related *study guides*.

Radiovision an audiovisual instructional system which uses special filmstrips, booklets, or other visual material linked with radio broadcasts.

Random Access Memory (RAM) a computing term for a fast, random-access *store* of the type found in the central processing units of computers.

Random access slide projector a slide projector which can show slides in the magazine in any order rather than merely in the sequence in which they were loaded into the magazine.

Random learning learning acquired incidentally, as opposed to learning acquired deliberately in a course or through study.

Rank order a list of learners' scores, etc given in order of merit, attainment or some other attribute(s).

Raster scan a type of scanning that involves crossing the area being covered in a series of close, parallel lines, one below (or above) the other; the process by which a television picture is produced.

Rating scale a numerical scale (generally with no more than five or six points) upon which aspects of an exercise, programme, course, etc can be scored as part of a diagnostic or evaluation process.

Rationale the underlying philosophy of a course, curriculum, etc.

Raw score a score which has not (so far) been modified by mathematical operations.

Readability a measure of the appropriateness of reading material to the age or ability of the reader.

Reader a projection device used to produce an eye-readable image of a *microcopy* on a small screen, which may be either opaque or translucent.

Reader-printer a microcopy reader with additional built-in facilities for producing an eye-legible hard copy of any page or section required.

Reading age a measure of the reading ability of an individual in terms of the *chronological age* of the average population to which he is equivalent in reading ability.

Read-out the display of output from a computer on the screen of a video display unit, as opposed to a hard-copy printout.

Real time the actual time over which a game, simulation or other exercise operates, as opposed to any simulated time scale built into its structure; see *real-time processing*.

Real-time processing computer processing of data as it arises, so that the information obtained can be of immediate use in analysing or controlling external events happening concurrently.

Rear projection see *back projection*.

Rearrangement test a test that involves arranging items in the correct order or pattern.

Recall test a type of *objective test* in which the subject is required to supply missing items of information (usually words, numbers or phrases) to complete statements.

Receiving an *affective* process that involves showing awareness of, and willingness to receive, certain stimuli such as the aesthetic properties of an object, system, etc; the lowest level (level 1) of Bloom's *affective domain*.

Reception learning an instructional technique in which the entire content of what is to be learned is presented to the learner in final form; sometimes called expository teaching.

Recitation a learning exercise and teaching procedure in which learners repeat orally or explain material learned by individual study or drill, or material previously presented by the teacher, and (in some cases) reply to questions on the material asked by the teacher.

Recognition test a type of recall test in which a learner has to recognize objects, symbols, patterns, words, etc previously encountered or learned.

Record card a card showing a learner's progress, attainment record, etc.

Reel-to-reel a term describing a process or machine in which tape or film moves from one open reel or spool to a separate take-up reel or spool during processing, play-back or projection.

Regular 8 an alternative name for *standard 8* cine film; see also *super 8*.

Reinforcement (a) in behavioural psychology, a process in which a *stimulus* presented immediately following a *response* increases the likelihood of the response being repeated when the same situation recurs; (b) the process of helping a learner to master new facts, principles, etc by repetition, rehearsal, demonstrating applications, etc.

Reliability (a) a measure of the consistency with which an item, test, examination, etc produces the same results under different but comparable conditions; (b) the capability of a device to function properly over a period of time.

Reliability coefficient a statistical measure used to quantify the *reliability* of a test or between two forms of a test.

Remedial class a class organized for pupils or students who need special help to catch up in a particular subject or subject area.

Remedial frame(s) a frame (or sequence of frames) in a *programmed learning* sequence that covers material previously covered in the programme, usually in order to help the learner master material that he did not succeed in mastering the first time (see Chapter 1).

Remedial instruction a specific unit (or system of units) of instruction based on comprehensive diagnostic findings and intended to overcome a particular learning deficiency (or set of learning deficiencies) in a student.

Remedial loop a loop in an instructional programme that employs *backward branching* whereby a learner is made to repeat a section he has failed to master or is exposed to other remedial material (see Chapter 1).

Remote terminal a computer terminal sited in a place convenient to a user rather than in the vicinity of a central processing unit; it may be anywhere from the next room to the other side of the world.

Repertoire assessment assessment of the nature and degrees of skill possessed by a learner prior to beginning a programme or course of instruction, ie assessment of his *entry skills*.

Reprography a term embracing all copying and microcopying processes using any form of radiation (including heat), all duplicating and office printing processes, and all ancillary operations connected with such processes.

Resource a system, set of materials or situation that is deliberately created or set up in order to enable an individual student to learn (see Chapter 9).

Resource-based learning a highly-structured, individualized, student-centred learning system that makes full use of appropriate resources, both material and human, in creating an effective learning situation (see Chapter 9).

Resource materials (a) the basic components of a package used in an exercise, programme, course, etc; (b) a general term for resources and instructional materials used by learners or teachers.

Resource(s) centre a place — which can be anything from part of a room to a complex of buildings — that is set up specially for the purpose of housing and using a collection of resources, both in printed and in non-printed form (see Chapter 9).

Resource(s) island a central area in a classroom where resources are available for use by pupils.

Resource(s) peninsula a position at one side of a classroom where resources are available for use by pupils.

Responding an *affective* process that involves showing an interest in an object, system, etc as opposed to merely being aware of it; level 2 of Bloom's *affective domain* (see Chapter 3).

Response (a) in behavioural psychology, any implicit or overt change in an organism's behaviour brought about by the application of a *stimulus*; (b) the behaviour a learner emits following an instructional *stimulus* (usually a question or request to perform some activity).

Response card, sheet a printed card or sheet used in an objective test as a vehicle for the person being tested to record his answers.

Response frame a frame in an *interactive videotex(t)* system that requires a response from the user.

Retention test a test administered some time after the completion of a course or programme of instruction in order to determine the extent to which knowledge, skills, etc have been retained by the learner.

Review items items or frames in a programmed learning sequence that cause the learner to repeat or review material, usually for reinforcement purposes.

Role play a technique (used in *games* and *simulations*) in which participants act out the parts of other persons or categories of persons.

Rotary stencil duplication a duplicating process in which a special perforated *master* (known as a mimeograph master or stencil) is first prepared and then attached to a rotary drum; the printing takes place by forcing ink through the holes in the master on to the copy paper; also known as *mimeographing*, or *stencil duplication*.

Rote learning a type of learning drill in which material is learned by simple repetition.

Routing page a *viewdata* term for a page whose function is to indicate a choice of other pages.

S

Scale an ordered series of symbols or numbers by means of which a measure of some aspect(s) of a person's behaviour or some aspect(s) or attribute(s) of a system can be given; see also *rating scale*.

Scaling adjustment of examination or other marks so that they conform to an agreed standard or yardstick, thus allowing meaningful comparisons or inferences to be made; see also *grading on the curve*.

Scenario background information relating to the setting of a *game*, *simulation* or other exercise.

Score a number or credit assigned to an educational or other datum indicating its position on a scale of quality and/or quantity.

Scrambled text, book a text (book) in which the sequence of pages does not follow logically and whose order of use is determined by the response of the reader to questions; a type of *branching programme*.

Self-assessment assessment of progress, attainment of objectives, etc by the actual learner, generally by using some sort of questionnaire or criterion-referenced test.

Self-completion questionnaire a questionnaire that is completed by the recipient or interviewee rather than by the interviewer.

Self-contained classroom a 'traditional' classroom of the type used in most primary and elementary schools in which one teacher is responsible for all aspects of the work of a class except for certain specialist activities.

Self-display materials another name for *non-projected visual aids*.

Self-help group a group of students on a distance learning course who get together in order to share ideas, problems and experience and generally help one another with the work of the course (see Chapter 6).

Self-help materials instructional materials or resources designed for use by an individual in order to help him carry out some specific task.

Self-instruction an instructional technique which involves the use by learners of individualized instructional materials or resources that require minimal (or no) intervention on the part of the teacher (see Chapter 5).

Self-pacing a method where the individual learner controls the speed at which he carries out a given programme or course of work, eg the *Keller Plan* (see Chapter 5).

Self-study centre another name for a *resources centre*.

Self-study material(s) another name for *self-instructional material(s)*.

Semantic differential technique a diagnostic technique involving the use of pairs of antonyms joined by a *rating scale* (see Chapter 8).

Seminar (a) a small class organized in order to discuss a particular topic; (b) a conference of specialists in a particular field; (c) a short, intensive course on a particular subject or topic.

Sentence completion a type of completion item in which the learner has to complete a sentence by adding a missing word (or words).

Sequential approach arrangement of instructional items in a planned and logical sequence.

Serial learning learning to make a series of responses in the correct order.

Shredding submitting possible *multiple-choice items* to a battery of diagnostic procedures in order to determine whether they are suitable for inclusion in a multiple-choice test or examination, ie a combination of item editing and item trial testing; see *validation*.

Silvered screen a metal projection screen with a silvered surface that produces a very high reflectivity in a forward direction; often used as a *daylight screen*.

Simulated case study a *case study* that is based on a simulated as opposed to a real situation.

Simulation (a) in general, any operating representation of a real system or process (or part thereof); (b) an educational, training or research exercise that incorporates such features; see also *participative simulation, predictive simulation, simulated case study, simulation game* (see Chapter 6).

Simulation game an exercise that includes all the essential characteristics of both a *game* and a *simulation*.

Single concept film loop (loop film) a loop film that illustrates a particular concept, idea, process, etc and can be shown or viewed at an appropriate point in an instructional programme.

Single-frame a term used to describe a filmstrip where the horizontal axis of the pictures is at right angles to the length of the film.

Single-track a term used to describe (a) a recording tape that carries only one recording track; (b) a set of programmed materials with only a single track through them, ie a *linear programme*.

Situational assessment assessment of a learner's ability to handle particular situations (often simulated) involving decision-making and other skills (see Chapter 7).

Sixteen millimetre (16mm) film a standard size of motion picture film 16mm wide.

Skill(s) analysis a detailed analysis of a task, job or activity in terms of the basic skills involved; also known as task analysis.

Skip branching a type of branching programme in which not all the frames are necessarily worked on, depending on the progress of the learner.

Slide a single positive image on transparent material (a *slide transparency*) held in a mount and designed for projection; see also *compact slide, lantern slide* (see Chapter 4).

Slide sequence a series of slides that are designed for consecutive showing or viewing in order to present a connected visual theme, with or without a spoken commentary; see also *tape-slide programme*.

Slow motion the technique of slowing down a motion picture film by running the camera faster than normal and then showing the resulting film at normal speed; cf *slow play.*

Slow play the technique of slowing down a motion picture film or videorecording by operating the projector or playback machine slower than normal; cf *slow motion.*

Small assembly session a session in an instructional programme in which the learners assemble in small groups to discuss a particular problem, aspect of the work, etc; see also *buzz session.*

Smart terminal a computer terminal which has a certain amount of in-built data processing ability, but not so much as an *intelligent terminal.*

Snowball group a discussion group which moves or is guided through successive phases of idea sharing, with one idea leading on to another.

Social/anthropological approach (to evaluation) a subjective approach to evaluation that is more concerned with studying the on-going process of education than with trying to measure specific outputs (see Chapter 8).

Soft copy computer output displayed on a *video display unit* or fed into a storage medium, as opposed to *hard copy.*

Soft keyboard a representation of a keyboard on the screen of a *video display unit* that can be used to input data into a computer by pointing a light pen at each required character in turn.

Software a general term for material which is used in conjunction with *hardware* (see Chapter 1), although its use is sometimes restricted to describe the programs that control computers; see also *courseware.*

Sound disc a vinyl or plastic disc bearing a sound recording by means of spiral grooves or tracks cut or pressed into it; commonly known as a record; see also *compact disc, microgroove.*

Sound film a motion picture film with a self-contained optical or magnetic *soundtrack.*

Sound filmstrip a *filmstrip* accompanied by an audiorecording, usually a tape cassette.

Sound synchronizer a device linking an audiotape recorder to an automatic slide or filmstrip projector which causes the projector to advance by means of signals recorded on the audiotape.

Soundtrack the optical or magnetic strip on a sound film that carries the sound signal; see also *magnetic soundtrack, optical soundtrack.*

Speech compressor an electronic device capable of compressing and expanding an *audio signal* (usually human speech) without changing the pitch.

Speed test a test in which the total number of items or questions answered is an important factor; cf *power test.*

Spirit duplicating a method of producing multiple copies of a document from a specially-prepared *master* carrying a reversed image by pressing the copy material, moistened with spirit, against the master.

Split screen (projection) projection or showing or two or more different images on different parts of the same screen.

Spot questions test or examination questions requiring short, usually factual answers rather than more discussive, essay-style answers (see Chapter 7).

S-R bond, connection, mechanism see *stimulus-response bond, mechanism.*

Stand-alone (capability) the capability of an item of equipment to function independently of any other equipment.

Standard 8 standard 8mm motion picture film, as opposed to *super 8* (see Chapter 4).

Start-up costs the total costs involved in launching a project, programme, etc, over and above any operating costs subsequently incurred.

Stem the introductory part of a *multiple-choice item* containing the information on the basis of which the candidate makes his choice of answer from the various options that follow (see Chapter 7).

Stencil a sheet of material in which an image is cut by mechanical or other means and through which ink, paint, etc can be forced to create an image on a receiving sheet.

Stencil duplication another name for *rotary stencil duplication.*

Step in *programmed learning*, one of the discrete stages into which the programme is broken down (see Chapter 1).

Step size in *programmed learning*, the size of a *step* measured in terms of (a) the length of time needed to complete it, (b) the number of words, (c) the amount of information contained (see Chapter 1).

Stereograph a pair of slides or transparencies designed to produce a three-dimensional effect when viewed using a suitable projector or viewer.

Stereophonic a term used to describe a sound recording or sound reproduction system that employs two discrete but related sound-tracks, channels or sources.

Stereoscope an optical device for viewing *stereographs.*

Stillitron a learner-response device consisting of a printed circuit board that is slipped under a page of a specially-printed book; a learner answers multiple-choice questions by pressing appropriate areas with a stylus, the correctness (or wrongness) of the answers being indicated by the illumination of a green (or red) light.

Still motion slide a stationary slide or transparency in which an illusion of motion is produced by use of polarized light, *moirée fringes* or some other technique.

Stimulus (a) in behavioural psychology, an external force, burst of energy, or other signal that is supplied to an organism in an attempt to activate sensory receptors and internal data processing systems and hence elicit a *response;* (b) in learning theory, a signal, message, question, etc that is given to a learner in an attempt to elicit a desired *response.*

Stimulus-response (SR) bond, connection, mechanism the link between a *stimulus* and the *response* that it elicits.

Stop motion the technique of exposing one frame of a motion picture film at a time in *time-lapse photography* or *animation* work.

Store a computer memory unit; see also *backing store, main store.*

Storyboard a series of sketches or pictures and any accompanying text used in the planning of an audiovisual programme.

Streaming dividing children of the same *chronological age* into separate classes on the basis of overall ability or ability in a particular subject.

Structural communication test a test in which the subject is presented with a grid containing a number of (correct) statements pertaining to a particular topic and has to select and arrange relevant pieces of information in response to questions on the topic (see Chapter 7).

Structured teaching putting together a lesson or series of lessons in a systematic, highly-organized way.

Student-centred approach, learning, teaching an approach to instruction that concentrates on the needs of the individual student, and in which the teacher and the host institution play supportive rather than central roles (see Chapter 2).

Student-paced learning aids, materials learning aids (materials) that are designed in such a way to allow each individual student to work at his own natural pace (see Chapter 9).

Study circle a group of people who meet in order to discuss and study a subject of common interest; see also *self-help group.*

Study guide direction or guidance provided for students to help them cope with the work associated with a course.

Study skills the set of skills that a learner needs to develop in order to study effectively.

Subject-centred a term applied to a teaching or learning approach which emphasizes the content of a syllabus or curriculum rather than the particular needs of individual learners.

Subject-specific a term applied to instruction, instructional materials, etc that are solely concerned with, or relevant to, the teaching of a single academic subject.

Summative evaluation evaluation carried out at the conclusion of a project, activity, etc in order to provide data for product validation or to determine the overall effectiveness of a course or other activity.

Super 8 a type of 8mm motion picture film with a larger image than *standard 8* (see Chapter 4).

Supervised correspondence course a correspondence course in which the students carry out all or part of their work at regular, supervised classes held in their locality.

Switched-star system a high-capacity *cable television* distribution system currently being developed in the UK; subscribers are connected via optical fibre cables to local distribution centres, which are, in turn, linked to the main distribution centre.

Syllabus an outline or brief description of the main points or areas covered by a text, lecture or course.

Synchronizing signal, pulse an audible or inaudible signal or pulse (stored on an audiotape or sound disc) used as a component of a synchronized sound/vision presentation in order to cause the frame to be advanced manually or automatically.

Synchronizing unit an electronic device that enables a pulsed *tape-slide programme* to be played using an ordinary taperecorder and automatic slide projector.

Syndicate a small group of course students or participants in an exercise who are separated from the rest of the students or participants in order to undertake a specific task or investigation.

Synthesis a *cognitive* process which involves the rearranging of elements, parts, items, etc into a new and integrated whole; level 5 of Bloom's *cognitive domain*.

System the structure or organization of an orderly whole, clearly showing the interrelationship between the different parts (sub-systems) and between the parts and the whole (see Chapter 1).

Systematic teaching structured teaching which is preplanned to produce specific learning outcomes; contrast with *opportunistic teaching*.

Systems approach a term used to describe the systematic application of educational technology to an educational or training problem, starting with the input (*entry behaviour*) and output (*terminal behaviour*) and determining how best to progress from the former to the latter (see Chapter 1).

T

T-group a group in which the members study their own social interactions and try to improve their interpersonal and social skills.

Tablet arm a writing surface attached to, or built into, the arm of a chair in order to facilitate note-taking and similar activities.

Tachistoscope a device similar to the shutter of a camera that permits momentary exposure of slides or portions of slides during a presentation or instructional programme.

Talking book a spoken text recorded either on audiotape or on a sound disc, eg for use with the visually handicapped.

Tape-slide programme, presentation an instructional programme or presentation in the form of a slide sequence accompanied by an audiotape, the two being synchronized by means of audible or inaudible cues recorded on the tape.

Target population that proportion of the total learner population selected for exposure to a specific unit of instruction, instructional product, etc.

Task an activity which forms an observable and/or measurable unit of work, has a direct and immediate outcome, and contributes directly to the accomplishment of a goal or purpose.

Taught course a course in which students learn by being taught prescribed course material, as distinct from a course based on project or research work.

Teacher's guide an explanatory handbook for teacher use produced to accompany a textbook or instructional package.

Teachers' resources centre a comprehensive *resources centre* operated for the benefit of teachers in a town or region; such centres generally provide advice and back-up services for teachers carrying out innovative work or producing resource materials, as well as providing a loan service of educational resources.

Teacher/institution centred approach the 'traditional' educational system in which instruction is almost entirely under the control of the host institution and teaching staff (see Chapter 2).

Teaching/learning unit (TLU) a package of instructional materials that incorporates both a teacher's guide and resource materials for learners.

Teaching machine a device which uses mechanical, electrical or electronic means to present an instructional programme to a learner in a manner controlled by the learner's responses to the various items of the programme.

Teaching point the smallest level of detail in an outline of material to be presented in an instructional programme.

Team project a project carried out by a co-operative group, often as part of the work of a course (see Chapter 6).

Team teaching a teaching technique in which two or more teachers share responsibilities for a given instructional programme with the same group of learners.

Teazle board, teazlegraph alternative names for a *hook-and-loop board.*

Telebeam projector another name for a *television projector.*

Telecourse another name for a *distance learning course.*

Telelecture an arrangement which enables a speaker or lecturer to communicate with several classes in different locations simultaneously, using public telephone links.

Telemotion a sophisticated audiovisual presentation technique involving the use of multiple projectors of various types behind a large back projection screen, together with other equipment.

Telephone instruction education or teaching in which practically all direct communication between the teacher and the student is carried out via the public telephone system; also known as telephone tutoring.

Teleprinter another name for a *line printer.*

Teletext another name for *broadcast videotex(t).*

Tele-type terminal another name for a *keyboard terminal.*

Television game an electronic game that uses an external television set to produce a large-scale video display.

(Television) monitor an electronic device which translates television signals into pictures on a cathode ray tube screen and sound; a *monitor* differs from a television receiver in that the signal is generally fed in by cable and the picture quality is higher; monitors are used mainly in television production and broadcasting, and as *video display units.*

Television projector an electronic device which projects television images on to a large screen, usually for viewing in large rooms or spaces and/or by large groups of people.

Telewriter a device which transmits hand-written or hand-drawn material over a telephone line for display or viewing elsewhere.

Terminal see *computer terminal.*

Terminal assessment assessment that is carried out at the end of a course (or section thereof).

Terminal behaviour the set of knowledge, skills, behaviours, etc that a learner is expected to have acquired by the end of a course or programme of instruction.

Terminal course a course in a subject which is not likely to be taught again during a student's subsequent studies.

Terminal frames frames that end or terminate a *programmed learning* sequence; such frames are often used to revise or summarize earlier material.

Test (a) a group of items, questions or tasks which a learner is required to tackle in order to produce a quantitative measurement of the extent to which he has acquired a particular set of knowledge, skills, etc or has a given set of qualities, attributes, etc; (b) any method by which the presence, quality or genuineness of an attribute, system, item, process, etc is determined.

Testing machine a machine that is designed to test rather than teach a learner.

Thermal copier a reprographic device that makes use of some type of thermographic process, ie makes use of heat for the formation of the image.

Throw the distance from a projector to the projection screen with which it is used.

Time chart a type of chronological wallchart used in the teaching of history, geology, etc, divisions of time being represented by spaces of corresponding width and events being depicted in those spaces.

Time lapse photography a technique for visualizing normally invisibly slow processes by shooting one frame of a motion picture film at a time at prescribed intervals, and then showing the resulting sequence at normal speed.

Time-sharing a system whereby several users may, through *remote terminals*, each use the facilities of the same large computer at the same time so that each appears to have exclusive use of his own computer.

Track (a) that discrete area of a film, videotape or (usually) audiotape on which a particular signal is recorded; (b) a term used in *programmed learning* — see *multiple track, single track*.

Transfer (a) a term used in behavioural psychology to denote the effects of previous experience on later learning — see *horizontal, negative, vertical transfer (of learning)*; (b) a term applied to film, lettering, images, etc that can be transferred from one sheet to another by pressure or other means — see *transfer film, lettering, type.*

Transfer film transparent or translucent film with a pressure-sensitive adhesive back that can be used to add colour, shading, etc to overhead transparencies.

Transfer lettering, type a generic term for sheets of letters which can be transferred to other material by application of pressure (or some other process) during the preparation of graphic material, etc.

Transfer of learning see *transfer.*

Translucent screen a type of screen with a translucent surface used in *back projection.*

Transverse scanning a video scanning system in which the head moves across the recording tape rather than along it as in *helical scanning.*

Tree-and-branch system a *cable television* distribution system in which subscribers are connected to the distribution centre by a branching system of coaxial cables.

True-false test a test in which the testee has to mark items as either 'true' or 'false'.

Tuning carrying out fine adjustments to a system in order to optimize its operation.

U

Underwear a term sometimes applied to those aspects of educational technology which underlie the use of *hardware* and *software*; but which cannot be placed in either category (see Chapter 1).

Unique answer question an examination or test question that has a single correct answer or solution, as opposed to an *open-ended* question.

Unit-perfection requirement where it is laid down that a learner must demonstrate mastery of a particular unit, stage or area of a course of instruction before being allowed to proceed to the next unit, stage or area; also known as *mastery requirement.*

Unit plan a type of curriculum that outlines relatively large units of teaching rather than detailing individual lessons, leaving the organization of the latter to the individual teacher.

Unobtrusive assessment assessment based on observation that is carried out without the knowledge of the individual or group of people being assessed (see Chapter 7).

Unobtrusive measure an evaluation tool where the actual measurement process is not immediately apparent to, or is remote from, the individual or group being observed (see Chapter 8).

Up-time the time (absolute or fractional) during which a learning resource (usually a device or system) is fully available for use; cf *down-time*.

Use life the maximum amount of time (or number of times) for which a system can be used under normal conditions before deteriorating past the point of usefulness.

User-oriented language a computer *programming language* that is designed for use by ordinary computer users rather than by specialist computer staff; see also *high-level programming language*.

V

Validation the demonstration of the effectiveness of instructional materials or systems by the use of appropriate *summative evaluation* techniques.

Validity the extent to which a test or other measuring instrument fulfils the purpose for which it is designed (see Chapter 7).

Valuing an *affective* process that involves accepting that an object, system, etc, has value; level 3 of Bloom's *affective domain*.

Variable speech a technique used in audio instruction whereby the listener can vary the rate at which spoken information is presented without altering the pitch or introducing distortion.

Velcro board a type of *hook-and-loop board*.

Velour paper paper with a velvet-like finish used in preparing felt-board display materials.

Vertical panel book a *programmed text* in which the pages are divided vertically into panels.

Vertical transfer (of learning) a form of transfer of learning in which a low-order learned skill, concept or fact is put to use in a higher-order or more complex situation of which it is a component.

Video (a) (adjective) a term applied to all visual aspects of television signals, equipment, etc; (b) (noun) a loose term for a *videorecording* or for any machine that can be used to record and/or play back such recordings (videocassette recorders, videotape recorders, etc).

Video cartridge a *cartridge* containing *videotape*.

Videocassette a *cassette* containing *videotape*.

Videodisc a disc on which visual images, with or without sound, are electronically or optically recorded; see also *contact videodisc, optical videodisc*.

Videodisplay unit (VDU) a television-like computer terminal on which verbal, numerical or graphical information generated by the computer and user can be displayed.

Video signal an electronic signal, either in *analogue* or *digital* form, representing a visual scene and capable of being used to reproduce that scene.

Videogram a pre-recorded *videotape* or *videocassette*.

Videorecording (a) a generic term for a medium on which both television pictures and sound are recorded and which can be played back electronically to reproduce both the pictures and the sound; see also *videotape* and *videodisc*; (b) a television signal so recorded; (c) the activity of producing such a recording.

Videotape special magnetic tape on which encoded television signals are (or may be) recorded.

Videotex(t) a generic term for electronic systems that make computer-stored information available via video display units or television sets; see also *broadcast videotex, interactive videotex*.

Viewdata an alternative name for *interactive videotex(t)*.

Visual aids visual materials (such as diagrams, maps, pictures and slides) used as aids to teaching or learning. see also *audiovisual aids*.

Visual display unit (VDU) another name for a *video display unit*.

Visual materials a generic name for instructional materials which communicate primarily through sight.

Viva, viva voce (examination) other names for an *oral examination*.

W

Wallchart a relatively large opaque sheet exhibiting information in graphic or tabular form designed to be attached to a wall for display purposes.

Washahead another name for *forward branching*.

Washback another name for *backward branching*.

Weighting the assignment of differential values to test items, scores, etc in order to give them the required degree of relative importance.

Whiteboard a marker board with a white surface.

Whole-class approach, method a form of teaching in which all the members of a class carry out the same activity.

Whole learning an analytical method of teaching a topic that involves starting by looking at the topic as a whole and then looking at its constituent elements.

Word processor a keyboard/microcomputer system that enables text to be composed, edited and filed; the text is held in the computer store, and any part can be called up, visually displayed, printed in *hard copy* form, or fed into a different system at any time.

Workbook a text produced as a study or learning guide, usually containing exercises, problems, practice materials, etc.

Work card a re-usable card carrying instructions relating to a particular piece of work, and (usually) giving background information relating to same.

Worksheet a sheet carrying instructions, information, etc relating to part of (or some aspect of) the work of an exercise; such sheets often incorporate spaces where information, answers, results, etc have to be filled in.

Workshop a practical session designed to illustrate the underlying principle, logistics or mechanics of an exercise, programme, etc without necessarily working all the way through it.

X

Xerography a widely-used name for *electrostatic copying.*

Z

Zig-zag book a *scrambled text* in which pages are divided into cut sections which can be turned forward or backward independent of one another.

Zimdex a cueing technique used in audio instruction in which numbers or pulses are recorded on one track of an audiocassette in order to mark or index the contents of the other (main) track.

Bibliography

Readers wishing to study any of the topics covered in the various chapters in greater depth may find the following books and articles of interest.

Chapter 1: The Nature of Educational Technology

Banathy, B (1968) *Instructional Systems*. Fearon, Palo Alto, California.

Beard, R (1972) *Teaching and Learning in Higher Education* (Second Edition). Penguin, Harmondsworth.

Bjerstedt, A (1972) *Educational Technology*. Wiley-Interscience, New York.

Bolam, R (1975) The management of educational change. In Houghton, Y, McHugh, R and Morgan, C (eds) *Management in Education*. Ward Lock Educational, London.

Briggs, L J (1970) *Handbook of Procedures for the Design of Instruction*. American Institutes for Research, Pittsburgh, Pennsylvania.

Bruner, J S (1960) *The Process of Education*. Harvard University Press, Cambridge, Massachusetts.

Bugelski, B R (1971) *The Psychology of Learning Applied to Teaching*. Bobbs-Merrill, New York.

Buzan, T (1979) *How to Study*. Encyclopaedia Britannica, London.

Callahan, R E (1962) *Education and the Cult of Efficiency*. University of Chicago Press, Chicago.

CET (1979) *The Contribution of Educational Technology to Higher Education in the 1990s*. Council for Educational Technology, London.

Champness, B and Young, I (1980) Social limits in educational technology. *European Journal of Education*, 15, 3, pp 229-39.

Clarke, J L (1981) *Educational Development: A Select Bibliography*. Kogan Page, London.

Cleary, A, Mayes, T and Packham, D (1976) *Educational Technology: Implications for Early and Special Education*. Wiley, London.

Cowan, J (1980) Is systematic curriculum design always feasible? *Programmed Learning and Educational Technology*, **17**, 2, pp 115-17.

Davies, I K and Hartley, J (eds) (1972) *Contributions to an Educational Technology*. Butterworths, London.

De Cecco, J P (1968) *The Psychology of Learning and Instruction*. Prentice-Hall, Englewood Cliffs, New Jersey.

Entwhistle N J and Nisbet, J D (1972) *Educational Research in Action*. University of London Press, London.

Elton, L R B (1977) Educational technology — today and tomorrow. In Hills, P and Gilbert, J (eds) *Aspects of Educational Technology* **XI**. Kogan Page, London.

Eraut, M and Squires, G (1973) *An Annotated Select Bibliography of Educational Technology* (Second Edition). Council for Educational Technology, London.

Gage, N L (1963) *Handbook of Research on Teaching*. Rand McNally, Chicago.

Gagné, R M (ed) (1962) *Psychological Principles in System Development*. Holt, Rinehart and Winston, New York.

Gagné, R M (1970) *The Conditions of Learning* (Second Edition). Holt, Rinehart and Winston, New York.

Gagné, R M and Briggs, L J (1979) *Principles of Instructional Design* (Second Edition). Holt, Rinehart and Winston, New York.

Galloway, C (1976) *Psychology for Teaching and Learning*. McGraw-Hill, New York.

Gibbs, G (1981) *Teaching Students to Learn: A Student-Centred Approach*. Open University Press, Milton Keynes.

Glock, M D (ed) (1971) *Guided Learning. Readings in Educational Psychology*. Wiley, New York.

Hartley, J and Davies, I K (1978) *Contributions to an Educational Technology*, **2**. Kogan Page, London.

Havelock, R G (1970) *A Guide to Innovation in Education*. University of Michigan, Michigan.

Hawkridge, D G (1981) The telesis of educational technology. *British Journal of Educational Technology*, **12**, 1, pp 4-18.

Houghton, V, McHugh, R and Morgan, C (eds) (1975) *Management in Education*. Ward Lock Educational, London.

Howe, A (ed) (1980) *International Yearbook of Educational Technology 1980/81*. Kogan Page, London.

Huczynski, A (1983) *Encyclopaedia of Management Development Methods*. Gower Press, Farnborough.

Lewis, B N (1980) The professional standing of educational technology. In Howe, A (ed) *International Yearbook of Educational and Training Technology 1980/81*. Kogan Page, London.

Morgan, R N (1978) Educational technology: adolescence to adulthood. *Educational Communication and Technology,* **26,** 2.

Nickson, M (1971) *Educational Technology. A Systematic Approach for Teachers.* Ward Lock Educational, London.

Osborne, C W (ed) (1982) *International Yearbook of Educational and Instructional Technology 1982/83.* Kogan Page, London.

Pfeiffer, J (1968) *New Look at Education: Systems Analysis in our Schools and Colleges.* Odyssey Press, New York.

Popham, W J and Baker, E L (1970) *Systematic Instruction.* Prentice-Hall, Englewood Cliffs, New Jersey.

Race, W P (1981) Help yourself to success — improving polytechnic students study skills. In Percival, F and Ellington, H I (eds) *Aspects of Educational Technology,* **XV.** *Distance Learning and Evaluation.* Kogan Page, London.

Reif, F (1978) Towards an applied science of education. *Instructional Science,* **7,** pp 1-14.

Richmond, W K (1969) A systems approach to educational reform: the Swedish example. In *The Education Industry.* Methuen, London.

Richmond, W K (1970) *The Concept of Educational Technology.* Weidenfeld and Nicolson, London.

Rogers, C (1969) *Freedom to Learn.* Merrill, Columbus, Ohio.

Romiszowski, A J (1974) *The Selection and Use of Instructional Media: A Systems Approach.* Kogan Page, London.

Romiszowski, A J (1981) *Designing Instructional Systems.* Kogan Page, London.

Romiszowski, A J (1983) *Producing Instructional Systems.* Kogan Page, London.

Rowntree, D (1976) *Learn How to Study.* McDonald and Jane's, London.

Rowntree, D (1982) *Educational Technology in Curriculum Development* (Second Edition). Harper and Row, London.

Saettler, P (1978) The roots of educational technology. *Programmed Learning and Educational Technology,* **15,** 1.

Skinner, B F (1968) *The Technology of Teaching.* Appleton-Century-Crofts, New York.

Stenhouse, L (1971) *An Introduction to Curriculum Development and Research.* Heinemann, London.

Tickton, S G (ed) (1970) *To Improve Learning.* Bowker, New York.

Travers, R M W (ed) (1973) *Second Handbook of Research on Teaching.* Rand McNally, Chicago.

Trott, A J, Strongman, H and Giddins, L (1983) *Aspects of Educational Technology,* **XVI.** *Improving Efficiency in Education and Training.* Kogan Page, London.

Unwin, D and McAleese, R (1978) *Encyclopaedia of Educational Media, Communications and Technology.* Macmillan, London.

UTMU (1976) *Improving Teaching in Higher Education.* University of London Teaching Methods Unit, London.

Chapter 2: Basic Educational Strategies

Allen, P S (1978) Developing a remedial Keller Plan course. *Studies in Higher Education,* **3**, 2.

Ausubel, D P and Robinson, F G (1969) *School Learning.* Holt, Rinehart and Winston, New York.

Bennett, S N (1976) *Teaching Styles and Pupil Progress.* Open Books, London.

Berstein, B (1971) Open schools, open society. In Cosin, B R *et al* (eds) *School and Society: A Sociological Reader.* Routledge and Kegan Paul, London.

Bremer, J and Von Moschzisker, M (1971) *The School Without Walls.* Holt, Rinehart and Winston, New York.

Coffey, J (1978) *Development of an Open Learning System in Further Education* (Working Paper 15). Council for Educational Technology, London.

Daly, D W and Robertson, S M (1978) *Keller Plan in the Classroom.* Scottish Council for Educational Technology, Glasgow.

Davies, T C (1977) *Open Learning Systems for Mature Students* (Working Paper 14). Council for Educational Technology, London.

Galton, M, Simon, B and Croll, P (1980) *Inside the Primary Classroom.* Routledge and Kegan Paul, London.

Gardner, D E M (1966) *Experiment and Tradition in Primary Schools.* Methuen, London.

Gnagey, W J, Chesebro, P A and Johnson, J A (1972) *Learning Environments.* Holt, Rinehart and Winston, New York.

Gross, N, Giacquinta, J B and Bernstein, M (1971) *Implementing Organizational Innovations.* Harper and Row, New York.

Haddon, F A and Lytton, H (1968) Teaching approach and the development of divergent thinking abilities in primary schools. *British Journal of Educational Psychology,* **38**, 2, pp 171-9.

Hooper, R S (ed) (1971) *The Curriculum: Context Design and Development.* Oliver and Boyd, Edinburgh.

Keller, F S (1968) Goodbye teacher . . . *Journal of Applied Behavioural Analysis,* **1**, pp 79-89.

Keller, F S and Sherman, J (1974) *The Keller Plan Handbook.* Benjamin, Menlo Park, California.

Mackenzie, N, Postgate, R and Scupham, J (1975) *Open Learning Systems and Problems in Post Secondary Education.* UNESCO Press, London.

Romiszowski, A J (1981) *Designing Instructional Systems.* Kogan Page, London.

Rowntree, D (1974) *Educational Technology in Curriculum Development.* Harper and Row, London.

Rowntree, D (1981) *Developing Courses for Students.* McGraw-Hill, London.

Spencer, D C (1980) *Thinking About Open Learning Systems* (Working Paper 19). Council for Educational Technology, London.

Weston, P B (1980) *Negotiating the Curriculum: A Study in Secondary Schooling.* NFER Publishing, Slough.

Chapter 3: Educational Objectives

Bandura, A (1970) *Principles of Behaviour Modification.* Holt, Rinehart and Winston, London.

Beard, R (1972) *Teaching and Learning in Higher Education.* Penguin, Harmondsworth.

Bloom, B S (ed) (1956) *Taxonomy of Educational Objectives. Book 1: Cognitive Domain.* Longman, London.

Bloom, B S, Hastings, J T and Madaus, J F (1971) *Handbook on Formative and Summative Evaluation of Student Learning.* McGraw-Hill, New York.

Bloom, B S, Krathwohl, D R and Masia, B (1964) *Taxonomy of Educational Objectives. Book 2: Affective Domain.* Longman, London.

Calder, J R (1980) In defense of the systematic approach to instruction and behavioural objectives. *Educational Technology,* **20**, pp 21-5.

Eisner, E W (1967) Educational objectives: help or hindrance? *School Review,* **75**, pp 250-60.

Harrow, A J (1972) *A Taxonomy of the Motor Domain.* McKay, New York.

Henrysson, S and Franke-Wikberg, S (1979) Long term effects of higher education. *International Newsletter,* **12**, pp 7-9. Society for Research into Higher Education.

Kapfer, M B (ed) (1971) *Behavioural Objectives in Curriculum Development.* Educational Technology Publications, Englewood Cliffs, New Jersey.

Macdonald-Ross, M (1973) Behavioural objectives — a critical review. *Instructional Science,* **2**, 1, pp 1-52.

Mager, R F (1962) *Preparing Instructional Objectives.* Fearon, Palo Alto, California.

Ormell, C P (1974) Bloom's taxonomy and the objectives of education. *Educational Research,* **17**, 1.

Ormell, C P (1974) Objections to Bloom's taxonomy. *Journal of Curriculum Studies,* **6**, pp 3-18.

Peters, R S (ed) (1969) *Proceedings of UTMU Conference on Objectives in Higher Education.* University of London Intitute of Education, London.

Plowman, P D (1971) *Behavioural Objectives.* Science Research Associates, Chicago.

Pring, R (1971) Bloom's taxonomy: a philosophical critique. *Cambridge Journal of Education,* 2, pp 83-91.

Rowntree, D (1973) Which objectives are most worthwhile? In Leedham, J F and Budgett, R E B (eds) *Aspects of Educational Technology,* VII. Pitman, London.

Rowntree, D (1982) *Educational Technology in Curriculum Development* (Second Edition). Harper and Row, London.

Seymour, W D (1954) *Industrial Training for Manual Operations.* Pitman, London.

Simpson, E (1971) Educational objectives in the psychomotor domain. In Kapfer, M B (ed) *Behavioural Objectives in Curriculum Development.* Educational Technology Publications, Englewood Cliffs, New Jersey.

Stenhouse, L (1975) Some limitations of the use of objectives in curriculum research and planning. *Paedagogica Europaea,* 6, pp 73-83.

Stones, E (1972) *Educational Objectives and the Teaching of Educational Psychology.* Methuen, London.

UTMU (1976) *Improving Teaching in Higher Education.* University of London Teaching Methods Unit, London.

Warren Piper, D J (1969) An approach to designing courses based on the recognition of objectives. In Peters, R S (ed) *Proceedings of UTMU Conference on Objectives in Higher Education.* University of London Institute of Education, London.

Chapter 4: Mass Instruction Techniques

Beard, R (1972) *Teaching and Learning in Higher Education.* Penguin, Harmondsworth.

Bligh, D A (1972) *What's the Use of Lectures?* Penguin, Harmondsworth.

Bligh, D A *et al* (1975) *Teaching Students.* Exeter University Teaching Services, Exeter.

Brown, G A (1978) *Lecturing and Explaining.* Methuen, London.

Dale, E (1969) *Audiovisual Methods in Teaching.* (Third Edition). Holt, Rinehart and Winston, New York.

Erickson, C W H (1972) *Fundamentals of Teaching with Audio-Visual Technology.* Collier-Macmillan, New York.

Hawkridge, D (1981) *Organizing Educational Broadcasting.* Croom Helm, London.

Henderson, J and Humphreys, F (1981) *The Audio Visual Handbook.* Kogan Page, London.

Johnstone, A H and Percival, F (1981) Attention breaks in lectures. *Education in Chemistry,* 13, 3, pp 49-50.

Kennedy, K (1972) *Film in Teaching.* Batsford, London.

McInnes, J (1980) *Video in Education and Training.* Focal Press, London.
McLeish, J (1968) *The Lecture Method* (Cambridge Monographs on Teaching Methods 1). Cambridge Institute of Education, Cambridge, UK.
McRae, R K (1975) *The Overhead Projector.* Association for the Study of Medical Education, Dundee.
Ogborn, J (ed) (1977) *Practical Work in Undergraduate Science.* Heinemann, London.
Powell, L S (1978) *A Guide to the Use of Visual Aids.* (Fourth Edition). British Association for Commercial and Industrial Education, London.
Powell, L S (1980) *A Guide to the Overhead Projector.* British Association for Commercial and Industrial Education, London.
Romiszowski, A J (1974) *The Selection and Use of Instructional Media.* Kogan Page, London.
Rowatt, R W (1980) *OHP — A Guide to the Use of the Overhead Projector.* Scottish Council for Educational Technology, Glasgow.
UTMU (1976) *Improving Teaching in Higher Education.* University of London Teaching Methods Unit, London.
Waters, C D J and Lawrie, N L (1981) The use of television equipment in Scottish secondary schools. In Percival, F and Ellington, H I (eds) *Aspects of Educational Technology,* **XV.** Kogan Page, London.

Chapter 5: Individualized Instructional Techniques

Barnet College of Further Education (1978) *Flexi-Study: A Manual for Local Colleges.* National Extension College, Cambridge, UK.
Bates, A W (1982) Learning from audio-visual media: the Open University experience. In *Teaching at a Distance: Research Supplement 1.* Open University, Milton Keynes.
Birch, D W and Cuthbert, R E (1981) *Costing Open Learning in Further Education.* Council for Educational Technology, London.
Bishop, L K (1971) *Individualizing Educational Systems.* Harper and Row, New York.
Block, J H (1971) *Mastery Learning: Theory and Practice.* Holt, Rinehart and Winston, New York.
Boud, D J (1981) *Developing Student Autonomy in Learning.* Kogan Page, London.
Boud, D J and Bridge, W (1974) Keller Plan: a case study in individualized learning. In *Towards Independence in Learning.* The Nuffield Foundation, London.
Bridge, W and Elton, L R B (eds) (1977) *Individual Study in Undergraduate Science.* Heinemann, London.
Butts, D (1981) Distance learning and broadcasting. In Percival, F and Ellington, H I (eds) *Aspects of Educational Technology,* **XV.** Kogan Page, London.

Clarke, J and Leedham, J (eds) (1976) *Aspects of Educational Technology*, **X**. *Individualized Learning*. Kogan Page, London.

Coffey, J (1978) *Development of an Open Learning System in Further Education: A Report* (Working Paper 15). Council for Educational Technology, London.

Daly, D W and Robertson, S M (eds) (1978) *Keller Plan in the Classroom*. Scottish Council for Educational Technology, Glasgow.

Davies, T C (1977) *Open Learning Systems for Mature Students*. (Working Paper 14). Council for Educational Technology, London.

Davies, W J K (1978) *Implementing Individualised Learning in Schools and Colleges* (Guidelines 4). Council for Educational Technology, London.

Davies, W J K (1980) *Alternatives to Class Teaching in Colleges and Schools* (Guidelines 9). Council for Educational Technology, London.

Gagné, R M (ed) (1967) *Learning and Individual Differences*. Macmillan, New York.

Goldschmid, B and Goldschmid, M L (1976) Peer teaching in higher education: a review. *Higher Education*, 5, 1, pp 9-33.

Graves, J and Graves, V (1979) *Designing a Tape-Slide Programme*. Association for the Study of Medical Education, Dundee.

Harding, A G (1973) The project: its place as a learning situation. *British Journal of Educational Technology*, 4, pp 216-32.

Harris, W J A and Williams, J D S (1977) *A Handbook on Distance Education* (Manchester Monograph 7). Manchester University, Manchester.

Heidt, E U (1976) *Instructional Media and the Individual Learner*. Kogan Page, London.

Heidt, E U (1980) Differences between media and differences between learners: can we relate them? *Instructional Science*, 9, pp 365-91.

Hills, P J (1976) *The Self-Teaching Process in Higher Education*. Croom Helm, London.

Holmberg, B (1977) *Distance Education — A Survey and Bibliography*. Kogan Page, London.

Holmberg, B (1981) *Status and Trends of Distance Education*. Kogan Page, London.

Keller, F S (1968) Goodbye teacher . . . *Journal of Applied Behavioural Analysis*, 1, pp 79-89.

Keller, F S and Sherman, J (1974) *The Keller Plan Handbook*. Benjamin, Menlo Park, California.

Lewis, R (1981) *How to Tutor in an Open Learning Scheme*. Council for Educational Technology, London.

Lewis, R (1981) *How to Write Self-Study Materials* (Guidelines 10). Council for Educational Technology, London.

Lewis, R and Jones, G (eds) (1980) *How to Write a Distance Learning Package: A Self-Study Pack for Authors*. Council for Educational Technology, London.

Lickley, A (1977) *Towards Individualized Learning in Teacher Education*. Council for Educational Technology, London.

Mackenzie, M L (1978) *Deciding to Individualize Learning: A Study of the Process*. Council for Educational Technology, London.

Mackenzie, N, Postgate, R and Scupham, J (1975) *Open Learning Systems for Post-Secondary Education*. UNESCO Press, London.

Manpower Services Commission (1981) *An 'Open Tech' Programme: A Consultative Document*. Manpower Services Commission, London.

Manwaring, G (1977) *Individualized Learning*. Dundee College of Education, Dundee (Audio-visual package).

Neil, M W (ed) (1981) *Education of Adults at a Distance. A Report of the Open University's Tenth Anniversary Conference*. Kogan Page, London.

Nuffield Foundation (1974) *Towards Independence in Learning*. The Nuffield Foundation, London.

Percival, F and Ellington, H I (eds) (1981) *Aspects of Educational Technology*, **XV**. *Distance Learning and Evaluation*. Kogan Page, London.

Postlethwait, S N, Novak, J and Murray, H (1971) *An Audio-Tutorial Approach to Learning*. Burgess, Minneapolis.

Romiszowski, A J (ed) (1976) *Programmed Learning and Educational Technology*, **13**, 1 (Special issue on 'Individualization in Higher Education').

Rowatt, R W (1980) *Slide-Tape — A Guide to the Production of Slide-Tape Programmes*. Scottish Council for Educational Technology, Glasgow.

Rowntree, D (ed) (1976) *Programmed Learning and Educational Technology*, **13**, 4 (Special issue on 'The Open University').

Rowntree, D and Conners, B (eds) (1980) *How to Develop Self-Instructional Teaching. A Self-Instructional Guide to the Writing of Self-Instructional Materials*. The Open University, Milton Keynes.

Ruskin, R S (ed) (1977) *Educational Technology*, **17**, 9 (Special issue on 'The Personalized System of Instruction (PSI)').

Spencer, D C (1977) *Independence in Learning* (Coombe Lodge Information Paper 1193). Coombe Lodge, Bristol.

Spencer, D C (1980) *Thinking About Open Learning Systems* (Working Paper 19). Council for Educational Technology, London.

SRHE (1976) *The Use of Project Methods in Higher Education*. Society for Research in Higher Education, London.

Stack, E M (1971) *The Language Laboratory and Modern Language Teaching* (Third Edition). Oxford University Press, London.

Twining, J (ed) (1982) *Open Learning for Technicians*. Stanley Thornes, Cheltenham.

Young, M *et al* (1980) *Distance Teaching for the Third World*. Routledge and Kegan Paul, London.

Chapter 6: Group Learning Techniques

Abercrombie, M L J (1979) *Aims and Techniques of Group Teaching* (Fourth Edition). Society for Research into Higher Education. Guildford.

Abercrombie, M L J and Terry, P M (1978) *Talking to Learn: Improving Teaching and Learning in Small Groups.* Society for Research into Higher Education, Guildford.

Argyle, M (1967) *The Psychology of Interpersonal Behaviour.* Penguin, Harmondsworth.

Boocock, S S and Schild, E O (eds) (1968) *Simulation Games in Learning.* Sage Publications, Beverly Hills, California.

Bramley, W (1979) *Group Tutoring: Concepts and Case Studies.* Kogan Page, London.

Brown, G A (1975) *Microteaching, A Programme of Teaching Skills.* Methuen, London.

Collier, K (1969) Syndicate methods: further evidence and comment. *Universities Quarterly,* 23, 4.

Ellington, H I, Addinall, E and Percival, F (1981) *Games and Simulations in Science Education.* Kogan Page, London.

Ellington, H I, Addinall, E and Percival, F (1982) *A Handbook of Game Design.* Kogan Page, London.

Ellington, H I, Addinall, E and Percival, F (1984) *Case Studies in Game Design.* Kogan Page, London.

Ellington, H I and Percival, F (1977) Educating 'through' science using multi-disciplinary simulation games. *Programmed Learning and Educational Technology,* 14, 2, pp 117-26.

Greenblat, C S and Duke, R D (1981) *Principles and Practice of Gaming-Simulation.* Sage Publications, Beverly Hills, California.

Hargie, O and Maidment, P (1978) *Microteaching in Perspective.* Blackstaff Press, Dundonald, Co Down.

Henry, N B (ed) (1960) *The Dynamics of Instructional Groups.* National Society for the Study of Education, New York.

Hill, W F (1977) *Learning Thru' Discussion.* Sage Publications, Beverly Hills, California.

Jones, K (1980) *Simulations: A Handbook for Teachers.* Kogan Page, London.

Jordan, W J J (1961) *Synectics.* Harper and Row, London.

Megarry, J (ed) (1977) *Aspects of Simulation and Gaming.* Kogan Page, London.

Megarry, J (1979) Developments in simulation and gaming. In Howe, A and Romiszowski, A J (eds) *International Yearbook of Educational and Instructional Technology 1978/9.* Kogan Page, London.

Ogborn, J (ed) (1977) *Small Group Teaching in Undergraduate Science.* Heinemann, London.

Pfeiffer, J W and Jones, J E (1969-1983) *Annual Handbooks for Group Facilitators.* University Associates, La Jolla, California.

Rowntree, D (1982) *Educational Technology in Curriculum Development* (Second Edition). Harper and Row, London.

Ruddock, J (1978) *Learning Through Small Group Discussion.* Society for Research into Higher Education, Guildford.

Simons, H, Squires, G and Ruddock, J (1976) *Small Group Teaching: Selected Papers.* The Nuffield Foundation, London.

Tansey, P J (ed) (1971) *Educational Aspects of Simulation.* McGraw-Hill, London.

Tansey, P J and Unwin, D (1969) *Simulation and Gaming in Education.* Methuen, London.

Taylor, J L and Walford, R (1978) *Learning and the Simulation Game.* Open University Press, Milton Keynes.

Teather, D L B (1978) Simulation and games. In Unwin, D and McAleese, R (eds) *Encyclopaedia of Educational Media, Communications and Technology.* Macmillan, London.

Twelker, P A (1971) Simulation and media. In Tansey, P J (ed) *Educational Aspects of Simulation.* McGraw-Hill, London.

UTMU (1972) *Varieties of Group Discussion in University Teaching.* London University Institute of Education.

Van Ments, M (1983) *Role-Play. A Handbook for Teachers.* Kogan Page, London.

Walton, H F (1973) *Small Group Methods in Medical Training* (Medical Education Booklet 1). Association for the Study of Medical Education, Dundee.

Wentworth, D R and Lewis, D R (1973) A review of research on instructional games and simulations in social science education. *Social Education* May, pp 432-48.

Chapter 7: Student Assessment

Belasco, J A and Trice, H M (1969) *The Assessment of Change in Training and Therapy.* McGraw-Hill, New York.

Clift, J C and Imrie, B W (1981) *Assessing Students, Appraising Teachers.* Croom Helm, London.

Cox, R (1972) Traditional examinations in a changing society. *Universities Quarterly,* **27**, 2.

Ebel, R L (1972) *Essentials of Educational Measurement.* Prentice-Hall, Englewood Cliffs, New Jersey.

Edwards, D (1979) A study of reliability of tutor-marked assignments in the Open University. *Assessment in Higher Education,* **5**, 1, pp 16-44.

Fairbrother, R (1975) The reliability of teachers' judgements of the abilities tested by multiple-choice items. *Educational Research,* **17**, 3, pp 202-10.

Gronlund, N E (1971) *Measurement and Evaluation in Teaching* (Second Edition). Macmillan, New York.

Harden, R M and Gleeson, F A (1979) *Assessment of Clinical Competence Using an Objective Structured Clinical Examination.* Association for the Study of Medical Education, Dundee.

Hartog, P and Rhodes, E C (1935) *An Examination of Examinations.* Macmillan, London.

Hoffman, B (1967) *The Tyranny of Testing.* Collier, New York.

Hudson, B (1973) *Assessment Techniques.* Methuen, London.

Illiffe, A H (1966) Objective tests. In Heyood, J and Illiffe, A H (eds) *Some Problems of Testing Academic Performance.* Department of Higher Education, University of Lancaster.

Ingenkamp, K (1977) *Educational Assessment.* NFER Publishing, Slough.

Klug, B (ed) (1975) *A Question of Degree: Assorted Papers on Assessment.* The Nuffield Foundation, London.

Knox, J D (1975) *The Modified Essay Question.* Association for the Study of Medical Education, Dundee.

Lennox, B (1974) *Hints on the Setting and Evaluation of Multiple Choice Questions of the One from Five Type.* Association for the Study of Medical Education, Dundee.

Miller, C and Parlett, M (1974) *Up to the Mark: A Study of the Examination Game.* Society for Research into Higher Education, Guildford.

Popham, W J (ed) (1971) *Criterion-Referenced Measurement.* Educational Technology Publications, Englewood Cliffs, New Jersey.

Rowntree, D (1977) *Assessing Students: How Shall We Know Them?* Harper and Row, London.

Rowntree, D (1982) *Educational Technology in Curriculum Development* (Second Edition). Harper and Row, London.

Satterly, D (1981) *Assessment in Schools.* Blackwell, Oxford.

SED (1979) *Issues in Educational Assessment.* HMSO, Edinburgh.

Sumner, R (1982) *Assessment in Schools.* Croom Helm, London.

Sumner, R and Bradley, K (1977) *Assessment in Transition.* NFER Publishing, Slough.

Sumner, R and Robertson, T S (1976) *Criterion-Referenced Measurement and Criterion-Referenced Tests: Some Published Work Reviewed.* NFER Publishing, Slough.

Tittle, C K and Miller, K M (1976) *Assessing Attainment.* Independent Assessment and Research Centre, London.

Tuckman, B W (1975) *Measuring Educational Outcomes: Fundamentals of Testing.* Harcourt Brace Jovanovich, New York.

Tyler, R W and Wolf, R M (eds) (1976) *Critical Issues in Testing.* McCutchan, Berkeley, California.

Wardrop, J L (1976) *Standardized Testing in the Schools: Uses and Roles.* Brooks/Cole, Monterey, California.

Webb, E J, Campbell, D T, Schwartz, R D and Sechrest, L (1969) *Unobtrusive Measures: Non-Reactive Research in the Social Sciences*. Rand McNally, Chicago.

Chapter 8: Evaluation

Beard, R (1972) *Teaching and Learning in Higher Education*. Penguin, Harmondsworth.

Becher, T (1981) Evaluation and educational technology. In Percival, F and Ellington, H I (eds) *Aspects of Educational Technology*, **XV**. Kogan Page, London.

Birch, D W and Cuthbert, R E (1981) *Costing Open Learning in Further Education*. Council for Educational Technology, London.

Bligh, D (1972) Evaluation of teaching in groups by interaction analysis. In *Varieties of Group Discussion in University Teaching*. University of London Institute of Education, London.

Bloomer, J (1975) Paradigms of evaluation. *SAGSET Journal*, **5**, 1, pp 36-7.

Bridge, W (1978) *Course Evaluation Package*. Joint Board of Clinical Nursing Studies, London.

Clift, J C and Imrie, B W (1981) *Assessing Students, Appraising Teachers*. Croom Helm, London.

Ebel, R L (1973) Evaluation and educational objectives. *Journal of Educational Measurement*, **10**, pp 273-9.

Ellington, H I (1981) Course development by error elimination — a Popperian approach. *Coombe Lodge Report: Course Monitoring and Evaluation*. Coombe Lodge, Bristol.

Eraut, M R (1970) The role of evaluation. In Taylor, G (ed) *The Teacher as a Manager*. Council for Educational Technology, London.

Falk, B and Lee Dow, K (1971) *The Assessment of University Teaching*. Society for Research in Higher Education, London.

Fielden, J and Pearson, P K (1978) *Costing Educational Practice*. Council for Educational Technology, London.

Fielden, J and Pearson, P K (1978) *The Cost of Learning with Computers: Report of the Financial Evaluation of the National Development Programme in Computer Assisted Learning*. Council for Educational Technology, London.

Flood-Page, C (1974) *Student Evaluation of Teaching: The American Experience*. Society for Research into Higher Education, London.

Gronlund, N E (1971) *Measurement and Evaluation in Teaching*. (Second Edition). Macmillan, New York.

Hamilton, D *et al* (1977) *Beyond the Numbers Game: A Reader in Educational Evaluation*. Macmillan, London.

Harlen, W (1975) *Evaluation in Curriculum Development: Twelve Case Studies*. Macmillan, London.

Harris, N D C and Bell, C D (1981) An evaluation resource pack: issues and implications. In Percival, F and Ellington, H I (eds) *Aspects of Educational Technology*, **XV**. Kogan Page, London.

Harris, N D C, Bell, C D and Carter, J E H (1981) *Signposts for Evaluating: A Resource Pack*. Council for Educational Technology, London.

Hawkridge, D G (1970) Design for evaluation studies. In *Evaluation Research: Strategies and Methods*. American Institutes for Research, Palo Alto, California.

Henderson, E S and Nathenson, M B (1976) Developmental testing: an empirical approach to course improvement. *Programmed Learning and Educational Technology*, **13**, 4, pp 31-42.

Knapper, C K (1980) *Evaluating Instructional Technology*. Croom Helm, London.

Lawless, C J (1981) Evaluating the process of learning. In Percival, F and Ellington, H I (eds) *Aspects of Educational Technology*, **XV**. Kogan Page, London.

McIntyre, D I (1980) Systematic observation of classroom activities. *Educational Analysis*, **2**, 2, pp 3-30.

Nathenson, M B and Henderson, E S (1980) *Using Student Feedback to Improve Learning Materials*. Croom Helm, London.

Nisbet, J D and Entwhistle, N J (1970) *Educational Research Methods*. University of London Press, London.

Oppenheim, A N (1966) *Questionnaire Design and Attitude Measurement*. Heinemann, London.

Pace, C R (1972) *Thoughts on Evaluation in Higher Education*. American College Testing Programme, Iowa.

Parlett, M and Hamilton, D (1972) *Evaluation as Illumination: A New Approach to the Study of Innovatory Programmes*. (Occasional Paper 9). Centre for Research in the Educational Sciences, University of Edinburgh.

Percival, F (1978) Evaluation procedures for simulation/gaming exercises. In McAleese, R (ed) *Perspectives on Academic Gaming and Simulation 3*. Kogan Page, London.

Percival, F (1981) The student questionnaire — a vehicle for on-going course development. *Coombe Lodge Report: Course Monitoring and Evaluation*. Coombe Lodge, Bristol.

Percival, F and Ellington, H I (eds) (1981) *Aspects of Educational Technology*, **XV**. *Distance Learning and Evaluation*. Kogan Page, London.

Popham, W J and Sirotnik, K A (1973) *Educational Statistics — Use and Interpretation*. Harper and Row, London.

Popper, K R (1972) *The Logic of Scientific Discovery* (Third Edition). Hutchinson, London.

Roebuck, M (1971) Floundering among measurements in educational technology. In Packham, D, Cleary, A and Mayes, T (eds) *Aspects of Educational Technology*, **V**. Pitman, London.

Rowntree, D (1982) *Educational Technology in Curriculum Development* (Second Edition). Harper and Row, London.

Scriven, M (1967) The methodology of evaluation. In Tyler, R W, Gagné, R and Scriven, M (eds) *Perspectives of Curriculum Evaluation*. Rand McNally, Chicago.

Stake, R E (1967) The countenance of educational evaluation. *Teachers College Record*, **68**, 7, pp 523-40.

Stake, R E (1978) *Evaluating the Arts in Education — A Responsive Approach*. Merrill, Columbus, Ohio.

Tyler, R W, Gagné, R and Scriven, M (1967) *Perspectives of Curriculum Evaluation*. Rand McNally, Chicago.

UTMU (1975) *Evaluating Teaching in Higher Education*. University of London Teaching Methods Unit, London.

UTMU (1976) *Improving Teaching in Higher Education*. University of London Teaching Methods Unit, London.

Walford, R (1975) Evaluation. *SAGSET Journal*, **5**, 1, pp 20-22.

Wittrock, N C and Wiley, D E (1970) *The Evaluation of Instruction*. Holt, New York.

Chapter 9: Resources Centres

Atherton, B (1980) *Adapting Spaces for Resource-Based Learning* (Guidelines 8). Council for Educational Technology, London.

Barker, A L and Cowan, J (1978) Cataloguing and retrieval of inter-related resource material. *British Journal of Educational Technology*, **9**, 1, pp 59-70.

Beswick, N J (1975) *Organising Resources: Six Case Studies*. Heinemann, London.

Beswick, N J (1977) *Resource-Based Learning*. Heinemann, London.

CET (1974) *Non-Book Materials: Cataloguing Rules* (Working Paper 11). Library Association/Council for Educational Technology, London.

Clarke, J (ed) (1975) *Programmed Learning and Educational Technology*, **12**, 3 (Special issue on 'Resource Centres in Education').

Clarke, J (1978) *Learning Resources for an Institution of Higher Education: A Feasibility Study*. Dundee College of Education, Dundee.

Clarke, J (1982) *Resource-Based Learning for Higher and Continuing Education*. Croom Helm, London.

Crabb, G (1975) Copyright and the resource centre. *Programmed Learning and Educational Technology*, **12**, 3, pp 191-8.

Davies, W J K (1977) *Learning Resources? An Argument for Schools* (Guidelines 1). Council for Educational Technology, London.

Davies, W J K (1978) *Implementing Individualized Learning in Schools and Colleges* (Guidelines 4). Council for Educational Technology, London.

Donovan, K G (1981) *Learning Resources in Colleges: Their Organization and Management.* Council for Educational Technology, London.

Dove, J (1975) *The Audio Visual. The Availability and Exploitation of Non-Print Material with Special Reference to Libraries.* Andre Deutsch, London.

Fairfax, O, Durham, J and Wilson, W (1976) *Audio-visual Materials: Development of a National Cataloguing and Information Service* (Working Paper 12). Council for Educational Technology, London.

Fothergill, R (1973) *Resource Centres in Colleges of Education.* (Working Paper 10). Council for Educational Technology, London.

Gordon, C (1978) *Resource Organization in Primary Schools* (Guidelines 5). Council for Educational Technology, London.

Hannabus, C S (1981) The impact of independent and open learning systems on UK libraries since 1970. In Percival, F and Ellington, H I (eds) *Aspects of Educational Technology,* **XV**. Kogan Page, London.

Holder, M L and Mitson, M L (1974) *Resource Centres.* Methuen Educational, London.

Library Association (1974) Libraries and resource centres. *Library Association Record,* **76**, 12, pp 250.

Manwaring, G (1976) Self-instructional biology — a resource centre for individualized learning. In Clarke, J and Leedham, J (eds) *Aspects of Educational Technology,* **X**. Kogan Page, London.

Matthews, J and Buckingham, D (1976) Resource-based learning: a pragmatic approach. *Studies in Higher Education,* **1**, 2, pp 156-68.

Noble, P (1980) *Resource-Based Learning in Post-Compulsory Education.* Kogan Page, London.

Poller, R C and Sealey, M E (1977) A learning aids laboratory. *Education in Chemistry,* pp 51-2, March.

Powell, L S (1974) Learning resources centres. *BACIE Journal,* **4**, 28, pp 42-4.

Raddon, R (1980) *An Annotated Bibliography on Educational Resource Organization and Related Topics.* Council for Educational Technology, London.

Routh, J C (1975) Independent learning systems and their implications for libraries. *Coombe Lodge Report,* **8**, 2, pp 52-7.

SCET (1973) *A Resources Centre is a State of Mind.* Scottish Council for Educational Technology, Glasgow.

SCET (1976) *The Setting Up of a Resources Centre: Book 1: Basic Ideas,* Malcolm, A H; *Book 2: Planning and Staffing,* Tucker, R N; *Book 3: Retreival Systems,* Malcolm, A H (ed). Scottish Council for Educational Technology, Glasgow.

SCET (1978) *Sources and Resources.* Scottish Council for Educational Technology, Glasgow.

Taylor, L C (1972) *Resources for Learning* (Second Edition). Penguin, Harmondsworth.

Wilson, G V (1980) *Audio-Visual Resources in Secondary Schools: Their Organization and Management*. Council for Educational Technology, London.

Chapter 10: Computers in Education

Ahmed, K, Ingram, D and Dickinson, C J (1980) *Software for Educational Computing*. MTP Press, Lancaster.

Ayscough, P B (1976) CAL — boon or burden? *Chemistry in Britain*, 12, 11, pp 348-53.

Baker, F B ((1978) *Computer Managed Instruction*. Educational Technology Publications, Englewood Cliffs, New Jersey.

Beech, G (ed) (1978) *Computer Assisted Methods in Science Education*. Pergamon, Oxford.

Beveridge, W T (1982) *Educational Computer Package Evaluation and Design*. Scottish Microelectronics Development Programme, Glasgow.

Bork, A (1981) *Learning with Computers*. Digital Press, Bedford, Massachusetts.

CET (1978) *Microelectronics: Their Implications for Education and Training*. Council for Educational Technology, London.

CET (1980) *Microcomputers: Their Uses in Primary Schools*. Council for Educational Technology, London.

CET (1981) *Thinking About Microcomputers: First Steps* (Information Sheet 1). Council for Educational Technology, London.

Crabb, G (1980) *Copyright and Computers*. Council for Educational Technology, London.

Dean, C and Whitlock, Q (1983) *A Handbook of Computer-Based Training*. Kogan Page, London.

Dyer, C A (1972) *Preparing for Computer Assisted Learning*. Educational Technology Publications, Englewood Cliffs, New Jersey.

Ellingham, D (1982) *Managing the Microcomputer in the Classroom*. Council for Educational Technology, London.

Ellis, A B (1974) *The Use and Misuse of Computers in Education*. McGraw-Hill, New York.

Evans, C (1981) *The Micro Millennium*. Washington Square Press/ Pocket Books, New York.

Fielden, J and Pearson, P K (1978) *The Cost of Learning with Computers. Report of the Financial Evaluation of the National Development Programme in Computer Assisted Learning*. Council for Educational Technology, London.

Gosling, W (1978) *Microcircuits, Society and Education* (Occasional Paper 8). Council for Educational Technology, London.

Gray, L (1983) Teachers' unions and the impact of computer-based technologies. In Megarry, J, Walker, D R F, Nisbet, S and Hoyle, E (eds)

Computers and Education (World Yearbook of Education 1982/83). Kogan Page, London.

Hawkridge, D (1982) *New Information Technology in Education.* Croom Helm, London.

Henderson, J and Humphreys, F (eds) (1982) *The Audio Visual and Micro-computer Handbook.* Kogan Page, London.

Hooper, R (1977) *The National Development Programme in Computer Assisted Learning. Final Report of the Director.* Council for Educational Technology, London.

Hooper, R and Toye, I (1975) *Computer Assisted Learning in the United Kingdom. Some Case Studies.* Council for Educational Technology, London.

Hunt, R and Shelley, J (1975) *Computers and Commonsense.* Prentice-Hall International, London.

Howe, J A M and Ross, P M (1981) *Microcomputers in Secondary Education.* Kogan Page, London.

Jones, R (1982) *Five of the Best: Computer Programs in Primary Schools.* Council for Educational Technology, London.

Jones, R (1982) *Microcomputers in the Primary School: A Before-You-Buy Guide.* Council for Educational Technology, London.

Kemmis, S, Atkin, R and Wright, E (1977) *How Do Students Learn? Working Papers on Computer Assisted Learning.* Centre for Applied Research in Education, University of East Anglia, Norwich.

Lecarme, O and Lewis, R (eds) (1975) *Computers in Education.* North Holland, Amsterdam.

Leiblum, M D (1974) *An Analytical and Comparative Study of Computer-Assisted Instruction Programming Languages, Their Characteristics and Usage.* Katholieke University, Nijmegen, The Netherlands.

Leiblum, M D (1977) A pragmatic approach to initiating a computer-assisted instruction service and some problems involved. In Hills, P J and Gilbert J K (eds) *Aspects of Educational Technology,* **XI**. Kogan Page, London.

McKenzie, J, Elton, L and Lewis, R (eds) (1978) *Interactive Computer Graphics in Science Teaching.* Ellis Horwood, Chichester.

McMahon (1978) Progress and prospects in computer-managed learning in the United Kingdom. *Programmed Learning and Educational Technology,* **15**, 2, pp 104-13.

Maddison, J (1982) *Information Technology and Education. An Annotated Guide to Printed, Audiovisual and Multimedia Resources.* The Open University Press, Milton Keynes.

Meadows, A J, Gordon, M and Singleton, A (1982) *Dictionary of New Information Technology.* Kogan Page, London.

Megarry, J (1983) Thinking, learning and educating: the role of the computer. In Megarry, J, Walker, D R F, Nisbet, S and Hoyle, E (eds) *Computers and Education (World Yearbook of Education 1982/83).* Kogan Page, London.

Megarry, J, Smart, N and Tomasso, C (1981) Microcomputers and
    Scottish education. In Percival, F and Ellington, H I (eds) *Aspects
    of Educational Technology,* **XV**. Kogan Page, London.
Megarry, J, Walker, D R F, Nisbet, S and Hoyle, E (eds) (1983)
    *Computers and Education (World Yearbook of Education 1982/
    83)*. Kogan Page, London.
O'Shea, T and Self, J (1982) *Learning and Teaching with Computers.*
    Harvester Press, Brighton.
Rushby, N J (ed) (1977) *Computer Managed Learning in the 1980s.
    A Future Study Report.* (Technical Report 16). National
    Development Programme in Computer Assisted Learning, London.
Rushby, N J (1979) *An Introduction to Educational Computing.*
    Croom Helm, London.
Rushby, N J (ed) (1981) *Selected Readings in Computer-Based
    Learning.* Kogan Page, London.
Shepherd , I D H, Cooper, Z A and Walker, D R F (1980) *Computer
    Assisted Learning in Geography.* Council for Educational
    Technology/Geographical Association, London.
Sledge, D (1980) *Microcomputers in Education: A Selection of
    Introductory Titles.* Council for Educational Technology, London.
Smith, C (ed) (1982) *Microcomputers in Education.* Ellis Horwood,
    Chichester.
Tawney, D (ed) (1978) *Learnings Through Computers.* Macmillan,
    London.

Chapter 11: A Glimpse into the Future

Brook, D and Race, P (1978) *Aspects of Educational Technology,* **XII**,
    Educational Technology in a Changing World. Kogan Page, London.
CET (1978) *Microelectronics: Their Implications for Education and
    Training.* Council for Educational Technology, London.
CET (1980) *Microcomputers: Their Uses in Primary Schools.* Council
    for Educational Technology, London.
Gosling, W (1978) *Microcircuits, Society and Education* (Occasional
    Paper 8). Council for Educational Technology, London.
Hawkridge, D (1982) *New Information Technology in Education.*
    Croom Helm, London.
Howe, J A M and Ross, P M (1981) *Microcomputers in Secondary
    Education.* Kogan Page, London.
Maddison, J (1982) *Information Technology and Education. An
    Annotated Guide to Printed, Audiovisual and Multimedia Resources.*
    The Open University Press, Milton Keynes.
Megarry, J (1978) Retrospect and prospect. In McAleese, W (ed)
    Perspectives on Academic Gaming and Simulation 3. Kogan Page,
    London.

Megarry, J, Walker, D R F, Nisbet, S and Hoyle, E (eds) (1982) *Computers and Education (World Yearbook of Education 1982/83).* Kogan Page, London.

Rushby, N J (ed) (1977) *Computer Managed Learning in the 1980s. A Future Study Report* (Technical Report 16). National Development Programme in Computer Assisted Learning, London.

Smith, C (ed) (1982) *Microcomputers in Education.* Ellis Horwood, Chichester.

Winterburn, R and Evans, L (1980) *Aspects of Educational Technology,* **XIV.** *Educational Technology to the Year 2000.* Kogan Page, London.

List of Organizations involved in the Educational Technology Field

The following list contains some of the main bodies which are involved in the educational technology field, together with the addresses at which they may be contacted. For convenience, the list is organized on a national basis, dealing in turn with the United Kingdom, the USA, Canada, Australia and New Zealand.

United Kingdom

Association for Educational and Training Technology (AETT). A UK-based international organization that is concerned with all aspects of educational and training technology; address: BLAT Centre, BMA House, Tavistock Square, London WC1.

British Universities Film Council (BUFC). A national organization that was formed to promote the use of film and other audiovisual materials in British universities and other institutions of higher education; address: 72 Dean Street, London W1V 5HB.

Council for Educational Technology for the United Kingdom (CET). The central organization in the UK for promoting the application of educational technology in all sectors of education and training; address: 3 Devonshire Street, London W1N 2BA.

Educational Foundation for Visual Aids (EFVA). An organization set up to produce educational films and filmstrips and provide advice on the use of visual media; address: 33 Queen Anne Street, London W1.

Educational Television Association (ETA). An organization set up to promote the use of television and allied media in education and training; address: 86 Micklegate, York YO1 1JZ.

Network of Practitioners of Educational and Training Technology (NPETT). An association of individuals and organizations that are involved in the use of educational technology; address: 2 Haigh House Hill, Lindley Moor, Huddersfield, W Yorks HD3 3SZ.

Scottish Council for Educational Technology (SCET). The main official organization responsible for promoting educational technology in Scotland; address: Dowanhill, 74 Victoria Crescent Road, Glasgow G12 9JN.

Society for the Advancement of Gaming and Simulation in Education and Training (SAGSET). A UK-based international organization that promotes the use of gaming and simulation techniques in all branches of education and training; address: c/o Centre for Extension Studies, University of Technology, Loughborough LE11 3TU.

USA

Agency for Instructional Television (AIT). An organization whose aim is to promote education through television throughout the USA and Canada; address: Box A, Bloomington, IN 47402.

Association for Computer-Based Instructional Systems. An American organization set up to facilitate exchange of information on the use of computers in education; address: Box 70189, Los Angeles, CA 90070.

Association for Educational Communications and Technology (AECT). A major American professional organization concerned with learning and educational technology; address: 1126 16th Street, NW, Washington, DC 20036.

Division of Educational Technology. The Division of the US Office of Education with responsibility for educational technology and related activities; address: 3116 ROB/3, US Office of Education, Washington, DC 20202.

Educational Film Library Association. An organization that acts as a national clearinghouse for information about educational 16mm films, videorecording and other non-print media; address: 17 W 60th Street, New York, NY 10023.

International Congress for Individualized Instruction. A US-based international body concerned with research and evaluation in the field of individualized instruction; address: c/o Biology Dept, Fordham University, Bronx, NY 10458.

International Council for Computers in Education. A US-based international body primarily concerned with the use of computers at pretertiary level; address: Dept of Computer and Information Science, University of Oregon, Eugene, OR 97403.

International Tape Exchange. A body that acts as a clearinghouse for the exchange of educational audiotapes; address: 834 Ruddiman Avenue, North Muskegon, MI 49445.

National Audiovisual Center (NAC). A federal body that acts as a national clearinghouse and distribution centre for all audiovisual materials produced by the US Government and its agencies; address: General Services Administration, Reference Section, Washington, DC 20409.

National Center for Audio Tapes (NCAT). A National bank and distribution centre for audiotapes produced by American schools, colleges, official organizations, etc; address: c/o Educational Media Center, Stadium, University of Colorado, Boulder, CO 80309.

National Information Center for Educational Media (NICEM). A national centre that publishes lists of currently-available non-print instructional materials; address: University of Southern California, University Park, Los Angeles, CA 90007.

National Society for Performance and Instruction (NSPI). An interdisciplinary professional organization for teachers, trainers, educational and training technologists, researchers and producers of hardware and software; address: Box 266, Charles Town, WV 25414.

National Video Clearinghouse Inc. A national reference centre for all available video software; address: PO Box 3, Syosset, NY 11791.

North American Simulation and Gaming Association (NASAGA). A body set up to promote the use of gaming and simulation techniques in the USA and Canada; address: c/o Dr W T Nichols, Box 100, Westminster College, New Wilmington, PA 16142.

Society for Computer Simulation. An organization set up to promote the use of computer simulation in education, training, research, etc; address: PO Box 2228, La Jolla, CA 92038.

University Film Association. A professional association of people interested in the use of film for instructional and communication purposes; address: 217 Flint Hall, University of Kansas, Lawrence, KS 66045.

Canada

Association for Media and Technology in Education in Canada (AMTEC). A national organization set up to promote the dissemination of educational technology research findings; address: PO Box 174, Station W, Toronto, Ontario, M6M 4Z2.

Teaching and Instructional Support Division. A government body set up to help schools select and use audiovisual media and equipment; address: Dept of Education, PO Box 2000, Charlottetown, PEI.

Australia

Australian Society of Educational Technology (ASET). A national body, with state chapters, promoting all aspects of educational technology in Australia; address: PO Box 143, Kensington, NSW 2033.

Modern Teaching Methods Association. An organization which runs an audiocassette library and promotes the use of 'modern' teaching methods; address: 101 Wallan, Victoria 3654.

New Zealand

Department of Education, Resources Development Division. A government organization responsible for promoting the use of learning resources in schools; address: Department of Education, Wellington.

National Film Library of New Zealand. An organization that maintains a bank of films for lending to schools and other bodies; address; PO Box 9583, 6th Floor, Cubewell House, Kent Terrace, Wellington.

Keyword Index

Note: This Keyword Index refers only to the main text of the book, *not* to the Glossary or Bibliography. Where more than one page reference is given under a particular heading, any particularly important reference is given in italics.